Essential Series

Springer
London
Berlin
Heidelberg
New York
Barcelona
Hong Kong
Milan
Paris
Singapore
Tokyo

Ian Chivers

Essential Visual C++ 6.0 *fast*

An Introduction to Windows Programming using the Microsoft Foundation Class Library

Springer

Ian Chivers, BSc, PGCEd, MBCS, CEng
Room 1AB, Basement Chesham Building, Kings College Strand Campus,
London WC2R 2LS, UK

Series Editor
John Cowell, BSc (Hons), MPhil, PhD
Department of Computer and Information Sciences, De Montfort University,
Kents Hill Campus, Hammerwood Gate, Kents Hill, Milton Keynes, MK7 6HP, UK

ISBN 1-85233-170-4 Springer-Verlag London Berlin Heidelberg

British Library Cataloguing in Publication Data
Chivers, I. D. (Ian David), 1952-
    Essential Visual C++ 6.0 fast : an introduction to Windows
    programming using the Microsoft Foundation Class Library
    1.C++ (Computer program language) 2.Visual programming
    languages (Computer science)
    I.Title
    005.133
    ISBN 1852331704

Library of Congress Cataloging-in-Publication Data
Chivers, I. D. (Ian David), 1952-
    Essential Visual C++ 6.0 fast : an introduction to Windows
    programming using the Microsoft Foundation Class Library / I.D.
    Chivers
        p.   cm.
    Includes bibliographical references (p.
    ISBN 1-85233-170-4 (alk. paper)
    1. Microsoft Visual C++. 2. Microsoft Windows (Computer file)
    3. Microsoft foundation class library. I. Title.
    QA76.73.C153C485 1999
    005.13'3—dc21   99-41996

Typeset by the author
Printed and bound by Creative Print & Design Group (Wales), Ebbw Vale
34/3830-543210 Printed on acid-free paper SPIN 10718786

Contents

1

Overview

'Where shall I begin, please your Majesty?' he asked.
'Begin at the beginning,' the King said, gravely, 'and go
on until you come to the end: then stop.'

Lewis Carroll, Alice's Adventures in Wonderland.

Aims

The aims of the chapter are to provide a background to the organisation of the book.

Overview

This chapter provides a coverage of a number of key concepts and ideas that will be used throughout the book.

The aim of the book is to provide an introduction to windows programming with the Microsoft Foundation Class (MFC) library. MFC is the class library that Microsoft has provided to put an object oriented interface to the windows application program interface (API).

There is a coverage of the core interface features that one sees on most windows programs.

This includes:

- The two key windows classes:

    - CFrameWnd – The class that provides the functionality of a windows single document interface or pop-up frame window.

- CWinApp – The base class from which you derive a windows application object. This is the class that initialises your application and runs it.
- Message Maps – Windows programs respond to messages caused by key presses, the mouse etc.
- Controls – Windows programs have a common look and feel and we take advantage of the support that the MFC provides for programming the following controls:
  - Menus.
  - Dialog boxes.
  - Message boxes.
  - List boxes.
  - Check boxes.
  - Grouping of controls.
  - Edit boxes.
  - Radio buttons.

Graphical output – Windows programs often involve graphical information. There is a coverage of:

- Device contexts.
- Text input and output (i/o).
- Simple graphics i/o.
- Displaying bitmaps.

The intention is to provide a complete example that highlights the essentials of each of the features introduced.

The material is intended to be a starting point. After reading the book and trying out the examples you should be in a position to effectively use the information provided by Microsoft within Developer Studio.

Microsoft Visual C++ 6 – What isn't covered

Visual C++ is a professional development tool. It offers support for programming a wide range of applications, from the very simple to the extremely complex and feature rich. It is not possible in an introductory book to cover all of what it is capable of. Each of the following is worthy of a book on its own, and you will find several books have been written on each of them.

COM

The Component Object Model (COM) is a platform independent, distributed, object oriented system for creating binary software components that can interact. COM is the foundation technology for both Microsoft's OLE (compound documents) and ActiveX (internet enabled components). COM is not an object oriented language, but a standard.

Active X

Active technologies (formerly called ActiveX) use the COM to enable software components to interact with one another in a networked environment, regardless of the language with which they were created. Active technologies can be used to create applications that run on the desktop or the Internet.

Active Template Library – ATL

ATL is the Active Template Library, a set of template-based C++ classes with which you can easily create small, fast COM objects.

Database management – ODBC

Open Database Connectivity (ODBC) is an API that gives you the ability to write applications that are independent of any particular database management system (DBMS). ODBC provides an API that different database vendors implement via ODBC drivers specific to a particular DBMS. Your program uses this API to call the ODBC Driver Manager, which passes the calls to the appropriate driver. The driver, in turn, interacts with the DBMS using Structured Query Language (SQL).

Database management – DAO

Data Access Objects (DAO) is an API that gives you the ability to write applications that are independent of any particular DBMS. DAO works with MDB files like those created by Microsoft Access, but you can also access ODBC data sources through DAO and the Microsoft Jet database engine.

It is possible to use DAO with third party database engines and Oterro from Rbase Technologies is an example of a database engine that can be programmed via Visual Basic and DAO.

Internet programming – ISAPI

ISAPI, the Internet Server Application Programming Interface, is a set of APIs used to write OLE Server extensions and filters for Web servers like Internet Information Server. MFC provides five classes that wrap ISAPI.

Wizards

Developer Studio comes with a range of wizards that will automate the production of many of the tasks involved in windows programming. They generate skeleton code for you. Before you can use this code you need to develop a basic understanding of what is involved in windows programming. After reading this book you should be in a position to try following the code generated.

In addition the wizards force you down a particular approach. This may well be inappropriate for many programs.

Assumptions

It is assumed that the reader:

- has a good grounding in C++ programming.
- has a basic understanding of object oriented programming.

Microsoft Visual C++ versions

Microsoft has released three Visual C++ versions. These are:

- Standard or Learning Edition.
- Professional Edition.
- Enterprise Edition.

The examples have been developed with the Enterprise Edition but most if not all of what is covered here would also apply to the other two editions.

Edition comparison

Table 1.1 *Edition Comparison*

Feature	Std.	Pro.	Ent.
License for distributing applications	Y,+	Y	Y
MFC database classes	Y	Y	Y
Active Template Library	Y	Y	Y
Automatic statement completion (new)	Y,+	Y,+	Y
Client-server applications development	Y	Y	Y
OLE DB templates (new)		Y,+	Y,+
Code optimisation		Y	Y
Profiler		Y	Y
Static linking to the MFC Library		Y	Y
Databound controls (RemoteData)		Y	Y
InstallShield		Y	Y
Custom AppWizard		Y	Y
Visual Database Tools		Y,+,*	Y
Extended Stored Procedure Wizard (new)			Y,+
Visual SourceSafe			Y
License for distributing applications	Y,+	Y	Y
MFC database classes	Y	Y	Y
Active Template Library	Y	Y	Y
Automatic statement completion (new)	Y,+	Y,+	Y,+
Client-server applications development	Y	Y	Y
OLE DB templates (new)		Y,+	Y,+
Code optimisation		Y	Y
Profiler		Y	Y
Static linking to the MFC Library		Y	Y
Databound controls (RemoteData)		Y	Y
InstallShield		Y	Y
Custom AppWizard		Y	Y
Visual Database Tools		Y,+,*	Y
Extended Stored Procedure Wizard (new)			Y
Visual SourceSafe			Y

Table 1.1 *Edition Comparison, continued*

Feature	Std.	Pro.	Ent.
SQL Debugging			Y
SQL Server 6.5 Developer Edition			Y
SQL Server 6.5 Service Pack #3			Y
Visual Modeler (new)			Y,+
ASA400 database access via OLE DB (new)			Y ,+
Microsoft Transaction Server			Y
Internet Information Server 4.0 (new)			Y,+

Notes:
"Y" means the feature is included.
"+" means the feature is new, or new for the edition.
"*" indicates that some but not all aspects of the feature are available for the edition.

Windows programming

Standard C++ programs have a main program and zero or more functions, of a variety of data types including void. Interaction with the user is generally achieved using cin and cout.

A windows program or application is typified by a window or rectangular area of the screen where the application displays output and receives input from the user. The first thing to do with a windows application is to create a window.

A window shares the screen with other windows, including those from other applications. Only one window at a time can receive input from the user. The user can use the mouse, keyboard, or other input device to interact with this window and the application that owns it. Most if not all windows programs will have to handle events from the keyboard and mouse.

Windows programs rely on message passing. A message is a structure or set of parameters used for communicating information or a request. Messages can be passed between the operating system and an application, different applications, threads within an application, and windows within an application.

User interface features

Windows programs are typified by:
- Menus.
- Toolbars.
- Dialog boxes.

Simple windows programs like Notepad have only a menu bar and a small number of dialog boxes. Wordpad is a little more complex and also has tools available. Word is a very feature rich program.

In this book we will be looking at programming a range of user interface features using the MFC library.

Working methods

There are a number of key issues involved in using the MFC library successful, and they include:

- Deciding what the program or application is going to do and look like.
- Identifying the classes from the MFC that will support the above.
- Working out which constructors to use.
- Working out what member functions will be needed.
- Working out what defaults can be used.
- Working out what application specific code you need to write.
- Developing an understanding of the above.

The on-line information provided is **the** source of information to achieve the above. The information you require is there and can be found, not necessarily easily in all cases, but it is there. The examples have been developed by following the above steps.

Visual Studio

The Visual Studio 6.0 family of development products includes:

- Visual Basic.
- Visual C++.
- Visual FoxPro.
- Visual InterDev.
- Visual J++.
- Visual SourceSafe.
- Microsoft Developer Network (MSDN) Library.

The primary access to Visual C++ is through Visual Studio. A good working knowledge of Visual Studio is essential, and we will look in more depth at Visual Studio in the next chapter.

The MSDN Library is a very valuable source of information. If you buy the Professional or Enterprise editions these CDs will be included.

Microsoft also make this information available at:

```
http://msdn.microsoft.com/library/default.htm
```

Their home page is given below.

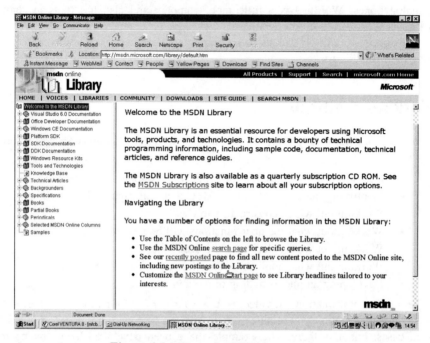

Figure 1.1 *Microsoft MSDN home page.*

If you have internet access and don't have the Professional or Enterprise editions then you are strongly advised to use this information resource. Microsoft have made a wealth of useful information available to you.

Development platforms

The examples in this book have been developed on a variety of platforms and include the following:

- Cyrix © 6x86 110 MHz processor, 32 Mb memory, 17 inch monitor, 32 speed CD rom.
- Intel © P120 MHz processor, 32 Mb memory, 17 inch monitor, 8 speed CD rom.
- Intel © PII 350 MHz processor, 64 Mb memory, 17 inch monitor, 32 speed CD rom.

The minimum recommendation is 32 Mb of memory and a 17 inch monitor at 1024*768. A good quality 15 inch monitor is adequate. If you don't have enough disk space to install all of the Developer Studio components and the Microsoft Developer Network documentation and examples then a high speed CD rom is recommended. A printer helps a lot.

Coda

Be prepared to devote some time to learning how to develop windows programs using the MFC. You can't gain an understanding of 50 years of program language development and a complex language like Visual C++ without some effort on your part.

Problems

Install Visual C++ 6!

Bibliography

The following are some sources that you will find useful:

- Zaratian B., *Visual C++ Programmer's Guide*, Microsoft Press.

    Good tutorial-based coverage of Visual C++. Comes with a CD with the source for all the sample programs.

- Kruglinski David J., Shepherd George, Wingo Scot, *Programming Microsoft Visual C++ 6, Fifth Edition*, Microsoft Press.

    Another good tutorial-based coverage of Visual C++. Also comes with a companion CD with the source for all of the sample programs.

- Prosise J., *Programming Windows 95 with MFC*, Microsoft Press.

    Good tutorial-based introduction to MFC. CD contains both source code and executables for all sample programs.

- MSDN Library – Twin CD.

    This is included with the Professional and Enterprise Editions of Visual Studio 6. This is an essential source of technical information. It contains product documentation, code samples, technical articles and utilities. It can be used as a replacement for many of the Microsoft books.

There are a number of Microsoft urls that you will find useful. The first is the Microsoft Developer Network (MSDN) home page.

`Http://www.msdn.microsoft.com/`

Another is the Microsoft Visual C++ home page.

```
Http://www.msdn.microsoft.com/visualc/
```

This provides details of the service packs that are available for Developer Studio. The book shop is worth a visit:

```
Http://www.msdn.microsoft.com/resources/books.asp
```

```
Http://mspress.microsoft.com/
```

MSDN on line documentation:

```
Http://www.msdn.microsoft.com/library/default.htm
```

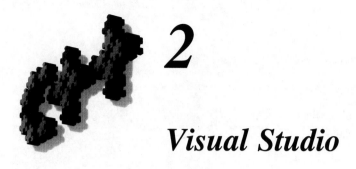

2

Visual Studio

'Don't panic.'

Douglas Adams, The Hitch-Hiker's Guide to the Galaxy

Aims

The aims of the chapter are to provide a quick introduction to the use of Visual Studio.

Visual Studio

This chapter looks at the environment within which Visual C++ exists.

Visual Studio 6.0 runs under Windows 95, Windows 98, Windows NT Workstation and Windows NT Server. It is expected that it will also work with future 32 bit versions of Windows.

To start Visual C++ 6.0 click on Start in the bottom left hand corner and then use the mouse to move down the following chain:

Programs | Microsoft Visual Studio 6.0 | Microsoft Visual C++ 6.0

This is shown below:

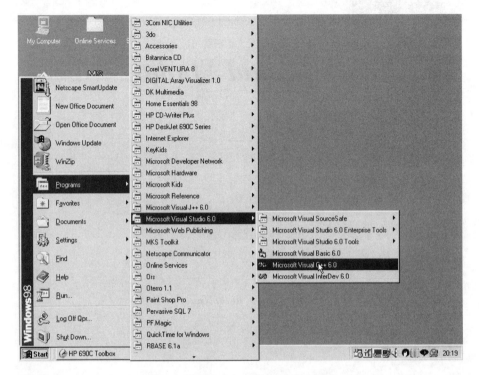

Figure 2.1 *Starting Visual C++ 6.0*

This is the typical set up we see when using windows. The exact layout will vary with the software installed and desktop options you have set.

This will bring up the following screen:

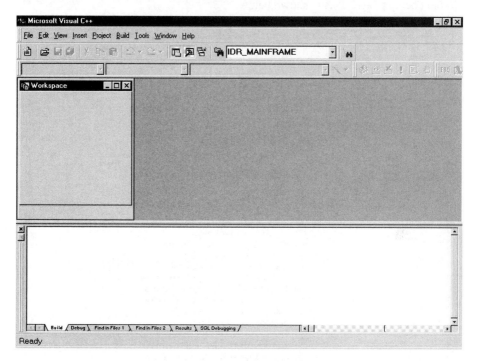

Figure 2.2 *Visual Studio opening screen.*

We have a typical windows application layout with menus and toolbars and three blank sub-windows.

On-line documentation

One of the key components of Visual Studio is the on-line documentation provided on the MSDN twin CDs. You have the option of installing this or running from the CDs. It is recommended that you install this documentation, as it provides detailed technical documentation on Developer Studio, Visual C++ and the MFC library.

Click on the Help menu and Contents to bring up the MSDN Library Visual Studio 6.0 opening page. This is shown below:

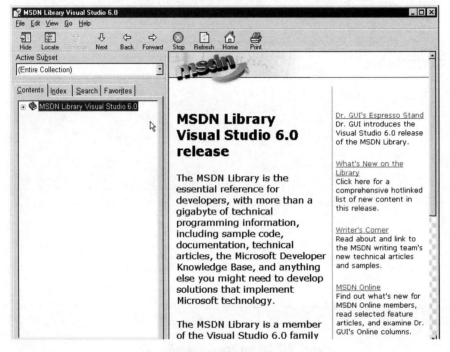

***Figure 2.3** On-line help.*

The key things to note here are in the top left hand corner of the screen. These are the:

- Active Subset
- (Entire Collection)

and left-hand windows just underneath with four tab options of:

- Contents – Index – Search – Favourites

and the Contents tab comes up by default. Click on the + sign by the MSDN Library Visual Studio book to provide a more detailed list of the documentation available. This will bring up the following window:

Click on the + sign by the side of the Visual C++ Documentation book, and then:

- Using Visual C++

and

- Reference.

This brings up the following screen:

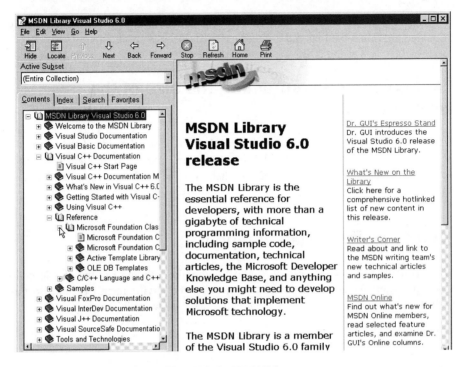

Figure 2.4 MSDN Library.

As you can see a wealth of on-line documentation is provided. You should use the information provided on the MFC as we look at the examples in later chapters. Each chapter will concentrate on examples using as small a working subset as possible of the MFC. It is worthwhile browsing round now to gain some familiarity with the organisation of the material provided. Good use is made of links to enable you to locate the exact information you require relatively quickly.

Right-hand mouse button

Clicking on the right-hand mouse button in the left had windows brings up a pop-up a menu box with the following three options:

- Close all.
- Print.
- Jump to URL.

This is a very useful interface option.

Mouse with middle roller

If you have a mouse with a middle roller facility clicking this provides a quick way of navigating round the material without having to use the scroll bars.

Expanding and contracting the size of the windows

Another useful feature is the ability to expand and contract the size of the windows. Move the mouse slowly from the left-hand window into the right-hand one and a double arrowed line will appear. You can then drag the bar left or right to adjust the size of the windows.

Simple program development

We will now look at using Visual Studio to compile, link and run the classic hello world program. As our main interest is in using the environment, we will do this with a conventional C++ program. Here is the program we will be using:

```cpp
#include <iostream.h>

int main()
{
    cout << " Hello world " << endl;
    return (0);
}
```

Stage 1 – File | New

Click on the File menu in the top left-hand corner and then New. This will bring up the following screen:

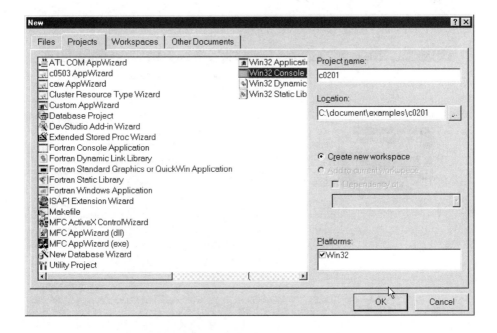

Figure 2.5 Starting a new project.

Four tabs are provided and if the Projects tab has not come up by default then click on it.

Stage 2 – Choose a project type

We are interested in a project of type:

- Win 32 Console application.

This option should be towards the bottom of the options provided.

Stage 3 – Choose a project name and location

Use the dialog boxes on the top right to choose both a project name and location. It is suggested that you choose a location first from which to base all projects. As you fill in the project name box the name will be added as a sub-directory of the location entry.

Stage 4 – Project type

Click OK and the following window appears:

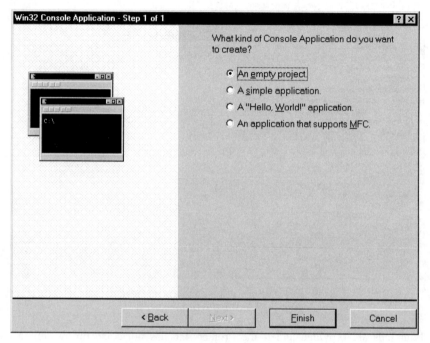

Figure 2.6 Selecting a project type.

You are presented with a choice of four radio buttons:

- An empty project.
- A simple application.
- A "Hello world" application.
- An application that supports MFC.

If the empty project button is not selected then choose it and click on Finish at the bottom.

Stage 5 – New project information

You should see something similar to that below:

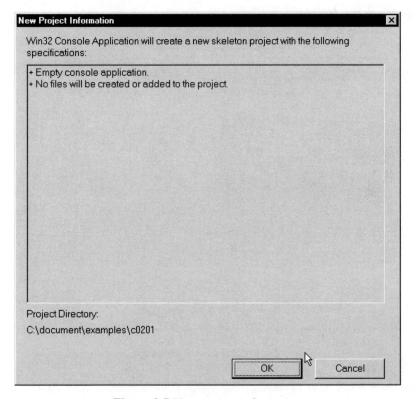

Figure 2.7 New project information.

The key features are:

- Win32 Console Application.
- Empty console application.
- No files will be created or added to the project.
- Project directory.

Click on OK.

Stage 6 – Visual Studio empty project

You should see a screen similar to that below:

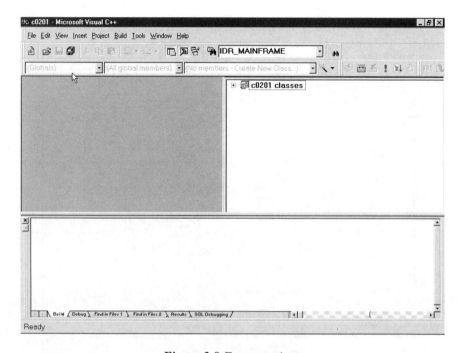

Figure 2.8 *Empty project.*

Some of the key features are:

- The window with the class information for the project.
- The additional windows.

Try moving the mouse over some of the items on the various toolbars. You will see a message pop up with a description of what the item on the toolbar does.

Don't worry at the moment about the complexity of the interface. This will become clearer after using the environment a couple of times.

Stage 7 – Project I Add to project I New

You will see a screen similar to the one below:

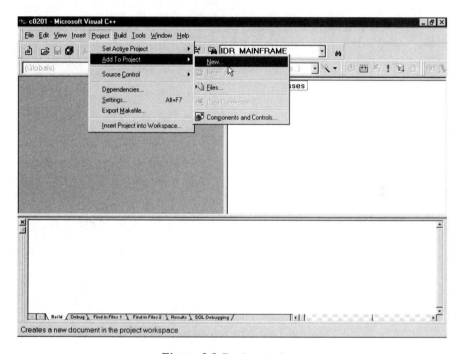

Figure 2.9 *Project options.*

Some of the key features are:

- The various drop down menu options, including:
  - Project.
  - Build.
  - Window.

We will cover some of these in later examples.

Stage 8 – New I Files/Projects/Other documents

You will see a screen similar to the one below:

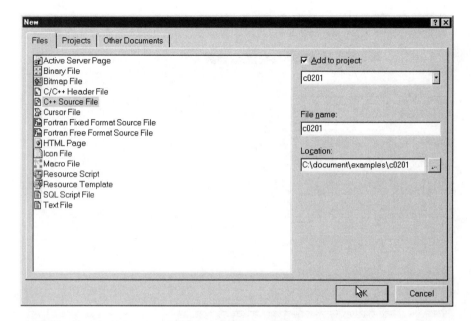

Figure 2.10 *File name.*

Ensure that the File tab is selected and that:

- C++ Source File.

is also selected.

Add the file name in the box marked. Take a note of the directory that the project is in.

Stage 9 – Visual Studio – Editor window:

You will have an empty editor window:

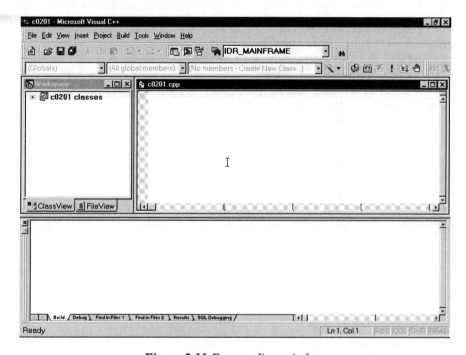

Figure 2.11 *Empty editor window.*

Some of the key features here are:

- The class window.
- The empty editor window.
- The bottom window with a variety of tabs including:
  - Build.
  - Debug.

The exact set of tabs will depend on which version of Developer Studio you have.

Stage 10 – Type in the program

You will see a screen similar to the one below:

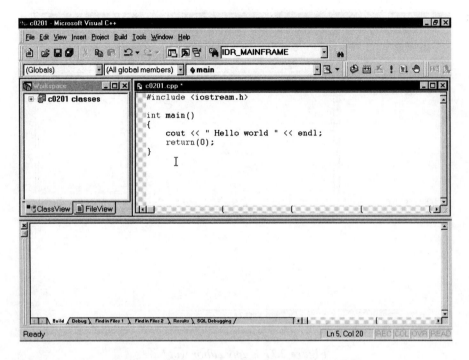

Figure 2.12 Sample program in editor window.

Note that the editor is semi-intelligent and that it will recognise the syntax of the C++ source. Certain language elements will be colour coded, and indentation will be applied automatically as you type the program in.

Stage 11 – Build | Execute

You will see something like the screen below:

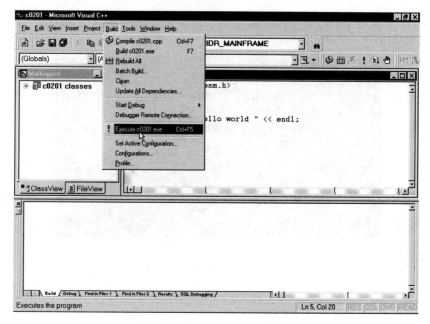

Figure 2.13 Build the program.

Stage 12 – This file does not exist

The following should appear:

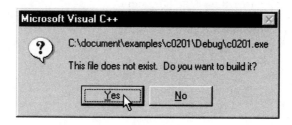

Figure 2.14 File does not exist.

Click button.

Stage 13 – DOS Console window

You should see the following:

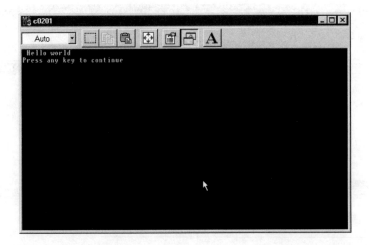

Figure 2.15 *Application running.*

Some of the features to note are:

- The DOS box that the program runs in.

The text message

- Press any key to continue.

This enables you to see the output from the program.

Pressing any key will terminate the program executing and return to Visual Studio.

A stand alone executable will also have been created that you can execute from the File Manager of from a DOS box.

Stage 14 – Back to Visual Studio

You will see something like that below:

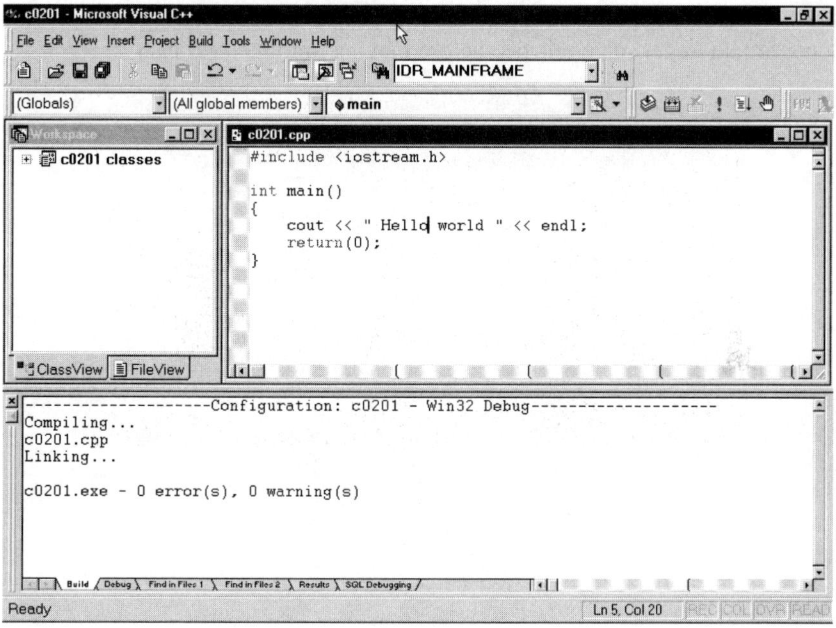

Figure 2.16 Visual Studio return screen.

The bottom window has the compile and link messages.

Summary

The quote at the start of the chapter by Douglas Adams sums it up quite beautifully:

Don't panic

There is a lot to assimilate. You have to get familiar with the following:

- The Developer Studio visual environment.
- The types of windows within the Developer Studio visual environment.
- The menu options.
- The toolbars.
- The change in status of items on the toolbars depending on the context of what you are doing.
- Projects.
- Types of projects.

- Project options.
- The location of the directories and sub-directories where Developer Studio organises your work files.
- Building your application.

It is recommended that you try creating a couple of simple programs within Developer Studio to get some practice before moving onto the next chapter.

3

Getting Started

'Though this be madness, yet there be method in't.'

Shakespeare

Aims

The chapter starts with a minimal MFC program. This example is used to introduce some of the essential information required to program using the MFC. This includes:

- CFrameWnd – The class that provides the functionality of a windows single document interface or pop-up frame window:
  - Associated constructor and parameters.
- CWinApp – The base class from which you derive a windows application object. This is the class that initialises your application and runs it:
  - Associated constructor and parameters.
- Message maps.
- Project options.
- Windows data types and naming conventions.

Getting started

We are going to look at a complete but minimal windows program that uses the MFC. This program serves as a basis to introduce the concepts necessary to develop windows programs using the MFC.

The program

The complete program is given below.

```
#include <afxwin.h>
class CMainWindow : public CFrameWnd
{
public :
    CMainWindow();
    DECLARE_MESSAGE_MAP()
};

CMainWindow::CMainWindow()
{
    Create(NULL , " Minimal MFC program or application");
}

class CMyApplication : public CWinApp
{
public :
    BOOL InitInstance();
};

BOOL CMyApplication::InitInstance()
{
    m_pMainWnd = new CMainWindow;
    m_pMainWnd->ShowWindow(m_nCmdShow);
    m_pMainWnd->UpdateWindow();

    return TRUE;
}

BEGIN_MESSAGE_MAP(CMainWindow,CFrameWnd)
END_MESSAGE_MAP()

CMyApplication Application;
```

Running the program

Start up Visual Studio and take the following steps to compile, link and run the program:

- **File | New project**.
- Choose Win 32 application.

- Type in the project name and location.

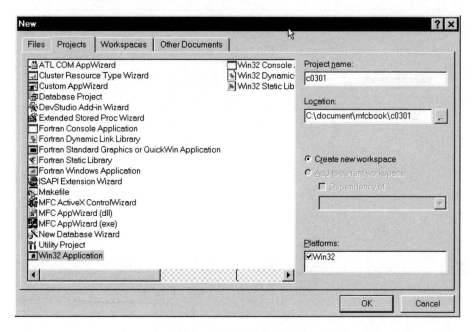

Figure 3.1 *New project.*

We have a number of project types available. The exact set will depend on what version of Developer Studio you have installed. The system on which the above example was done also has Compaq's Visual Fortran installed.

Ensure that

- Win32 Application.

is selected.

Click OK.

- A number of project types are available.

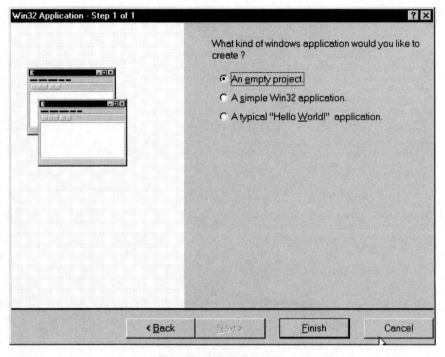

Figure 3.2 Empty project.

Select:

- An empty project.

Notice that you have the option of going back to the previous screen if you have made a mistake or want to check what you have done.

We will look at the second project option later.

The following window will appear.

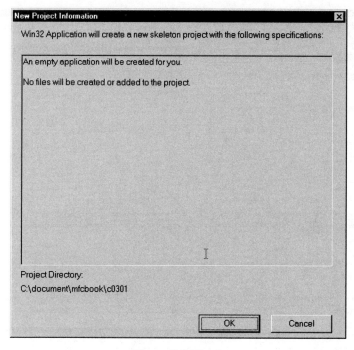

Figure 3.3 Finish.

Key features are:

- Win32 Application.
- An empty application.
- No files will be created.

The location of the project directory is also provided.
Click OK

- The following window will appear.

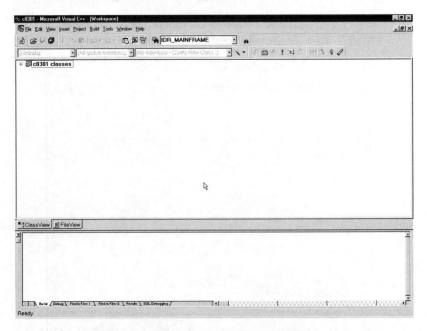

Figure 3.4 *Developer Studio empty project.*

The appearance may not match exactly.
The key features are:

- Two or more windows should appear.
- Each window will have tabs at the bottom that offer ways of bringing up a wealth of information about the project.

It is possible to use the Window menu to arrange the windows that appear. Click on that menu option to see what is available.

Also try switching between ClassView mode and FileView mode.

- Project menu I Add to project I New.
- Choose C++ source file.
- Type in the file name. Make a note of where Developer Studio puts things.
- A window should appear similar to the following one:

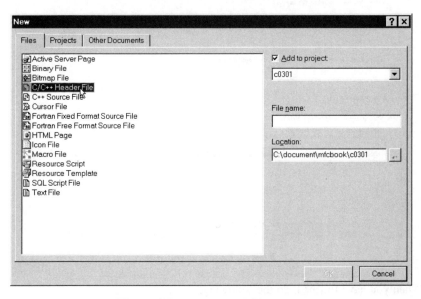

Figure 3.5 *Location and file setting.*

Now type in the program in the editor window. There are a number of things to note as you type the program in:

- C++ keywords are highlighted in a different colour.
- The Visual C++ Text editor uses IntelliSense® to make writing your code easier and more error-free. IntelliSense options include Statement Completion, which provides quick access to valid member functions or variables, including globals, via the Members list.

You end up with a window like the following:

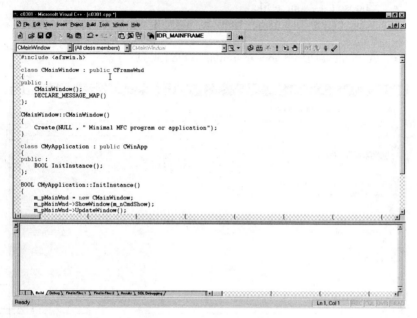

Figure 3.6 C++ source.

When you have finished, do the following:
- **Project menu | Settings**.

You will see the following window:

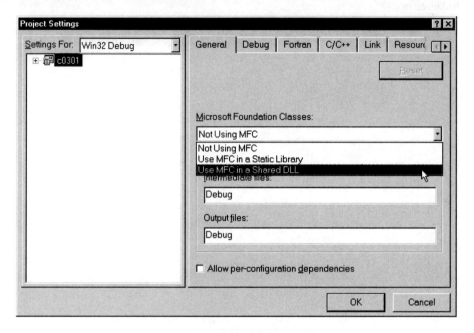

Figure 3.7 *Using MFC in a Shared DLL*

Ensure that under the General tab:

- Use MFC in a Shared Dll is chosen under Microsoft Foundation Classes.

Now choose the Build menu and select Execute filename.exe.
This will then:

- Compile.
- Link.

and

- Run.

the program.

You should see something like the window below if there are no compilation or linker errors.

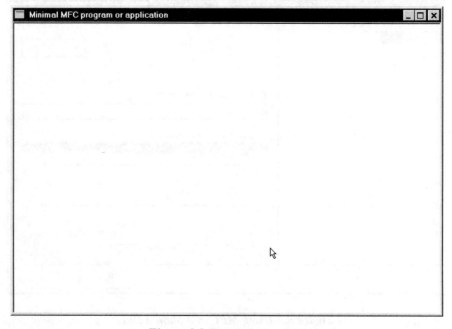

Figure 3.8 Program running.

The window can be:

- Minimised.
- Maximised.

and

- Closed.

Now locate the directory where the executable is and have a look at the size. On one system used the .exe file is about 100Kb.

Now go back to Visual Studio and in the Project settings menu choose MFC in a Static Library. Rebuild the executable and have a look at the file size. On one system the file was about 1.2 Mb

Static linking provides an executable that does not require the MFC Dlls. However, except for very simple programs you also need to explicitly include a number of header and resource files. To simplify the program examples always choose:

- Use MFC in a Shared Dll

in the project options when building your executable. The required information is then obtained behind the scenes.

Let us now look at each line of the program in more depth.

```
#include <afxwin.h>
```

The MFC Library can be divided into two major sections:

- The MFC classes

and

- macros and globals.

If a function or variable is not a member of a class, it is a global function or variable. This header file makes available all of the necessary globals and macros. These can be used and shared between all MFC classes. This avoids unnecessary duplication throughout the MFC hierarchy.

```
class CMainWindow : public CFrameWnd
```

The CFrameWnd class provides the functionality of a windows single document interface (SDI) overlapped or pop-up frame window and member functions for managing the window. To create a window for your application you:

- Derive a class from CFrameWnd.
- Add member variables to the derived class to store data specific to your application.
- Implement message-handler member functions and a message map in the derived class to specify what happens when messages are directed to the window.
- Construct a frame window.

In this example we do it directly using Create.
CFrameWnd is three levels into the MFC hierarchy.
CObject is the MFC root. The tree is shown below.

- Cobject -> CCmdTarget -> Cwnd -> CFrameWnd

If you want more information on the complete hierarchy then use the help menu and contents to bring up the MSDN on-line documentation. Look under Reference beneath the C++ documentation.

This is shown below:

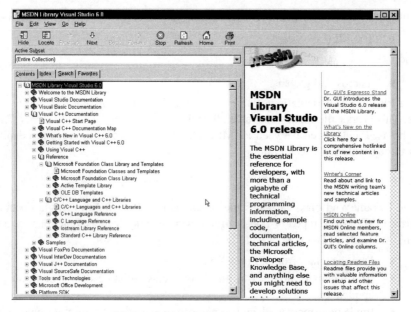

Figure 3.9 On-line documentation.

Have a browse around to gain some familiarity with the material. It will be necessary to locate and refer to information throughout the sample programs and also as you develop your own applications.

```
public :
```

Standard C++ declaration.

```
CMainWindow();
```

Constructor prototype. Body given later.

```
DECLARE_MESSAGE_MAP()
```

Each CCmdTarget-derived class in your program must provide a message map to handle messages. You must include a DECLARE_MESSAGE_MAP macro at the end of your class declaration. Then in the source file that defines the member functions for the class, use the BEGIN_MESSAGE_MAP macro, macro entries for each of your message-handler functions, and the END_MESSAGE_MAP macro. In this simple example we don't handle any messages.

```
CMainWindow::CMainWindow()
```

This is the actual constructor.

```
Create(NULL , " Minimal MFC program or application");
```

Call to create and initialise the windows frame window associated with the CFrameWnd object. This makes the window visible.

The first argument, if NULL, uses the predefined default CFrameWnd attributes.

The second argument points to a null-terminated character string that represents the window name. Used as text for the title bar.

There are a number of additional arguments. We accept the defaults in this simple example. We will look at other parameters in later examples. More information can be found in the on-line MSDN documentation.

```
class CMyApplication : public CWinApp
```

The main application class in MFC encapsulates the initialisation, running, and termination of an application for windows. An application built on the framework must have one (and only one) object of a class derived from CWinApp – in this case CMyApplication. This object is constructed before windows are created. (CWinApp is derived from CWinThread, which represents the main thread of execution for your application, which might have one or more threads.)

```
public :
```

Standard C++ declaration.

```
BOOL InitInstance();
```

Windows allows several copies of the same program to run at the same time. Application initialisation is conceptually divided into two sections: one-time application initialisation that is done the first time the program runs, and instance initialisation that runs each time a copy of the program runs, including the first time. The framework's implementation of WinMain calls this function. We will come back to WinMain later.

We override InitInstance to construct the main window object and set the CWinThread::m_pMainWnd data member to point to that window.

```
BOOL CMyApplication::InitInstance()
```

See above.

```
m_pMainWnd = new CMainWindow;
```

Use this data member to store a pointer to your thread's main window object. The MFC library will automatically terminate your thread when the window referred to by m_pMainWnd is closed. If this thread is the primary thread for an application, the application will also be terminated. If this data member is NULL, the main window for the application's CWinApp object will be used to determine when to terminate the thread. m_pMainWnd is a public variable of type CWnd*. Typically, you set this member variable when you override InitInstance.

The CWinThread data member m_pMainWnd points to the new window.

```
m_pMainWnd->ShowWindow(m_nCmdShow);
```

Sets the visibility state of the window. ShowWindow must be called only once per application for the main window with CWinApp::m_nCmdShow.

```
m_pMainWnd->UpdateWindow();
```

Updates the client area by sending a WM_PAINT message if the update region is not empty. The UpdateWindow member function sends a WM_PAINT message directly, by-passing the application queue. We will return to the WM_PAINT message and concept of an application queue later.

```
return TRUE;
```

It has worked!

```
BEGIN_MESSAGE_MAP(CMainWindow,CFrameWnd)
```

In the source file that defines the member functions for your class, start the message map with the BEGIN_MESSAGE_MAP macro, then add macro entries for each of your message-handler functions, and complete the message map with the END_MESSAGE_MAP macro. There are no other entries in this example.

```
END_MESSAGE_MAP()
```

See above.

```
CMyApplication Application;
```

The CWinApp class is the base class from which you derive a windows application object. The class hierarchy is given below. CObject is the MFC root.

- Cobject -> CCmdTarget -> CWinThread -> CWinApp

An application object provides member functions for initialising your application (and each instance of it) and for running the application. Each application that uses the Microsoft Foundation classes can only contain one object derived from CWinApp. This object is constructed when other C++ global objects are constructed and is already available when windows calls the WinMain function, which is supplied by the MFC library.

Windows data types and naming conventions

Microsoft invented a naming convention for data types, variables, parameters and functions. Consider the following prototype:

CWnd::Create
virtual BOOL Create(LPCTSTR lpszClassName, LPCTSTR lpszWindowName,
DWORD dwStyle, const RECT& rect, CWnd* pParentWnd,
UINT nID, CCreateContext* pContext = NULL);

The capitalised terms refer to their own data types.

Some of the commonly used windows Software Development Kit (SDK) and MFC data types are given in Table 3.1 below.

Table 3.1 *Windows SDK and MFC data types*

Name	Description
BOOL	A Boolean value.
BSTR	A 32-bit character pointer.
BYTE	An 8-bit integer that is not signed.
COLORREF	A 32-bit value used as a colour value.
DWORD	A 32-bit unsigned integer or the address of a segment and its associated offset.
LONG	A 32-bit signed integer.
LPARAM	A 32-bit value passed as a parameter to a window procedure or callback function.
LPCSTR	A 32-bit pointer to a constant character string.
LPCTSTR	A 32-bit pointer to a constant character string that is portable for Unicode and DBCS.
LPSTR	A 32-bit pointer to a character string.
LPTSTR	A 32-bit pointer to a character string that is portable for Unicode and DBCS.
LPVOID	A 32-bit pointer to an unspecified type.
LRESULT	A 32-bit value returned from a window procedure or callback function.
UINT	A 32-bit unsigned integer on Win32.
WNDPROC	A 32-bit pointer to a window procedure.
WORD	A 16-bit unsigned integer.
WPARAM	A value passed as a parameter to a window procedure or callback function. 32 bits on Win32.
Variable prefixes include:	
b	boolean
c	character
C	class

Table 3.1 Windows SDK and MFC data types, continued

Name	Description
dw	long unsigned integer
f	16 bit – used as flags
fn	function
h	handle
l	long integer
lp	long pointer
lpsz	long pointer to null-terminated string
n	short integer
p	pointer
pt	long integer – screen co-ordinates
rgb	long integer holding rgb colour values
sz	pointer to null-terminated string
w	short unsigned integer

It may not be perfect but it is used through all of their documentation.

Summary of steps in creating a windows program

Decide what user interface features you want.
Determine what classes offer support for those features.
Look at the constructors for these classes..
Look at what defaults we can accept.
Look at the member functions for these classes.
Derive a windows class from CFrameWnd – this creates your window.
Derive an applications class from CWinApp – this starts the program running.
Define a message map – windows programs respond to messages.
Override InitInstance – create a window, display it and handle repaints.
Instantiate your application class.

4

Messages

'Why, sometimes I've believed as many as six impossible things before breakfast.'

Lewis Carroll, Alice Through the Looking-Glass.

Overview

Windows is a message based operating system. It is essential to develop an understanding of message handling to write windows programs or applications. We will look at handling:

- Keyboard input and associated message handlers.
- Left and right mouse button presses and associated message handlers.
- Device contexts.
- Repainting the client window.

Messages

Interaction with a windows program or application is achieved using the keyboard and mouse, and messages lie at the heart of this process. Windows itself is a message based operating system and a large part of windows programming involves message handling. Each time an event such as a keystroke or mouse click occurs, a message is sent to the application, which must then handle the event.

The MFC library offers a programming model optimised for message-based programming. Message maps are used to designate which functions will handle various messages for a particular class. Message maps contain one or more macros that specify which messages will be handled by which functions.

In the example in the last chapter you met the following three message map macros.

DECLARE_MESSAGE_MAP Declares that a message map will be used in a class to map messages to functions – must be in the class declaration. It must be at the end of the class declaration.

BEGIN_MESSAGE_MAP Begins the definition of a message map – must be in the class implementation.

END_MESSAGE_MAP Ends the definition of a message map – must be in the class implementation.

These macros are necessary for any windows program, but in this case the program didn't actually respond to any messages.

This program will extend the previous example and show how to handle the following types of messages:

- Character input from the keyboard.
- Left and right mouse button presses.
- Repainting the client screen.

Working methods again

In the first chapter we looked at a working method to help us with windows programming. We will apply the following steps:

- Decide what we want to do.
- Identify the MFC classes that will support that.
- Identify the constructors to use.
- Work out what member functions will be needed.
- Work out what defaults we can accept.
- Write the application specific code.

The application

In this example only one file is required. Later examples will require several.

The program

The complete program is given below.

```
#include <afxwin.h>
#include <string.h>
```

```
class CMainWindow : public CFrameWnd
{
public :
   CMainWindow();
   afx_msg void OnChar(UINT ch, UINT count, UINT flags);
   afx_msg void OnPaint();
   afx_msg void OnLButtonDown(UINT flags, CPoint loc);
   afx_msg void OnRButtonDown(UINT flags, CPoint loc);
   DECLARE_MESSAGE_MAP()
};

CMainWindow::CMainWindow()
{
   Create(NULL , " Minimal Message handling");
}

class CMyApplication : public CWinApp
{
public :
   BOOL InitInstance();
};

BOOL CMyApplication::InitInstance()
{
   m_pMainWnd = new CMainWindow;
   m_pMainWnd->ShowWindow(m_nCmdShow);
   m_pMainWnd->UpdateWindow();

   return TRUE;
}

BEGIN_MESSAGE_MAP(CMainWindow,CFrameWnd)
   ON_WM_CHAR()
   ON_WM_PAINT()
   ON_WM_LBUTTONDOWN()
   ON_WM_RBUTTONDOWN()
END_MESSAGE_MAP()

char line[80]=" Output line of text";
char textline[80];
int wx=1,wy=1;
int charcount=0;
```

```
afx_msg void CMainWindow::OnChar(UINT ch, UINT count,
UINT flags)
{
    textline[charcount]=char(ch);
    charcount++;
    wx=1;
    wy=1;
    strcpy(line,textline);
    InvalidateRect(NULL);
    if (charcount==79) charcount=0;
    return;
}

afx_msg void CMainWindow::OnPaint()
{
    CPaintDC dc(this);
    dc.TextOut(wx,wy,line,strlen(line));
    return;
}
afx_msg void CMainWindow::OnLButtonDown(UINT flags,
CPoint loc)
{
    strcpy(line," Left Button");
    wx=loc.x;
    wy=loc.y;
    InvalidateRect(NULL);
    return;
}
afx_msg void CMainWindow::OnRButtonDown(UINT flags,
CPoint loc)
{
    strcpy(line," Right button");
    wx=loc.x;
    wy=loc.y;
    InvalidateRect(NULL);
    return;
}

CMyApplication Application;
```

Running the program

A convenient working practice is to copy the source for one of the earlier examples and use this as a basis for the current example. Copy with a new name and directory.

Start up Visual Studio and repeat the steps taken in the example in chapter three, i.e.

- **File menu | New project.**
  - Choose Win 32 application: Type in the project name and location. Take care to use the name and location used in the copy.
  - Choose the project type: An empty project.
- **Project menu | Add to project | Files**.
  - You should be in the directory specified above and the copied source file should be there. Click on the file.

Now modify the program in the editor window. When you have finished do the following:

- **Project menu | Settings**.

You will see the following window:

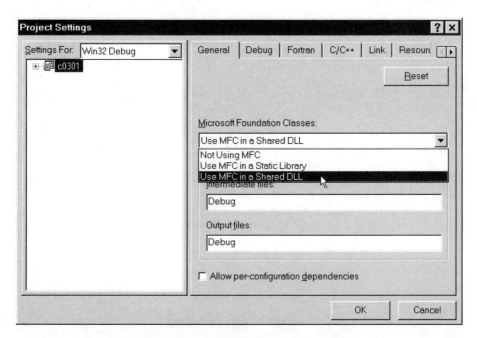

Figure 4.1 *Using MFC in a Shared DLL.*

Ensure that under the General tab:

- Use MFC in a Shared Dll

is chosen under Microsoft Foundation Classes.
Now choose the:

- Build menu.

and select:

- Execute filename.exe.

This will then:

- Compile.
- Link.

and

- Run.

the program.
You should see something like the window below if there are no compilation or linker errors.

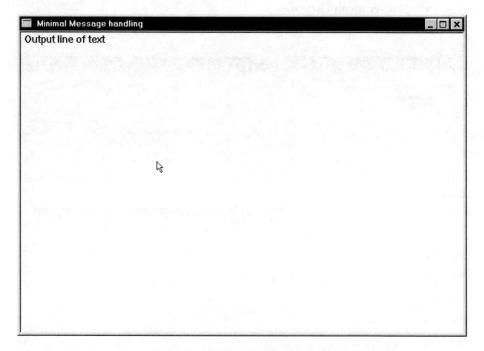

Figure 4.2 *Program running.*

The window can be:

- Minimised.
- Maximised.

and

- Closed.

Experiment with typing in some text and using the mouse.
The client region will respond to the mouse and keyboard actions.

The C++ source

```
#include <afxwin.h>
```

Including this file will ensure that most of the MFC support information is available to your program. All examples in this book will include this file.

To look at the contents of this file use the right mouse button when on this line in the source file and choose:

- Open Document <afxwin.h>

from the options available. This will display the file in a window. Have a look at the wealth of information contained.

```
#include <string.h>
```

We are going to be doing some text i/o so need this header file.

```
afx_msg void OnChar(UINT ch, UINT count, UINT flags);
```

This is the function prototype for the first of the four messages we will be handling in this program. The function processes a key press. More details are given below.

CWnd::OnChar

afx_msg void OnChar(UINT nChar, UINT nRepCnt, UINT nFlags);

Parameters

- nChar:
  - Contains the character code value of the key.
- nRepCnt:
  - Contains the repeat count, the number of times the keystroke is repeated when user holds down the key.
- nFlags:
  - Contains the scan code, key-transition code, previous key state, and context code,

The OnChar function is part of the CWnd base class. The CWnd class provides the base functionality of all window classes in the MFC library. CFrameWnd inherits from CWnd, and our class CMainWindow in turn inherits from CFrameWnd.

```
afx_msg void OnPaint();
```

This is the function prototype for the second of the four messages we will be handling. The framework calls this member function when Windows or an application makes a request to repaint a portion of an application's window. The WM_PAINT message is sent when the UpdateWindow or RedrawWindow member function is called.

In this example we force all i/o through the OnPaint function.

```
afx_msg void OnLButtonDown(UINT flags, CPoint loc);
```

This is the function prototype for the third of the four messages we will be handling. The framework calls this member function when the user presses the left mouse button

```
afx_msg void OnRButtonDown(UINT flags, CPoint loc);
```

This is the function prototype for the last of the four messages we will be handling. The framework calls this member function when the user presses the right mouse button.

```
BEGIN_MESSAGE_MAP(CMainWindow,CFrameWnd)
```

This macro takes two arguments. The first is the class handling the messages. The second is the base class from which this class is derived.

```
ON_WM_CHAR()
```

Map entry for the OnChar function.

```
ON_WM_PAINT()
```

Map entry for the OnPaint function.

```
ON_WM_LBUTTONDOWN()
```

Map entry for the LButtonDown function.

```
ON_WM_RBUTTONDOWN()
```

Map entry for the RButtonDown function.

For each map entry there is a corresponding function. Note the naming conventions. The map entries are all in upper case. The function names use mixed case with capitalisation.

```
char line[80]=" Output line of text";
```

Global variable. Holds the text output to the client window.

```
char textline[80];
```

Global variable. Holds character representation of the keys pressed.

```
int wx=1,wy=1;
```

Global variable. The windows x-coordinate and y-coordinate.

```
int charcount=0;
```

Global variable. Used to control the position of the character pressed in the textline string.

```
afx_msg void CMainWindow::OnChar(UINT ch, UINT count,
UINT flags)
```

Actual function header.

```
textline[charcount]=char(ch);
```

Convert and copy key pressed into textline.

```
charcount++;
```

Increment charcount.

```
wx=1;
```

Reset x-coordinate.

```
wy=1;
```

Reset y-coordinate.

```
strcpy(line,textline);
```

Copy the characters typed.

```
InvalidateRect(NULL);
```

Force a call of OnPaint. Complete details are given in a later chapter.

```
if (charcount==79) charcount=0;
```

Provide for overwriting of textline.

```
afx_msg void CMainWindow::OnPaint()
```

Function header.

```
CPaintDC dc(this);
```

The CPaintDC class is a device context class derived from CDC. It performs a CWnd::BeginPaint at construction time and CWnd::EndPaint at destruction time. A CPaintDC object can only be used when responding to a WM_PAINT message, usually in your OnPaint message-handler member function

A device context is a windows data structure containing information about the drawing attributes of a device such as a display or a printer. All drawing calls are made through a device-context object, which encapsulates the windows APIs for drawing lines, shapes, and text. Device contexts allow device-independent drawing in windows. Device contexts can be used to draw to the screen, to the printer, or to a metafile.

We will cover this whole area in much greater depth in a later chapter.

```
dc.TextOut(wx,wy,line,strlen(line));
```

He above writes a character string at the specified location using the currently selected font.

```
afx_msg void CMainWindow::OnLButtonDown(UINT flags,
CPoint loc)
```

Function header.

The CPoint class is similar to the windows POINT structure. The POINT data structure has the following form:

```
typedef struct tagPOINT
{
  LONG x;
  LONG y;
} POINT;
```

```
strcpy(line," Left Button");
```

Copy text.

```
wx=loc.x;
```

Set windows x-location.

```
wy=loc.y;
```

Set windows y-location.

```
InvalidateRect(NULL);
```

Force a call to OnPaint.

```
afx_msg void CMainWindow::OnRButtonDown(UINT flags,
CPoint loc)
```

Function header.

```
strcpy(line," Right button");
```

Copy string.

```
wx=loc.x;
```

Set window x-coordinate.

```
wy=loc.y;
```

Set window y-coordinate.

```
InvalidateRect(NULL);
```

Force a call of OnPaint.

Summary

Adding message handling involves the following stages:

- Adding the message handling functions to CMainWindow.
- Adding the corresponding message macros to the message map.
- Overriding each of the message handling functions.

In this example we route all i/o through the OnPaint function.

We generate the OnPaint message by calling the InvalidateRect function.

InvalidateRect is in the CWnd base class. It takes two arguments and when the first is NULL the entire client window area is updated.

Experiment with the characters typed in. Compare the length of the line when using full stops with upper case w. We will look in more depth at text i/o in a later chapter.

When doing i/o we need to use a device context. As all i/o is restricted to OnPaint we have a very simple example of how to set up and use a device context. We create an object of type CPaintDC and then use the TextOut function to write some text to the screen.

We have the following sequence:

- User action, keyboard, mouse etc.
- Windows event generated.
- Temporary storage in a hardware input queue.
- Message passed to the appropriate thread message queue – Windows is a multithreaded operating system.

- Message taken from queue and passed to WinMain.
- WinMain loops retrieving and despatching messages.

The MFC library manages to encapsulate quite a lot of complexity!

5

Controls: Menus

'Winnie-the-Pooh read the two notices very carefully,
first from left to right, and afterwards,
in case he had missed some of it, from right to left.'

A. A. Milne, Winne-the-Pooh.

Overview

There are a number of user interface features that characterise most windows programs, and the three most commonly used are menus, toolbars and dialog boxes. In
this chapter we look at drop down menus. The following concepts are covered:

- Resources – menus:
    - Menu names.
    - Menu types.
    - Menu ID.
    - Menu resource file.
    - Menus and the message map.
    - Short cut keys – accelerators.
- Message boxes.
- Left and right mouse button presses.
- Repainting the client window.
- Programming resources versus using the resource editors.

Menus

Windows programs have evolved to have a consistent user interface. Take a look at:

- Notepad
- Wordpad
- Word

to see a progression from very simple to quite complex.
You will find the following in most windows programs:

- Drop down menus.
- Tool bars.
- Dialog boxes.
- Controls, including:

  - Radio buttons.
  - Push buttons.
  - Check boxes.
  - List boxes.
  - Edit boxes.

- Scroll bars.

This program will extend an earlier example and show how to add the common menus:

- File.
- Edit.
- View.
- Help.

These are seen in many windows programs. We will address this problem by programming the menus directly.

Resources

A menu is classified as a resource. Resources contain text and graphics that determine the visual user interface. Resources include:

- Accelerator tables – key board short cuts.
- Binary data information.
- Bitmaps, icons, and other image files.
- Cursors.
- Dialog boxes.
- HTML pages.
- Menus.
- String tables – menu hints etc.

- Toolbar resources.
- Version information.

You can edit all of the windows resources that your application uses and open a resource (.rc) file in text format. Resources have many commands and procedures in common. Once you learn how to use menus, you know the steps for creating and working with many of the other resources.

The application

This program is made up of three files. As the examples get more complex it is necessary to organise things in terms of components. The components are:

- An include file that is used within both the resource file and the program. This file contains macro definitions of the menu ID values.
- A resource file.
    - Menus, dialog boxes and icons are all resources. They are maintained separately to your program and are compiled during the build process and added to your executable file. You must add the resource file to your project.
- The C++ source file or program:
    - This is the program source.

Let us look at each in turn.

The menu ID file – menuids.h

The information in this file is required by both the resource file and the program. It contains the macro definitions of the menu ID values. Each menu has both a name and associated value. The names comprise a number of parts. The middle says which menu it is part of and the last which option within that menu. The numbers are arbitrary, and must lie between 1 and 65,565.

```
#define ID_MA_FILE_NEW            10
#define ID_MA_FILE_OPEN           11
#define ID_MA_FILE_SAVE           12
#define ID_MA_FILE_SAVE_AS        13
#define ID_MA_FILE_PAGE_SETUP     14
#define ID_MA_FILE_PRINT          15
#define ID_MA_APP_EXIT            16

#define ID_MA_EDIT_UNDO           20
#define ID_MA_EDIT_CUT            21
```

```
#define  ID_MA_EDIT_COPY              22
#define  ID_MA_EDIT_PASTE             23
#define  ID_MA_EDIT_DELETE            24

#define  ID_MA_VIEW_NORMAL            30
#define  ID_MA_VIEW_ZOOM              31

#define  ID_MA_APP_HELP               40
#define  ID_MA_APP_ABOUT              41
```

The naming convention has been chosen not to conflict with that used by Microsoft. We will look at what Microsoft use in some of their header files.

The resource file

The resource file in this example is a plain text file. It is given the same file name prefix as the program source and a file name extension of rc, i.e. c0501.rc is the filename. There is a simple syntax to statements that make up the resource file.

```
include  "menuids.h"

DEFAULTMENU  MENU
{
    POPUP  "&File"
    {
        MENUITEM  "&New\tCntl+N"         ,  ID_MA_FILE_NEW
        MENUITEM  "&Open\tCntl+O"        ,  ID_MA_FILE_OPEN
        MENUITEM  "&Save\tCntl+S"        ,  ID_MA_FILE_SAVE
        MENUITEM  "Save &as"             ,  ID_MA_FILE_SAVE_AS
        MENUITEM  SEPARATOR
        MENUITEM  "Page Set&up"        ,  ID_MA_FILE_PAGE_SETUP
        MENUITEM  "&Print\tCntl+P"     ,  ID_MA_FILE_PRINT
        MENUITEM  SEPARATOR
        MENUITEM  "&Exit"              ,  ID_MA_APP_EXIT
    }
    POPUP  "&Edit"
    {
        MENUITEM  "&Undo\tCntl+Z"      ,  ID_MA_EDIT_UNDO
        MENUITEM  "Cu&t\tCntl+X"       ,  ID_MA_EDIT_CUT
        MENUITEM  "&Copy\tCntl+C"      ,  ID_MA_EDIT_COPY
        MENUITEM  "&Paste\tCntl+V"     ,  ID_MA_EDIT_PASTE
        MENUITEM  "&Delete"            ,  ID_MA_EDIT_DELETE
    }
    POPUP  "&View"
```

```
   {
      MENUITEM  "&Normal"                 ,  ID_MA_VIEW_NORMAL
      MENUITEM  "&Zoom"                   ,  ID_MA_VIEW_ZOOM
   }
  POPUP  "&Help"
   {
      MENUITEM  "&Help"                   ,  ID_MA_APP_HELP
      MENUITEM  "&About"                  ,  ID_MA_APP_ABOUT
   }
}

DEFAULTMENU ACCELERATORS
{
    "N",  ID_MA_FILE_NEW,      VIRTKEY,CONTROL
    "O",  ID_MA_FILE_OPEN,     VIRTKEY,CONTROL
    "S",  ID_MA_FILE_SAVE,     VIRTKEY,CONTROL
    "P",  ID_MA_FILE_PRINT,    VIRTKEY,CONTROL
    "Z",  ID_MA_EDIT_UNDO,     VIRTKEY,CONTROL
    "X",  ID_MA_EDIT_CUT,      VIRTKEY,CONTROL
    "C",  ID_MA_EDIT_COPY,     VIRTKEY,CONTROL
    "V",  ID_MA_EDIT_PASTE,    VIRTKEY,CONTROL
}
```

DEFAULTMENU is the name of the menu. It is used twice. The first identifies the menus, and the second identifies the short cut or accelerator keys. This name will also be used in the C++ source file.

We use { and } to bracket sections.

We have four pop-up menus. These will appear on the windows menu bar.

Within each of these we have MENUITEMs. Each menu item has some associated text and activation mechanism. Some of the menu items have short cut keys as well as the standard activation mechanism. Each menu also has an associated menu name and hence menu ID.

The & character is used to indicate what ALT key will activate the menu item. We also see the use of the SEPARATOR menu item to put a bar between sections of the menus.

Finally we have the ACCELERATOR section where we define the short cut key combinations.

The C++ source file

```
#include  <afxwin.h>
#include  "menuids.h"

class CMainWindow : public CFrameWnd
{
```

```cpp
public :
    CMainWindow();

    afx_msg void OnNew();
    afx_msg void OnOpen();
    afx_msg void OnSave();
    afx_msg void OnSaveas();
    afx_msg void OnPageSetup();
    afx_msg void OnPrint();
    afx_msg void OnExit();

    afx_msg void OnUndo();
    afx_msg void OnCut();
    afx_msg void OnCopy();
    afx_msg void OnPaste();
    afx_msg void OnDelete();

    afx_msg void OnNormal();
    afx_msg void OnZoom();

    afx_msg void OnHelp();
    afx_msg void OnAbout();

    DECLARE_MESSAGE_MAP()
};

CMainWindow::CMainWindow()
{
    Create(  NULL ,
             " Minimal Menu program " ,
             WS_OVERLAPPEDWINDOW ,
             rectDefault ,
             NULL ,
             "DEFAULTMENU");
    LoadAccelTable("DEFAULTMENU");
}

class CMyApplication : public CWinApp
{
public :
    BOOL InitInstance();
};

BOOL CMyApplication::InitInstance()
{
```

```
    m_pMainWnd = new CMainWindow;
    m_pMainWnd->ShowWindow(m_nCmdShow);
    m_pMainWnd->UpdateWindow();

    return TRUE;
}

BEGIN_MESSAGE_MAP(CMainWindow,CFrameWnd)

    ON_COMMAND(ID_MA_FILE_NEW          ,OnNew)
    ON_COMMAND(ID_MA_FILE_OPEN         ,OnOpen)
    ON_COMMAND(ID_MA_FILE_SAVE         ,OnSave)
    ON_COMMAND(ID_MA_FILE_SAVE_AS      ,OnSaveas)
    ON_COMMAND(ID_MA_FILE_PAGE_SETUP   ,OnPageSetup)
    ON_COMMAND(ID_MA_FILE_PRINT        ,OnPrint)
    ON_COMMAND(ID_MA_APP_EXIT          ,OnExit)

    ON_COMMAND(ID_MA_EDIT_UNDO         ,OnUndo)
    ON_COMMAND(ID_MA_EDIT_CUT          ,OnCut)
    ON_COMMAND(ID_MA_EDIT_COPY         ,OnCopy)
    ON_COMMAND(ID_MA_EDIT_PASTE        ,OnPaste)
    ON_COMMAND(ID_MA_EDIT_DELETE       ,OnDelete)

    ON_COMMAND(ID_MA_VIEW_NORMAL       ,OnNormal)
    ON_COMMAND(ID_MA_VIEW_ZOOM         ,OnZoom)

    ON_COMMAND(ID_MA_APP_HELP          ,OnHelp)
    ON_COMMAND(ID_MA_APP_ABOUT         ,OnAbout)

END_MESSAGE_MAP()

afx_msg void CMainWindow::OnNew()
{ MessageBox("New","New"); }

afx_msg void CMainWindow::OnOpen()
{ MessageBox("Open","Open"); }

afx_msg void CMainWindow::OnSave()
{ MessageBox("Save","Save"); }

afx_msg void CMainWindow::OnSaveas()
{ MessageBox("Saveas","Saveas"); }

afx_msg void CMainWindow::OnPageSetup()
{ MessageBox("PageSetup","PageSetup"); }
```

```
afx_msg void CMainWindow::OnPrint()
{  MessageBox("Print","Print");}

afx_msg void CMainWindow::OnExit()
{  MessageBox("Exit","Exit");}

afx_msg void CMainWindow::OnUndo()
{  MessageBox("Undo","Undo");}

afx_msg void CMainWindow::OnCut()
{  MessageBox("Cut","Cut");}

afx_msg void CMainWindow::OnCopy()
{  MessageBox("Copy","Copy");}

afx_msg void CMainWindow::OnPaste()
{  MessageBox("Paste","Paste");}

afx_msg void CMainWindow::OnDelete()
{  MessageBox("Delete","Delete");}

afx_msg void CMainWindow::OnNormal()
{  MessageBox("Normal","Normal");}

afx_msg void CMainWindow::OnZoom()
{  MessageBox("Zoom","Zoom");}

afx_msg void CMainWindow::OnHelp()
{  MessageBox("Help","Help");}

afx_msg void CMainWindow::OnAbout()
{  MessageBox("About","About");}

CMyApplication Application;
```

Running the program

Copy the source for one of the earlier examples and use this as a basis for the current example. Copy with a new name and directory.

Start up Visual Studio and repeat the steps taken in the earlier examples.

- **File menu | New project**.
  - Choose Win 32 application. Type in the project name and location. Take care to use the name and location used in the copy.
  - Choose the project type: An empty project.
- **Project menu | Add to project | Files**.
  - You should be in the directory specified above and the copied source file should be there. Click on the file.
  - Repeat for the resource file.

Now modify the program in the editor window.
When you have finished do the following:

- Project menu:
  - Settings.

Ensure that under the General tab Use MFC in a Shared Dll is chosen under Microsoft Foundation Classes.

Now choose the Build menu and select Execute filename.exe. This will then compile, link and run the program. You should see something like the window below if there are no compilation or linker errors.

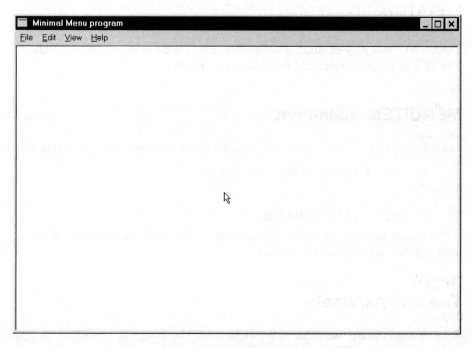

Figure 5.1 Program running.

The window can be minimised, maximised and closed as before. The menus can be activated. The end result is a simple message box. Let us now look at some of the lines of the source files in more depth.

The resource file

The following resources share a common syntax:

- Menus.
- Dialog boxes.
- List boxes.
- Check boxes.
- Edit boxes.
- Radio buttons.
- Combo boxes.

We will look in some depth at this syntax in this chapter, and cover it more briefly when looking at the other controls.

MENU statement

The MENU resource-definition statement specifies the contents of a menu resource. This defines the appearance and functionality of a menu.

MENUITEM statement

The MENUITEM resource-definition statement creates a menu item. The syntax is:

- MENUITEM text, result, [[option list]]

and

- MENUITEM SEPARATOR

The second form inserts a dividing bar between two active menu items. We look at each parameter of the statement in turn.

The text parameter

A string that indicates the name of the menu item. The string can contain the escape characters \t and \a. The \t character inserts a tab in the string and is used to align text in columns. Tab characters should be used only in menus, not in menu bars.

(For information on menus, see POPUP Resource.) The \a character aligns all text that follows it flush right to the menu bar or pop-up menu.

The result parameter

A number that specifies the result generated when the user selects the menu item. This parameter takes an integer value. Menu-item results are always integers; when the user clicks the menu-item name, the result is sent to the window that owns the menu.

The option list parameter

This parameter specifies the appearance of the menu item. This optional parameter takes one or more redefined menu options, separated by commas or spaces. The menu options are as follows:

- CHECKED Menu item has a check mark next to it.
- GRAYED Menu item is initially inactive and appears on the menu in gray or a lightened shade of the menu-text colour. This option cannot be used with the INACTIVE option.
- HELP Identifies a help item.
- INACTIVE Menu item is displayed but it cannot be selected. This option cannot be used with the GRAYED option.
- MENUBARBREAK Same as MENUBREAK except that for pop-up menus, it separates the new column from the old column with a vertical line.
- MENUBREAK Places the menu item on a new line for static menu-bar items. For menus, it places the menu item in a new column with no dividing line between the columns.

POPUP resource

The POPUP resource-definition statement creates a menu item that can contain menu items and sub-menus. The syntax is:

- POPUP text, [[option list]]   {   item-definitions   .   .   . }

We will look at each parameter in turn.

The text parameter

A string that contains the name of the menu. This string must be enclosed in double quotation marks (").

The option list parameter

This parameter specifies redefined menu options that specify the appearance of the menu item. This optional parameter can be one or more of the following:

- CHECKED Menu item has a check mark next to it. This option is not valid for a top-level menu.
- GRAYED Menu item is initially inactive and appears on the menu in gray or a lightened shade of the menu-text colour. This option cannot be used with the INACTIVE option.
- HELP Identifies a help item.
- INACTIVE Menu item is displayed but it cannot be selected. This option cannot be used with the GRAYED option.
- MENUBARBREAK Same as MENUBREAK except that for pop-up menus, it separates the new column from the old column with a vertical line.
- MENUBREAK Places the menu item on a new line for static menu-bar items. For menus, it places the menu item in a new column with no dividing line between the columns.

The ACCELERATORS statement

This defines the short cut keys for the program. These have been chosen to conform to the naming convention used by Microsoft and found increasingly in most Windows applications. This helps minimise the learning curve required for your program or application.

The C++ source file

```
#include <afxwin.h>
#include "menuids.h"
```

Standard include files. The first contains the MFC support information we require. The second contains details of the menu items we will be handling.

```
class CMainWindow : public CFrameWnd
{
public :
    CMainWindow();

    afx_msg void OnNew();
    afx_msg void OnOpen();
    afx_msg void OnSave();
    afx_msg void OnSaveas();
    afx_msg void OnPageSetup();
    afx_msg void OnPrint();
    afx_msg void OnExit();

    afx_msg void OnUndo();
    afx_msg void OnCut();
    afx_msg void OnCopy();
    afx_msg void OnPaste();
    afx_msg void OnDelete();

    afx_msg void OnNormal();
    afx_msg void OnZoom();

    afx_msg void OnHelp();
    afx_msg void OnAbout();

    DECLARE_MESSAGE_MAP()
};
```

This is the basic window for our application derived from CFrameWnd. We then have the function prototypes for the message handlers for each of the menu items we will use in this application.

```
Create( NULL ,
        " Minimal Menu program " ,
        WS_OVERLAPPEDWINDOW ,
        rectDefault ,
        NULL ,
        "DEFAULTMENU"); }
```

Create the window for our application. In the first example we only provided two arguments to this function. In this example we override the defaults. Let us look at each parameter in turn.

WS_OVERLAPPEDWINDOW

Windows can come in a variety of styles. Specifying this parameter creates an overlapped window with the following attributes:

- WS_OVERLAPPED – The window has a caption and a border.
- WS_CAPTION – The window has a title bar.
- WS_SYSMENU – The window has a menu in the title bar.
- WS_THICKFRAME – The window has a thick frame that can be used to size the window.
- WS_MINIMIZEBOX – The window has a minimize box.
- WS_MAXIMIZEBOX – The window has a maximise box.

This is a common style to choose.

```
rectDefault
```

Allows windows to choose the initial size and position.

```
NULL
```

Specifies the parent window of this frame window. This parameter is NULL for top-level frame windows.

```
"DEFAULTMENU"
```

Identifies the name of the menu resource to be used with the window. We obviously use the same name for the menus as we used in the resource file.

```
LoadAccelTable("DEFAULTMENU");
```

We load the accelerator table. Note that we use same name for the table as we used in the resource file.

```cpp
class CMyApplication : public CWinApp
{
public :
    BOOL InitInstance();
};

BOOL CMyApplication::InitInstance()
{
    m_pMainWnd = new CMainWindow;
    m_pMainWnd->ShowWindow(m_nCmdShow);
    m_pMainWnd->UpdateWindow();
    return TRUE;
}
```

Here we derive our applications class from CWinApp and now in InitInstance we create the window, make it visible and cause a repaint if we do anything to the window.

```
BEGIN_MESSAGE_MAP(CMainWindow,CFrameWnd)

  ON_COMMAND( ID_MA_FILE_NEW     ,   OnNew)
  ON_COMMAND( ID_MA_FILE_OPEN    ,   OnOpen)
  ON_COMMAND( ID_MA_FILE_SAVE    ,   OnSave)
    stuff deleted
END_MESSAGE_MAP()
```

This is the message map for our application.

```
ON_COMMAND( id, memberFxn )
```

Parameters:

- id – The command ID.
- memberFxn – The name of the message-handler function to which the command is mapped.

This macro is usually inserted in a message map manually as in this case or automatically by ClassWizard. It indicates which function will handle a command message from a command user-interface object such as a menu item or toolbar button.

When a command-target object receives a windows WM_COMMAND message with the specified ID, ON_COMMAND will call the member function memberFxn to handle the message.

```
afx_msg void CMainWindow::OnNew()
{
  MessageBox("New","New");
}

afx_msg void CMainWindow::OnOpen()
{
  MessageBox("Open","Open");
}
stuff deleted
```

These are the functions that actually handle the menu choices. In this example we only invoke a message box. A message box is a very simple way of telling the user that something has happened. The function prototype is given below.

```
CWnd::MessageBox
int MessageBox(    LPCTSTR lpszText,
                   LPCTSTR lpszCaption = NULL,
                   UINT nType = MB_OK );
```

The return value specifies the outcome of the function. It is 0 if there is not enough memory to create the message box.

The three parameters are:

- lpszText: Points to a CString object or null-terminated string containing the message to be displayed.
- lpszCaption: Points to a CString object or null-terminated string to be used for the message-box caption. If lpszCaption is NULL, the default caption "Error" is used.
- nType: Specifies the contents and behaviour of the message box.

The default behaviour is MB_OK. Other options include:

- MB_ABORTRETRYIGNORE – The message box contains three pushbuttons: Abort, Retry, and Ignore.
- MB_OK – The message box contains one pushbutton: OK.
- MB_OKCANCEL – The message box contains two pushbuttons: OK and Cancel.
- MB_RETRYCANCEL – The message box contains two pushbuttons: Retry and Cancel.
- MB_YESNO – The message box contains two pushbuttons: Yes and No.
- MB_YESNOCANCEL – The message box contains three pushbuttons: Yes, No, and Cancel.

It creates and displays a window that contains an application-supplied message and caption, plus a combination of the predefined icons and pushbuttons described in the Message-Box Styles list. Use the global function AfxMessageBox instead of this member function to implement a message box in your application.

Summary

Adding menus involves the following stages:

- Creating the menu ID file that gives the menus names and associated IDs. Care must be taken here not to choose names used internally by Developer Studio. We will look at this in more detail below.
- Create a resource file that has the menus and accelerators keys you want. Choose short cut keys that are consistent with those used by Microsoft.
- Write the associated functions for each of the menu items in your program.

Menus are an essential part of most windows programs.

Wizards and resource editors

So far we have directly programmed our examples. This has been done to minimise the amount of information you are required to learn. It is possible to use the wizards and resource editors and we will look briefly at using these tools now.

Wizards

Open a new project. Chose:

- MFC AppWizard (DLL)

from the project options. Just accept all of the default options. When you have finished you should have a screen similar to the one below.

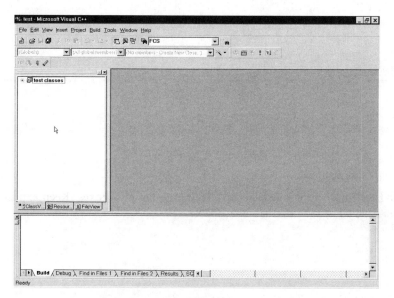

Figure 5.2 Exploring Developer Studio.

The first thing of interest is the Work space window. There are three tabs shown:

- Class View.
- Resource View.
- File View.

Start with the Class tab. You should see a screen similar to the one below:

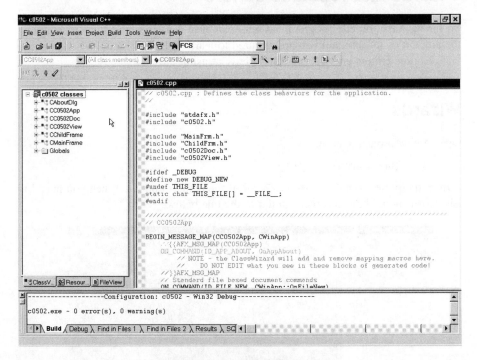

Figure 5.3 Class view.

Expand the information available by clicking on the plus boxes. Keep expanding until you have all of the information available.

Repeat for the File tabs. You should see a screen similar to the one below:

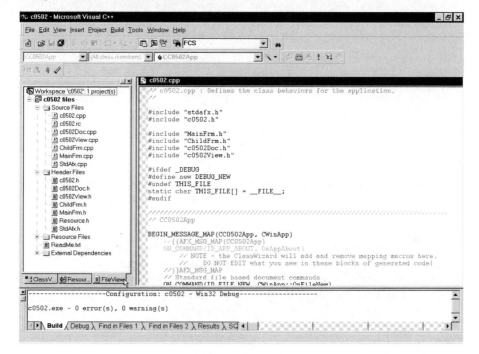

Figure 5.4 *File view*

As you can see the Wizard provides a considerable amount of code. Some twenty or so files are created. One of the files created is:

- readme.txt

and excerpts from this file are shown below.

. . .

```
This file contains a summary of what you will find in
each of the files that make up your c0502 application.
```

```
C0502.dsp
```

```
    This file (the project file) contains information at
    the project level and is used to build a single
    project or subproject. Other users can share the
    project (.dsp) file, but they should export the
    makefiles locally.
```

```
c0502.h
```

```
    This is the main header file for the application. It
```

includes other project specific headers (including
Resource.h) and declares the C0502App application
class.

c0502.cpp
   This is the main application source file that
   contains the application class CC0502App.

c0502.rc
   This is a listing of all of the Microsoft Windows
   resources that the program uses. It includes
   the icons, bitmaps, and cursors
   that are stored in the RES subdirectory. This file
   can be directly edited in Microsoft Visual C++.

c0502.clw
   This file contains information used by ClassWizard
   to edit existing classes or add new classes.
   ClassWizard also uses this file to store
   information needed to create and
   edit message maps and dialog data maps and to create
   prototype member functions.

res\c0502.ico
   This is an icon file, which is used as the
   application's icon. This icon is included by
   the main resource file c0502.rc.

res\c0502.rc2
   This file contains resources that are not edited by
   Microsoft Visual C++. You should place all
   resources not editable by the resource editor
   in this file.
...
For the main frame window:

MainFrm.h, MainFrm.cpp
   These files contain the frame class CMainFrame,
   which is derived from CMDIFrameWnd and controls
   all MDI frame features.

res\Toolbar.bmp

   This bitmap file is used to create tiled images
   for the toolbar. The initial toolbar and status

bar are constructed in the CMainFrame class.
Edit this toolbar bitmap using the resource editor,
and update the IDR_MAINFRAME TOOLBAR array
in c0502.rc to add toolbar buttons.
...
For the child frame window:

ChildFrm.h, ChildFrm.cpp
    These files define and implement the
    CChildFrame class, which supports the child
    windows in an MDI application.
...
AppWizard creates one document type and one view:

c0502Doc.h, c0502Doc.cpp - the document
    These files contain your CC0502Doc class. Edit these
    files to add your special document data and to
    Implement file saving and loading
    (via CC0502Doc::Serialize).

c0502View.h, c0502View.cpp - the view of the document
    These files contain your CC0502View class.
    CC0502View objects are used to view CC0502Doc
    objects.

res\c0502Doc.ico
    This is an icon file, which is used as the icon for
    MDI child windows for the CC0502Doc class.
    This icon is included by the main resource file
c0502.rc.
...
Other standard files:

StdAfx.h, StdAfx.cpp

    These files are used to build a precompiled
    header (PCH) file named c0502.pch and a
    precompiled types file named
    StdAfx.obj.

Resource.h

    This is the standard header file, which defines new
    resource IDs. Microsoft Visual C++ reads and updates
    this file.

. . .

There is rather too much to assimilate. You must develop a basic grounding first before using the various Wizards provided.

There are two other files to look.

The c0503.rc file

This is the resource file and can be found in your work directory.

The afxres.h file

This is one of the afx include files, and can be found in:

• C:\Program Files\Microsoft Visual Studio\VC98\Include

or similar, depending on how you installed Developer Studio.

The latter file contains a large number of #DEFINEs and you should examine the file carefully to see the naming convention adopted by Microsoft.

The resource editor

A resource editor is provided in Developer Studio. It supports working with the following resource types:

• Accelerators.
• Bitmaps.
• Cursors.
• Dialog boxes.
• HTML.
• Icons.
• Menus.
• String Tables.
• Toolbars.
• Versions.

You need to know what is happening behind the scenes to be able to use the resource editors effectively. You also have to write the C++ code to go with the resources.

6

Controls: Dialog Boxes

'Plenty of practice' he went on repeating, all the time that Alice was getting him on his feet again. 'Plenty of practice.'

Lewis Carroll, The White Knight in Alice Through the Looking Glass.

Overview

One of the most widely used user interface features to a windows program is a dialog box. There is a coverage of using a menu to activate the dialog box, and simple use of message boxes to show what is happening.

Dialog boxes

In the previous chapters we have seen how to handle user interaction with a windows program through the keyboard, mouse and menus. In this and the following chapter we will look at using a simple dialog box. We will use message boxes again to show what is happening. We will do this by actually programming the dialog boxes and controls.

In the MFC framework, a dialog box has two components:

- A dialog-template resource that defines the dialog box's controls and placement. The dialog resource stores a dialog template from which windows creates the dialog window and displays it. The template specifies the dialog box's characteristics, including its size, location, style, and the types and positions of the dialog box's controls. You normally use a dialog template stored as a resource.

- A dialog class, derived from CDialog, to provide a programmatic interface for managing the dialog box. A dialog box is a window and will be attached to a windows window when visible.

When the dialog window is created, the dialog-template resource is used as a template for creating child window controls for the dialog box.

The application

This program is made up of three files. The three files are:

- An include file that is used within both the resource file and the program. This file contains macro definitions of the menu ID values.
- The resource file. Menus and dialog boxes are both resources. They are maintained separately to your program and are compiled during the build process and added to your executable file. You must add the resource file to your project.
- The C++ source file or program. This is the program source.

We will look at each file in turn.

The menu ID file

```
#define  ID_MENU_DIALOG     100
#define  ID_A_EXIT          200
#define  ID_A_HELP          210
#define  ID_DIALOG_START    300
#define  ID_DIALOG_STOP     310
#define  ID_DIALOG_CON      320
#define  ID_DIALOG_EXIT     330
```

We will provide access to the dialog box through a menu.

The resource file

The syntax of the commands in this file are similar to those from the previous chapter.

```
#include  <afxres.h>
#include  "menuids.h"
```

```
ControlExampleMenu MENU
{
   POPUP "&Dialog"
   {
     MENUITEM "&Activate Dialog Box" ,ID_MENU_DIALOG
     MENUITEM "&Exit"                ,ID_A_EXIT
   }
     MENUITEM "&Help"                 ,ID_A_HELP
}

DialogExample DIALOG 10,10,200,100

CAPTION "Control Example - Simple Dialog Box"

STYLE DS_MODALFRAME | WS_CAPTION | WS_POPUP | WS_SYSMENU
{
   DEFPUSHBUTTON "Start" , ID_DIALOG_START , 30, 20, 30,
20,
     BS_DEFPUSHBUTTON |
     WS_TABSTOP

   PUSHBUTTON "Stop" , ID_DIALOG_STOP , 70, 20, 30, 20,
     WS_CHILD |
     WS_TABSTOP |
     WS_VISIBLE

   PUSHBUTTON "Continue" , ID_DIALOG_CON ,110, 20, 30,
20,
     WS_CHILD |
     WS_TABSTOP |
     WS_VISIBLE
   PUSHBUTTON "Exit" , ID_DIALOG_EXIT , 30, 50, 30, 20,
     WS_CHILD |
     WS_TABSTOP |
     WS_VISIBLE
}
```

The C++ source file

```
#include <afxwin.h>
#include "menuids.h"

class CMainWindow : public CFrameWnd
{
```

```
public :
   CMainWindow();

   afx_msg void OnMenuDialog();
   afx_msg void OnAppExit();
   afx_msg void OnAppHelp();

   DECLARE_MESSAGE_MAP()
};

CMainWindow::CMainWindow()
{
   Create(  NULL ,
            " Control Example - Simple dialog box " ,
            WS_OVERLAPPEDWINDOW ,
            rectDefault ,
            NULL ,
            "ControlExampleMenu");
}

class CMyApplication : public CWinApp
{
public :
   BOOL InitInstance();
};

BOOL CMyApplication::InitInstance()
{
   m_pMainWnd = new CMainWindow;
   m_pMainWnd->ShowWindow(m_nCmdShow);
   m_pMainWnd->UpdateWindow();

   return TRUE;
}
class CDialogExample : public CDialog
{
public :
   CDialogExample(   char *DialogName ,
                     CWnd *Owner)
   : CDialog(  DialogName,
               Owner) {}

   afx_msg void DialogStart();
   afx_msg void DialogStop();
   afx_msg void DialogCon();
```

```
   afx_msg void DialogExit();

   DECLARE_MESSAGE_MAP()
};

BEGIN_MESSAGE_MAP(CMainWindow,CFrameWnd)

   ON_COMMAND( ID_MENU_DIALOG , OnMenuDialog )
   ON_COMMAND( ID_A_EXIT       ,  OnAppExit)
   ON_COMMAND( ID_A_HELP       ,  OnAppHelp)

END_MESSAGE_MAP()

afx_msg void CMainWindow::OnMenuDialog()
{
   CDialogExample dialog("DialogExample",this);
   dialog.DoModal();
}

afx_msg void CMainWindow::OnAppExit()
{
   int reply;
   reply=MessageBox(" Exit?","Exit",MB_YESNO);
   if (reply==IDYES) SendMessage(WM_CLOSE);
}

afx_msg void CMainWindow::OnAppHelp()
{
 MessageBox("Minimal Dialog example","Help");
}

BEGIN_MESSAGE_MAP(CDialogExample,CDialog)
   ON_COMMAND(ID_DIALOG_START , DialogStart)
   ON_COMMAND(ID_DIALOG_STOP ,  DialogStop)
   ON_COMMAND(ID_DIALOG_CON    , DialogCon)
   ON_COMMAND(ID_DIALOG_EXIT ,  DialogExit)
END_MESSAGE_MAP()

afx_msg void CDialogExample::DialogStart()
{
   MessageBox("Start"," pressed");
}
afx_msg void CDialogExample::DialogStop()
{
   MessageBox("Stop"," pressed");
```

```
}
afx_msg void CDialogExample::DialogCon()
{
    MessageBox("Continue"," pressed");
}
afx_msg void CDialogExample::DialogExit()
{
    int reply;
    reply=MessageBox(" Exit?","Exit",MB_YESNO);
    if (reply==IDYES) SendMessage(WM_CLOSE);
}

CMyApplication Application;
```

Running the example

Create a new sub-directory for this project. Use Notepad to create the menu ID file and resource file. Copy over one of the old C++ source files to use as a skeleton for this example. Start up Visual Studio and take the following steps to compile link and run the program:

- **File menu I New project:**
    - Choose Win 32 application: Type in the project name and location. Take care to use the name and location used in the copy.
    - Choose the project type: An empty project.
- **Project menu I Add to project I Files;.**
    - You should be in the directory specified above and the copied source file should be there. Click on the file.
    - Repeat for the resource file.

Now modify the program in the editor window.

When you have finished ensure that under the Project menu and settings option General tab:

- Use MFC in a Shared DLL.

is chosen under Microsoft Foundation Classes.

Now choose the Build menu and select Execute filename.exe. This will then compile, link and run the program. You should see something like the window below if there are no compilation or linker errors:

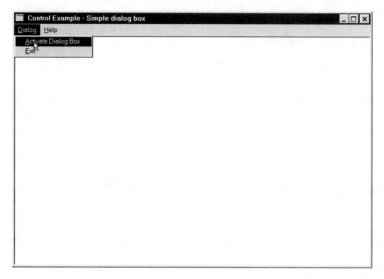

Figure 6.1 *Dialog example.*

Choosing the Dialog menu option followed by the dialog box brings up a window with four buttons.

Let us now look at each file in turn.

The menu ID file

This file contains the macro definitions of the menu IDs and dialog box IDs.

The resource file

This file contains the menu and dialog box information. We will only look at the dialog box information here as the previous example introduced menus. We include afxres.h as we need access to DS_MODALFRAME.

```
DialogExample DIALOG 10,10,200,100
```

Identify the resource as a dialog box, provide a name and give x and y initial values and a width and height in pixels. The name will be used in the C++ source to link to the correct resources.

```
CAPTION "Control Example - Simple dialog box"
```

Prove a caption for the dialog box.

```
STYLE DS_MODALFRAME | WS_CAPTION | WS_POPUP | WS_SYSMENU
```

Choose the style of the box.

```
DS_MODALFRAME
```

This creates a dialog box with a modal dialog box frame that can be combined with a title bar and window menu by specifying the WS_CAPTION and WS_SYSMENU styles.

```
WS_CAPTION
```

This creates a window that has a title bar (implies the WS_BORDER style).

```
WS_POPUP
```

This creates a pop-up window. It cannot be used with the WS_CHILD style.

```
WS_SYSMENU
```

This creates a window that has a window menu in its title bar. Used only for windows with title bars. If used with a child window, this style creates a close button instead of a window menu.

```
DEFPUSHBUTTON "Start" , ID_DIALOG_START ,30,20,30,20,
```

Identifies this as the default button, with Start caption, linked to the ID_DIALOG_START ID, x=30 and y=20 initial position with width=30 and height=20.

```
BS_DEFPUSHBUTTON |
```

This creates a button that has a heavy black border. The user can select this button by pressing the ENTER key. This style enables the user to quickly select the most likely option (the default option).

```
WS_TABSTOP
```

This specifies one of any number of controls through which the user can move by using the TAB key. The TAB key moves the user to the next control specified by the WS_TABSTOP style. This style is valid only for controls.

```
PUSHBUTTON "Stop" , ID_DIALOG_STOP , 70, 20, 30, 20,
```

The PUSHBUTTON resource-definition statement creates a push-button control. The control is a round-cornered rectangle containing the given text. The text is centred in the control. The control sends a message to its parent whenever the user chooses the control.

```
WS_CHILD |
```

This creates a child window. It cannot be used with the WS_POPUP style. The | character is used to separate the options.

```
WS_VISIBLE
```

This creates a window that is initially visible. This applies to overlapping and pop-up windows. For overlapping windows, the y parameter is used as a parameter for the ShowWindow function. The others are similar to the above.

The C++ source file

```
#include <afxwin.h>
#include "menuids.h"
```

Standard include files.

```
class CMainWindow : public CFrameWnd
{
public :
    CMainWindow();

    afx_msg void OnMenuDialog();
    afx_msg void OnAppExit();
    afx_msg void OnAppHelp();

    DECLARE_MESSAGE_MAP()
};

CMainWindow::CMainWindow()
{
    Create( NULL ,
            " Control Example - Simple dialog box " ,
            WS_OVERLAPPEDWINDOW ,
            rectDefault ,
            NULL ,
            "ControlExampleMenu");
}
```

The code for the main application window, with three message handlers, and the same constructor as in the previous example, inheriting from CFrameWnd.

```
class CMyApplication : public CWinApp
{
public :
   BOOL InitInstance();
};

BOOL CMyApplication::InitInstance()
{
   m_pMainWnd = new CMainWindow;
   m_pMainWnd->ShowWindow(m_nCmdShow);
   m_pMainWnd->UpdateWindow();

   return TRUE;
}
```

The code for the application with the same override of InitInstance as the previous example, inheriting from CWinApp.

```
class CDialogExample : public CDialog
```

The start of the code for the dialog box, inheriting from the CDialog class.

```
public :
   CDialogExample(    char *DialogName ,
                         CWnd *Owner)
    : CDialog(        DialogName,
                      Owner) {}
```

The dialog box constructor in turn calls the base class constructor. See the OnMenuDialog routine for details of the dialog name.

```
   afx_msg void DialogStart();
   afx_msg void DialogStop();
   afx_msg void DialogCon();
   afx_msg void DialogExit();
```

Message handlers for the dialog box.

```
   DECLARE_MESSAGE_MAP()

BEGIN_MESSAGE_MAP(CMainWindow,CFrameWnd)

   ON_COMMAND( ID_MENU_DIALOG , OnMenuDialog )
   ON_COMMAND( ID_A_EXIT       ,  OnAppExit)
   ON_COMMAND( ID_A_HELP       ,  OnAppHelp)

END_MESSAGE_MAP()
```

Message map for the main window.

```
afx_msg void CMainWindow::OnMenuDialog()
```

Message handler.

```
CDialogExample dialog("DialogExample",this);
```

Identifies the name of the dialog (as in the resource file) and the window owner.

```
dialog.DoModal();
```

You call this member function to invoke the modal dialog box and return the dialog-box result when done. This member function handles all interaction with the user while the dialog box is active: the user cannot interact with other windows until the dialog box is closed.

```
afx_msg void CMainWindow::OnAppExit()
{
    int reply;
    reply=MessageBox(" Exit?","Exit",MB_YESNO);
    if (reply==IDYES) SendMessage(WM_CLOSE);
}
```

Message handler. In this example we use the fact that the MessageBox function returns an integer value and we compare the result with the predefined value for IDYES. We then explicitly close the message box.

```
afx_msg void CMainWindow::OnAppHelp()
{ MessageBox("Minimal Dialog example","Help"); }
```

Message handler.

```
BEGIN_MESSAGE_MAP(CDialogExample,CDialog)
    ON_COMMAND(ID_DIALOG_START ,   DialogStart)
    ON_COMMAND(ID_DIALOG_STOP  ,   DialogStop)
    ON_COMMAND(ID_DIALOG_CON       ,  DialogCon)
    ON_COMMAND(ID_DIALOG_EXIT  ,   DialogExit)
END_MESSAGE_MAP()
```

Message map for the dialog box.

```
afx_msg void CDialogExample::DialogStart()
{  MessageBox("Start"," pressed"); }
```

Message handler.

```
afx_msg void CDialogExample::DialogStop()
{  MessageBox("Stop"," pressed");}
```

Message handler.

```
afx_msg void CDialogExample::DialogCon()
{  MessageBox("Continue"," pressed");}
```

Message handler.

```
afx_msg void CDialogExample::DialogExit()
{
    int reply;
    reply=MessageBox(" Exit?","Exit",MB_YESNO);
    if (reply==IDYES) SendMessage(WM_CLOSE);
}
```

Message handler. We again use the fact that MessageBox returns an integer result and use this to close the message box. We compare against the predefined value for IDYES and explicitly close the message box.

```
CMyApplication Application;
```

Create the application.

Summary

This example combined a menu bar, a dialog box and message boxes. An examination of windows programs shows that they are typified by the above user interface features.

You need to:

- Add the menu IDs to the ID file.
- Define the appearance of the both the menus and the push-buttons in the resource file.
- Write the code to handle the both the menu selections and which buttons have been selected.

We also see the importance of the use of three files that make up the overall application. These are:

- The menu ID file
- The resource file
- The C++ source file

This enables the application to be worked on in stages. This becomes a necessity as we become familiar with the MFC library and want to add more and more user interface features to our applications.

7

Controls: List Boxes

'We have to go to another language in order to think clearly about the problem.'

Samuel R. Delany, Babel-17.

Overview

A list box presents the user with the opportunity to choose from a list of items. They are used quite heavily in windows applications.

List boxes

We have now seen how to handle user interaction via:

- The keyboard.
- The mouse.
- Menus.
- Dialog boxes.
- Message boxes.

In this chapter we will look at list boxes. These are used when the user can choose from several items.

There are two main ways of making list box selections. The first is by clicking on the item in the list. The second is to make a selection and using OK and Cancel buttons. This example will include both.

The application

This program is made up of three files. The three files are:

- The include file that is used within both the resource file and the program. This file contains macro definitions of the menu ID values.
- The resource file. This example has both menus and a list box.
- The C++ source file or program. This is the program source.

We will look at each file in turn.

The menu ID file

```
#define ID_MENU_DIALOG      100

#define ID_A_EXIT           200
#define ID_A_HELP           210

#define ID_LISTBOX          300
#define ID_SELECTAGE        310
```

The resource file

```
#include <afxres.h>
#include "menuids.h"

ControlExampleMenu MENU
{
   POPUP "&Dialog"
   {
     MENUITEM "&Activate Dialog Box"   ,  ID_MENU_DIALOG
     MENUITEM "&Exit"                  ,  ID_A_EXIT
   }
   MENUITEM "&Help"                    ,  ID_A_HELP
}

DialogExample DIALOG 10,10,200,120

CAPTION "Control Example - List box"

STYLE DS_MODALFRAME | WS_CAPTION | WS_POPUP | WS_SYSMENU
{
   LISTBOX ID_LISTBOX , 100 , 10 , 50 , 50 ,
```

```
          LBS_NOTIFY   |
          WS_BORDER         |
          WS_CHILD     |
          WS_TABSTOP   |
          WS_VISIBLE   |
          WS_VSCROLL

      PUSHBUTTON "Select age range: " , ID_SELECTAGE ,
          10 , 10 , 80 ,15,
          WS_CHILD     |
          WS_TABSTOP   |
          WS_VISIBLE

}
```

The C++ source file

```cpp
#include <afxwin.h>
#include "menuids.h"

class CMainWindow : public CFrameWnd
{
public :
    CMainWindow();

    afx_msg void OnMenuDialog();
    afx_msg void OnAppExit();
    afx_msg void OnAppHelp();

    DECLARE_MESSAGE_MAP()
};

CMainWindow::CMainWindow()
{
    Create(NULL ,
        " Control Example - List box" ,
        WS_OVERLAPPEDWINDOW ,
        rectDefault ,
        NULL ,
        "ControlExampleMenu");
}

class CMyApplication : public CWinApp
{
```

```
public :
   BOOL InitInstance();
};

BOOL CMyApplication::InitInstance()
{
   m_pMainWnd = new CMainWindow;
   m_pMainWnd->ShowWindow(m_nCmdShow);
   m_pMainWnd->UpdateWindow();

   return TRUE;
}

BEGIN_MESSAGE_MAP(CMainWindow,CFrameWnd)

   ON_COMMAND( ID_MENU_DIALOG    ,   OnMenuDialog)
   ON_COMMAND( ID_A_EXIT             ,   OnAppExit)
   ON_COMMAND( ID_A_HELP            ,   OnAppHelp)

END_MESSAGE_MAP()

class CDialogExample : public CDialog
{
public :
   CDialogExample(char *DialogName ,
      CWnd *Owner)
      : CDialog(DialogName,
      Owner) {}

   BOOL OnInitDialog();

   afx_msg void OnSelect();

   DECLARE_MESSAGE_MAP()
};

afx_msg void CMainWindow::OnMenuDialog()
{
   CDialogExample dialog("DialogExample",this);
   dialog.DoModal();
}

afx_msg void CMainWindow::OnAppExit()
{
   int reply;
```

```
      reply=MessageBox(" Exit?","Exit",MB_YESNO);
      if (reply==IDYES) SendMessage(WM_CLOSE);
}

afx_msg void CMainWindow::OnAppHelp()
{  MessageBox("Dialog example ","Help");}

BEGIN_MESSAGE_MAP(CDialogExample,CDialog)
   ON_COMMAND( ID_LISTBOX     , OnSelect      )
   ON_COMMAND( ID_SELECTAGE   , OnSelect      )
END_MESSAGE_MAP()

BOOL CDialogExample::OnInitDialog()
{
   CDialog::OnInitDialog();

   CListBox *lbptr = (CListBox *)
GetDlgItem(ID_LISTBOX);

   lbptr->AddString(" 0 -  9");
   lbptr->AddString("10 - 19");
   lbptr->AddString("20 - 29");
   lbptr->AddString("30 - 39");
   lbptr->AddString("40 - 49");
   lbptr->AddString("50 - 59");
   lbptr->AddString("60 - 69");
   lbptr->AddString("70 - 79");
   lbptr->AddString("Over 80");

   return true;
}

afx_msg void CDialogExample::OnSelect()
{
   CListBox *lbptr = (CListBox *)
GetDlgItem(ID_LISTBOX);

   char str[10];
   char errormessage[]="None ";

   int i;

   i = lbptr->GetCurSel();

   if (i==LB_ERR)
```

```
{
    MessageBox("Error!","No age selected");
    strcpy(str,errormessage);
}
else
{
    lbptr->GetText(i,str);
    MessageBox(" It worked ",str);
}

    MessageBox(str, "Age range selected");

}

CMyApplication Application;
```

Running the example

Follow the steps used in the previous examples. Choose the menu option and you should then see a window like the one below.

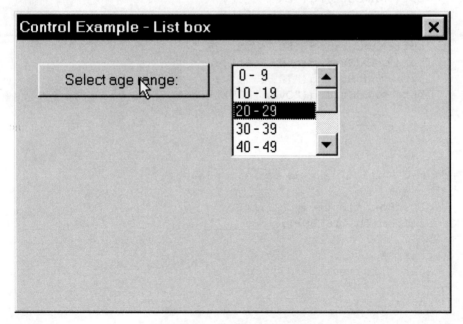

Figure 7.1 List box example.

Let us now look at each file in turn.

The menu ID file

We have access to the list box through a menu.

The resource file

```
DialogExample DIALOG 10,10,200,120
```

Gives the resource a name. This is used in the C++ source file.

```
CAPTION "Control Example - List box"
```

Text that appears when we run the program and activate the dialog box control.

```
STYLE DS_MODALFRAME | WS_CAPTION | WS_POPUP | WS_SYSMENU
```

Styles for the dialog box.

```
LISTBOX ID_LISTBOX , 100 , 10 , 50 , 50 ,
```

Identifies this as a list box resource and defines the layout and size. ID_LISTBOX is the ID that handles the list box.

```
LBS_NOTIFY | WS_BORDER | WS_CHILD | WS_TABSTOP |
WS_VISIBLE | WS_VSCROLL
```

Set the styles for the list box. The new one here is:

```
LBS_NOTIFY
```

and this means that the parent window receives an input message whenever the user clicks or double-clicks a string.

```
PUSHBUTTON "Select age range: " , ID_SELECTAGE ,
     10 , 10 , 80 ,15,
     WS_CHILD    |
     WS_TABSTOP |
     WS_VISIBLE
```

This creates a push-button with text caption and defines the layout and style of the button. ID_SELECTAGE is the ID that handles the selection.

The C++ Source File

We will only look at the new features in this example.

```
BOOL CDialogExample::OnInitDialog()
```

This member function is called in response to the WM_INITDIALOG message. This message is sent to the dialog box during the Create, CreateIndirect, or DoModal calls, which occur immediately before the dialog box is displayed. We override this member function to perform the list box initialisation. The overridden version must first call the base class OnInitDialog but can disregard its return value. You will normally return TRUE from this overridden member function. Windows calls the OnInitDialog function via the standard global dialog-box procedure common to all MFC library dialog boxes, rather than through your message map, so you do not need a message-map entry for this member function.

```
CDialog::OnInitDialog();
```

This must be called before any other processing.

```
CListBox *lbptr = (CListBox *) GetDlgItem(ID_LISTBOX);
```

GetDlgItem returns a pointer to the specified control – ID_LISTBOX. The pointer returned is then cast to the type of control identified by the argument – in this case a list box.

```
lbptr->AddString(" 0 -   9");
lbptr->AddString("10 -  19");
lbptr->AddString("20 -  29");
lbptr->AddString("30 -  39");
lbptr->AddString("40 -  49");
lbptr->AddString("50 -  59");
lbptr->AddString("60 -  69");
lbptr->AddString("70 -  79");
lbptr->AddString("Over 80");
```

Add each string in turn to the list box.

```
afx_msg void CDialogExample::OnSelect()
```

The select event occurs when a menu item has been selected but not yet activated.

```
CListBox *lbptr = (CListBox *) GetDlgItem(ID_LISTBOX);
```

GetDlgItem returns a pointer to the ID_LISTBOX control and the pointer returned is then cast to the type of control identified by the argument.

```
char str[10];
char errormessage[]="None ";
```

Variables that handle the text output to the user.

```
int i;   i = lbptr->GetCurSel();
```

GetCurSel returns the zero-based index of the currently selected item. It is LB_ERR if no item is currently selected or if the list box is a multiple-selection list box. It should not be called for a multiple-selection list box.

```
if (i==LB_ERR)
    {
        MessageBox("Error!","No age selected");
        strcpy(str,errormessage);
    }
```

Handle the case of no selection.

```
else
    {
        lbptr->GetText(i,str);
        MessageBox(" It worked ",str);
    }
    MessageBox(str, "Age range selected");
```

This handles the case of a valid selection. GetText has two prototypes:

- int GetText(int nIndex, LPTSTR lpszBuffer) const.

and

- void GetText(int nIndex, CString& rString) const.

The return value is the length (in bytes) of the string, excluding the terminating null character. If nIndex does not specify a valid index, the return value is LB_ERR.

The nIndex parameter specifies the zero-based index of the string to be retrieved. The lpszBuffer parameter points to the buffer that receives the string. The buffer must have sufficient space for the string and a terminating null character. The size of the string can be determined ahead of time by calling the GetTextLen member function. The rString parameter is a reference to a CString object. The first form gets a string from a list box. The second form fills a CString object with the string text.

OnInitDialog and LBN_DBLCLK

After the dialog box and all of its controls are created but just before the dialog box (of either type) appears on the screen, the dialog object's OnInitDialog member function is called. For a modal dialog box, this occurs during the DoModal call. For a modeless dialog box, OnInitDialog is called when Create is called.

An application sends the LBN_DBLCLK notification message when the user double-clicks a string in a list box. The parent window of the list box receives this notification message through the WM_COMMAND message.

List box handlers and member functions

The following:

- ON_LBN_DBLCLK.
- ON_LBN_ERRSPACE.
- ON_LBN_KILLFOCUS.
- ON_LBL_SELCHANGE.
- ON_LBL_SETFOCUS.

are some of the list box handlers.
The following:

- GetDlgItem.
- AddString.
- GetCurSel.
- GetText.
- DeleteString.
- FindString.
- SetCurSel.
- InsertString.
- GetCount.

are some of the list box member functions.

Summary

We have the following steps:

- Handle the initial use of the dialog:
  - OnInitDialog.
  - Obtain a pointer to the control and cast to the correct type.
  - Add strings to the list box: lbptr->AddString.
- Handle selection:
  - OnSelect.
  - Obtain a pointer to the dialog item and cast to the correct type.
  - Determine which item was selected: lbptr->GetCurSel().
  - Handle the item selected – simple message box in this case.
- Add the IDs for the list box to the ID file.
- Define the appearance of the dialog box and list box in the resource file.

8

Controls: Check Box with Grouping

'Round numbers are always false.'

Samuel Johnson

Overview

A check box presents the user with the opportunity to choose zero or more items and they are often grouped together.

Check box with grouping

We have now seen how to handle user interaction via:

- The keyboard.
- The mouse.
- Menus.
- Dialog boxes.
- List boxes.

In this chapter we will look at check boxes and grouping. These are used when the user can choose one or more items. We will also see how to group the check boxes.

The application

This program is made up of three files. The three files are:

- The include file that is used within both the resource file and the program. This file contains macro definitions of the menu ID values.
- The resource file. This example has a menu.
- The C++ source file or program.

We will look at each file in turn.

The menu ID file

```
#define  ID_MENU_DIALOG     100

#define  ID_A_EXIT          200
#define  ID_A_HELP          210

#define  IDD_1              300
#define  IDD_2              400
#define  IDD_3              500
#define  IDD_4              600
#define  IDD_5              700
#define  IDD_6              800

#define  IDD_GB1            900
#define  IDD_GB2            910

#define  IDD_D_OK           1000
```

The resource file

```
#include <afxres.h>
#include "menuids.h"

ControlExampleMenu MENU
{
  POPUP "&Dialog"
  {
      MENUITEM "&Activate Dialog Box" ,   ID_MENU_DIALOG
      MENUITEM "&Exit"                ,   ID_A_EXIT
  }
      MENUITEM "&Help"                ,   ID_A_HELP
```

```
}
DialogExample DIALOG 10,10,200,220
CAPTION "Control Example - Check box with grouping"
STYLE DS_MODALFRAME | WS_CAPTION | WS_POPUP | WS_SYSMENU
{
   AUTOCHECKBOX "Microsoft Word "               ,
      IDD_1   , 10,10,90,10
   AUTOCHECKBOX "Corel WordPerfect"             ,
      IDD_2   , 10,30,90,10
   AUTOCHECKBOX "Corel Ventura Publisher",
      IDD_3   , 10,50,90,10
   GROUPBOX "Word processing and DTP"           ,
      IDD_GB1    ,1,1,100,70
   AUTOCHECKBOX "Access"                        ,
      IDD_4   , 10,100,90,10
   AUTOCHECKBOX "Oracle"                        ,
      IDD_5   , 10,120,90,10
   AUTOCHECKBOX "Rbase"                         ,
      IDD_6   , 10,140,90,10
   GROUPBOX "Database Management"           ,
      IDD_GB2      , 1,90,100,70
   PUSHBUTTON "Details OK?"                     ,
      IDD_D_OK         , 10,180,70,15,
      WS_CHILD   | WS_TABSTOP | WS_VISIBLE
}
```

The C++ source file

```cpp
#include <afxwin.h>
#include "menuids.h"

class CMainWindow : public CFrameWnd
{
public :
   CMainWindow();

   afx_msg void OnMenuDialog();
   afx_msg void OnAppExit();
   afx_msg void OnAppHelp();

   DECLARE_MESSAGE_MAP()
};

CMainWindow::CMainWindow()
```

```
{
    Create(NULL ,
        " Control Example - Check boxes and grouping" ,
        WS_OVERLAPPEDWINDOW ,
        rectDefault ,
        NULL ,
        "ControlExampleMenu");
}

class CMyApplication : public CWinApp
{
public :
    BOOL InitInstance();
};

BOOL CMyApplication::InitInstance()
{
    m_pMainWnd = new CMainWindow;
    m_pMainWnd->ShowWindow(m_nCmdShow);
    m_pMainWnd->UpdateWindow();
    return TRUE;
}

BEGIN_MESSAGE_MAP(CMainWindow,CFrameWnd)
    ON_COMMAND( ID_MENU_DIALOG    , OnMenuDialog)
    ON_COMMAND( ID_A_EXIT         , OnAppExit)
    ON_COMMAND( ID_A_HELP         , OnAppHelp)
END_MESSAGE_MAP()

class CDialogExample : public CDialog
{
public :
    CDialogExample(char *DialogName ,
        CWnd *Owner)
        : CDialog(DialogName,Owner) {}
    afx_msg void DetailsOK();
    DECLARE_MESSAGE_MAP()
};

afx_msg void CMainWindow::OnMenuDialog()
{
    CDialogExample dialog("DialogExample",this);
    dialog.DoModal();
}
```

```
afx_msg void CMainWindow::OnAppExit()
{
    int reply;
    reply=MessageBox(" Exit?","Exit",MB_YESNO);
    if (reply==IDYES) SendMessage(WM_CLOSE);
}
afx_msg void CMainWindow::OnAppHelp()
{ MessageBox("Dialog example","Help"); }

BEGIN_MESSAGE_MAP(CDialogExample,CDialog)
    ON_COMMAND(IDD_D_OK   ,DetailsOK)
END_MESSAGE_MAP()

afx_msg void CDialogExample::DetailsOK()
{
    int cb1status=0,cb2status=0,cb3status=0,
    cb4status=0,cb5status=0,cb6status=0;
    CButton *cb1ptr = (CButton *) GetDlgItem(IDD_1);
    CButton *cb2ptr = (CButton *) GetDlgItem(IDD_2);
    CButton *cb3ptr = (CButton *) GetDlgItem(IDD_3);
    CButton *cb4ptr = (CButton *) GetDlgItem(IDD_4);
    CButton *cb5ptr = (CButton *) GetDlgItem(IDD_5);
    CButton *cb6ptr = (CButton *) GetDlgItem(IDD_6);;
    cb1status = cb1ptr->GetCheck();
    cb2status = cb2ptr->GetCheck();
    cb3status = cb3ptr->GetCheck();
    cb4status = cb4ptr->GetCheck();
    cb5status = cb5ptr->GetCheck();
    cb6status = cb6ptr->GetCheck();
    if (cb1status !=0)MessageBox("Word", " Selected");
    if (cb2status !=0)
        MessageBox("WordPerfect", " Selected");
    if (cb3status !=0)MessageBox("Ventura"," Selected");
    if (cb4status !=0)MessageBox("Access"," Selected");
    if (cb5status !=0)MessageBox("Oracle"," Selected");
    if (cb6status !=0)MessageBox("Rbase"," Selected");
}

CMyApplication Application;
```

Running the program

Repeat the steps from the earlier examples and compile and run the program.

You will see the following:

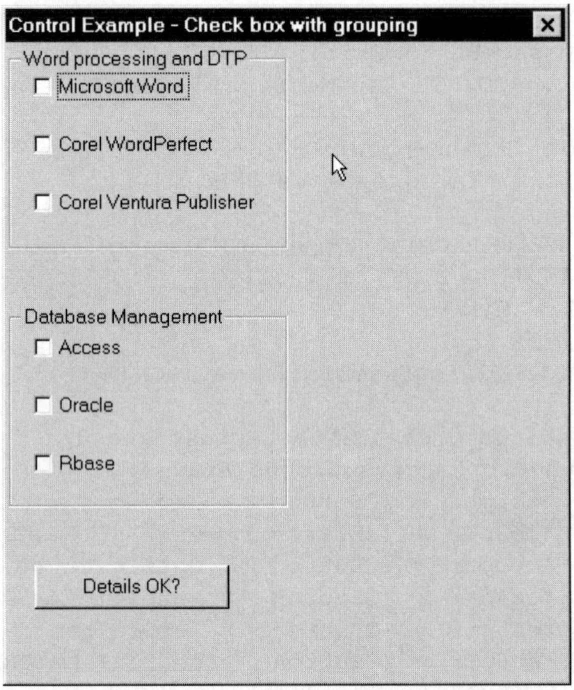

Figure 8.1 Check box example.

Experiment with the boxes to see what happens.

The menu ID file

This file contains the macro definitions of the menu IDs, dialog box IDs and check box IDs.

The resource file

```
AUTOCHECKBOX "Microsoft Word "                    ,
    IDD_1   , 10,10,90,10
AUTOCHECKBOX "Corel WordPerfect"                   ,
    IDD_2   , 10,30,90,10
AUTOCHECKBOX "Corel Ventura Publisher",
    IDD_3   , 10,50,90,10
```

```
GROUPBOX "Word processing and DTP"          ,
     IDD_GB1    ,1,1,100,70
```

We have three check boxes and group them with an appropriate text message.

```
AUTOCHECKBOX "Access"
     IDD_4   , 10,100,90,10
AUTOCHECKBOX "Oracle"                        ,
     IDD_5   , 10,120,90,10
AUTOCHECKBOX "Rbase"                       ,
     IDD_6   , 10,140,90,10
GROUPBOX "Database Management"              ,
     IDD_GB2    , 1,90,100,70
```

Three more check boxes, again grouped.

```
PUSHBUTTON "Details OK?"
   ,
     IDD_D_OK           , 10,180,70,15,
     WS_CHILD    | WS_TABSTOP | WS_VISIBLE
```

Simple conformation of details.

The C++ source

```
afx_msg void CDialogExample::DetailsOK()

{
   int cb1status=0,cb2status=0,cb3status=0,
       cb4status=0,cb5status=0,cb6status=0;
```

Variables to handle the check box status.

```
CButton *cb1ptr = (CButton *) GetDlgItem(IDD_1);
CButton *cb2ptr = (CButton *) GetDlgItem(IDD_2);
CButton *cb3ptr = (CButton *) GetDlgItem(IDD_3);
CButton *cb4ptr = (CButton *) GetDlgItem(IDD_4);
CButton *cb5ptr = (CButton *) GetDlgItem(IDD_5);
CButton *cb6ptr = (CButton *) GetDlgItem(IDD_6);
```

We use GetDlgItem to return a pointer to the check box control, which is then cast to the correct control type – in this case CButton.

```
cb1status = cb1ptr->GetCheck();
cb2status = cb2ptr->GetCheck();
cb3status = cb3ptr->GetCheck();
```

```
cb4status = cb4ptr->GetCheck();
cb5status = cb5ptr->GetCheck();
cb6status = cb6ptr->GetCheck();
```

Pick up the status of each check box.

```
if (cb1status !=0 )
   MessageBox("Word", " Selected ");
if (cb2status !=0)
   MessageBox("WordPerfect", " Selected ");
if (cb3status !=0 )
   MessageBox("Ventura", " Selected ");
if (cb4status !=0)
   MessageBox("Access", " Selected ");
if (cb5status !=0 )
   MessageBox("Oracle", " Selected ");
if (cb6status !=0)
   MessageBox("Rbase", " Selected ");
```

Work through each check box and display a message if the check box was selected.

Summary

You need to:

- Define the check box IDs in the ID file.
- Define the appearance of the check boxes in the resource file.
- Handle the selections in the C++ code.

Within the source code that handles the selections you need to:

- Create variables to handle the status of each check box.
- Use GetDlgItem to obtain a pointer to each check box control.
- Cast to the appropriate type.
- Use GetCheck to see if the item has been selected.
- Process the items selected – in this case simple message boxes are used.

You should use the on-line help to get more information about the MFC classes being used in the examples. It takes time to learn how to use the information provided. Have a look for the classes, constructors and default values and parameters.

9

Controls: Edit Boxes, Radio Buttons, Plain Text

'A good notation has a subtlety and suggestiveness which at times make it seem almost like a live teacher.'

Bertrand Russell.

Overview

There are a number of other controls that are frequently used as part of the user interface to a windows program. In this chapter we look at:

- Edit boxes.
- Radio buttons.
- Static controls – plain text.

Edit boxes, radio buttons and plain text

We have now seen how to handle user interaction via the keyboard, the mouse, menus, dialog boxes and list boxes.

In this chapter we complete the coverage of the frequently used controls or user interface features. The three new controls introduced here are:

- Edit boxes – used to handle user entered text.
- Radio buttons – mutually exclusive choices.
- Static controls – plain text.

The application

This program is made up of the typical three files, i.e. the ID file, the resource file and the C++ source file.

We will look at each in turn.

The ID file

```
#define  ID_MENU_DIALOG      100

#define  ID_A_EXIT           200
#define  ID_A_HELP           210

#define  ID_TEXT_F           300
#define  IDD_F               310
#define  ID_TEXT_L           400
#define  IDD_L               410
#define  ID_TEXT_T           500
#define  IDD_T               510
#define  ID_TEXT_S           600
#define  IDD_RB1             610
#define  IDD_RB2             620
#define  ID_TEXT_A           700
#define  IDD_A               710
#define  IDD_D_OK            800
```

The resource file

```
#include <afxres.h>
#include "menuids.h"

ControlExampleMenu MENU
{
   POPUP "&Dialog"
   {
   MENUITEM "&Activate Dialog Box" ,  ID_MENU_DIALOG
   MENUITEM "&Exit",                      ID_A_EXIT
```

```
   }
   MENUITEM "&Help",                              ID_A_HELP
}


DialogExample DIALOG 10,10,200,150

CAPTION "Control Example - edit box, radio buttons and
plain text"

STYLE DS_MODALFRAME | WS_CAPTION | WS_POPUP | WS_SYSMENU
{
   LTEXT "Firstname: " ,   ID_TEXT_F   ,   10,10,40,10
   EDITTEXT                      IDD_F    ,   50,10,80,10

   LTEXT "Lastname:   "     ,   ID_TEXT_L ,  10,30,40,10
   EDITTEXT                      IDD_L    ,   50,30,80,10

   LTEXT "Title:      "     ,   ID_TEXT_T  , 10,50,40,10
   EDITTEXT                      IDD_T     ,  50,50,80,10

   LTEXT "Sex:           "  ,   ID_TEXT_S  ,  10,70,40,10
   AUTORADIOBUTTON "Male" ,     IDD_RB1     ,  50,70,35,10
   AUTORADIOBUTTON "Female" ,  IDD_RB2   ,   80,70,35,10

   LTEXT "Age:          " ,  ID_TEXT_A   ,   10,90,40,10
   EDITTEXT                      IDD_A     ,   50,90,80,10

   PUSHBUTTON "Details OK?"    ,  IDD_D_OK  ,
   10,110,70,15,
           WS_CHILD |
           WS_TABSTOP |
           WS_VISIBLE

}
```

The C++ source file

```
#include <afxwin.h>
#include "menuids.h"

class CMainWindow : public CFrameWnd
{
public :
   CMainWindow();
```

```
   afx_msg void OnMenuDialog();
   afx_msg void OnAppExit();
   afx_msg void OnAppHelp();

   DECLARE_MESSAGE_MAP()
};

CMainWindow::CMainWindow()
{
   Create(NULL ,
   " Control Example - Edit Box, Radio Buttons and a
static control" ,
   WS_OVERLAPPEDWINDOW ,
   rectDefault ,
   NULL ,
   "ControlExampleMenu");
}

class CMyApplication : public CWinApp
{
public :
   BOOL InitInstance();
};

BOOL CMyApplication::InitInstance()
{
   m_pMainWnd = new CMainWindow;
   m_pMainWnd->ShowWindow(m_nCmdShow);
   m_pMainWnd->UpdateWindow();

   return TRUE;
}

BEGIN_MESSAGE_MAP(CMainWindow,CFrameWnd)

   ON_COMMAND(  ID_MENU_DIALOG   ,  OnMenuDialog)
   ON_COMMAND(  ID_A_EXIT    ,   OnAppExit)
   ON_COMMAND(  ID_A_HELP    ,   OnAppHelp)

END_MESSAGE_MAP()

class CDialogExample : public CDialog
{
public :
```

```
   CDialogExample(char *DialogName ,
   CWnd *Owner)
    : CDialog(DialogName,
       Owner) {}

   afx_msg void DetailsOK();

DECLARE_MESSAGE_MAP()
};

afx_msg void CMainWindow::OnMenuDialog()
{
   CDialogExample dialog("DialogExample",this);
   dialog.DoModal();
}

afx_msg void CMainWindow::OnAppExit()
{
   int reply;
   reply=MessageBox(" Exit?","Exit",MB_YESNO);
   if (reply==IDYES) SendMessage(WM_CLOSE);
}

afx_msg void CMainWindow::OnAppHelp()
{
   MessageBox("Dialog example","Help");
}

BEGIN_MESSAGE_MAP(CDialogExample,CDialog)
   ON_COMMAND(IDD_D_OK   ,DetailsOK)
END_MESSAGE_MAP()

afx_msg void CDialogExample::DetailsOK()
{
   CEdit *editboxfptr = (CEdit *) GetDlgItem(IDD_F);
   char firstname[80];
   int i;

   i = editboxfptr->GetWindowText(firstname,sizeof
firstname-1);

   MessageBox(firstname, " First name ");

   CEdit *editboxlptr = (CEdit *) GetDlgItem(IDD_L);
   char lastname[80];
```

```
    i = editbox1ptr->GetWindowText(lastname,sizeof
lastname-1);

    MessageBox(lastname, " Last name ");

    CEdit *editboxpttr = (CEdit *) GetDlgItem(IDD_T);
    char title[80];

    i = editboxpttr->GetWindowText(title,sizeof title-1);

    MessageBox(title, " Title");

    int rb1status=0,rb2status=0;
    CButton *rb1ptr = (CButton *) GetDlgItem(IDD_RB1);
    CButton *rb2ptr = (CButton *) GetDlgItem(IDD_RB2);;
    rb1status = rb1ptr->GetCheck();
    rb2status = rb2ptr->GetCheck();
    if (rb1status !=0 )
       MessageBox("Male", " Sex");
    else if (rb2status !=0)
       MessageBox("Female", " Sex");

    CEdit *editboxaptr = (CEdit *) GetDlgItem(IDD_A);
    char age[80];

    i = editboxaptr->GetWindowText(age,sizeof age-1);

    MessageBox(age, " Age");

}
CMyApplication Application;
```

Running the program

Compile and run the program. You will see a window as shown below:

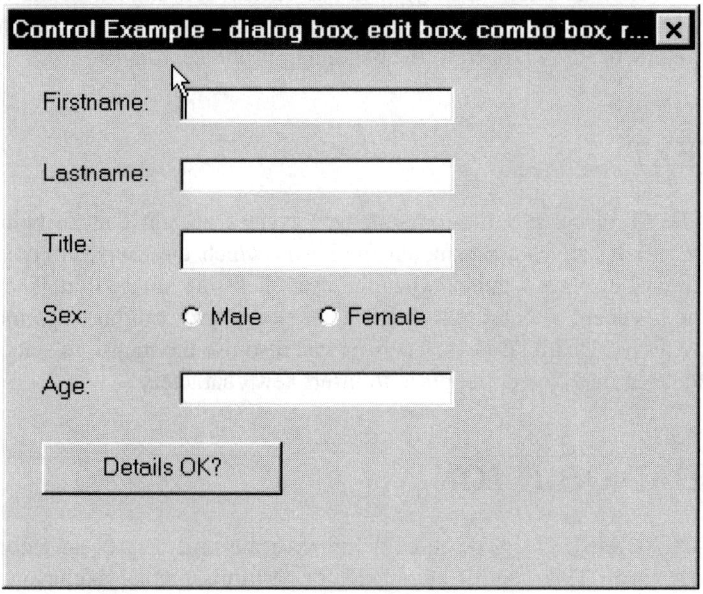

Figure 9.1 *Edit Box, radio buttons and text boxes.*

Experiment by typing into the various boxes to see what happens.

The menu ID file

This is as in the previous examples. We have IDs for the:

- Menus.
- Static text controls.
- Edit boxes.
- Radio buttons.

The resource file

This is very similar to the previous examples. The new features are:

- LTEXT – simple text display.
- EDITTEXT – user entered text.
- AUTORADIOBUTTON – simple choice of one or more items.

LTEXT

The LTEXT resource-definition statement creates a left-aligned text control. The control is a simple rectangle displaying the given text left-aligned in the rectangle. The text is formatted before it is displayed. Words that would extend past the end of a line are automatically wrapped to the beginning of the next line.

EDITTEXT

The EDITTEXT resource-definition statement creates an edit control belonging to the EDIT class. It creates a rectangular region in which the user can type and edit text. The control displays a cursor when the user clicks the mouse in it. The user can then use the keyboard to enter text or edit the existing text. Editing keys include the BACKSPACE and DELETE keys. The user can also use the mouse to select characters to be deleted or to select the place to insert new characters.

AUTORADIOBUTTON

The AUTORADIOBUTTON resource-definition statement creates an automatic radio button control. This control automatically performs mutual exclusion with the other AUTORADIOBUTTON controls in the same group. When the button is chosen, the application is notified with BN_CLICKED.

The C++ source file

The key in this example is that we only have one message handler for the new controls of this example. This is the Details OK button.

```
afx_msg void CDialogExample::DetailsOK()
```

Function prototype.

```
CEdit *editboxfptr = (CEdit *) GetDlgItem(IDD_F);
```

Obtain a pointer to the resource and cast to the appropriate type.

```
char firstname[80];
```

Variable used to hold the user entered text.

```
int i;
```

Variable used to hold the return value of GetWindowText.

```
i = editboxfptr->GetWindowText(firstname,sizeof
firstname-1);
```

GetTextWindow is used to return the user entered text in the first parameter. There are two function prototypes and these are:

- int GetWindowText(LPTSTR lpszStringBuf, int nMaxCount) const.

and

- void GetWindowText(CString& rString) const.

The return value specifies the length, in bytes, of the copied string, not including the terminating null character. It is 0 if CWnd has no caption or if the caption is empty.

Copies the CWnd caption title (if it has one) into the buffer pointed to by lpszStringBuf or into the destination string rString. If the CWnd object is a control as in this example, the GetWindowText member function copies the text within the control instead of copying the caption.

```
MessageBox(firstname, " First name ");
```

Simple use of a MessageBox to display the text entered.

We then see a repeat for the last name and title.

```
int rb1status=0,rb2status=0;
```

Two variables used to hold the status of the radio buttons.

```
CButton *rb1ptr = (CButton *) GetDlgItem(IDD_RB1);
CButton *rb2ptr = (CButton *) GetDlgItem(IDD_RB2);
```

Obtain a pointer to the control and cast to the appropriate type. In this case CButton.

```
rb1status = rb1ptr->GetCheck();
rb2status = rb2ptr->GetCheck();
```

Pick up the status of the radio buttons. The function prototype is:

- int GetCheck( ) const.

The return value from a button control created with the:

- BS_AUTOCHECKBOX.
- BS_AUTORADIOBUTTON.
- BS_AUTO3STATE.
- BS_CHECKBOX.
- BS_RADIOBUTTON.
- BS_3STATE.

Style is one of the following values:

- 0 Button state is unchecked.
- 1 Button state is checked.
- 2 Button state is indeterminate (applies only if the button has the BS_3STATE or BS_AUTO3STATE style).

If the button has any other style, the return value is 0.

```
if (rb1status !=0 )
   MessageBox("Male", " Sex");
else if (rb2status !=0)
   MessageBox("Female", " Sex");
```

Simple display using MessageBox to show the button selected.

Summary

The following steps are required:

- Add the IDs to the menu ID file.
- Define the layout in the resource file.
- Add the source code to handle the controls used.

10

Common Controls

'All the persons in this book are real and none is fictitious even in part.'

Flann O'Brien, The Hard Life.

Overview

This chapter introduces the so-called common controls that were introduced with Windows 95.

Common controls

The windows operating system has always provided a number of windows common controls. These control objects are programmable, and the Visual C++ dialog editor supports adding them to your dialog boxes. The MFC library supplies classes that encapsulate each of these controls, as shown in the table Windows Common Controls and MFC Classes. (Some items in the table have related articles that describe them further. For controls that lack articles, see the documentation for the MFC class.)

Class CWnd is the base class of all window classes, including all of the control classes. The windows common controls are supported in the following environments:

- Windows 95.
- Windows NT, version 3.51 and later.

- Win32s, version 1.3 (Visual C++ version 4.2 and later do not support Win32s) .

The older common controls — check boxes, combo boxes, edit boxes, list boxes, option buttons, pushbuttons, scroll bar controls, and static controls — were available in earlier versions of Windows as well.

This chapter looks briefly at the controls that were introduced with Windows 95. These controls are given the name *common controls*. A common control is a standardised child window that an application uses in conjunction with another window to perform i/o. The following table provides brief details of them all.

Table 10.1 Common Controls

Control	MFC Class	Description
Animation	CAnimateCtrl	displays successive frames of an AVI video clip
Date and time	CDateTimeCtrl	allows the user to choose a specific date or time value picker
Extended combobox	CComboBoxEx	a combo box control with the ability to display images
Header	CHeaderCtrl	button that appears above a column of text; controls width of text displayed
Hotkey	CHotKeyCtrl	window that enables user to create a "hot key" to perform an action quickly
Image list	CImageList	collection of images used to manage large sets of icons or bitmaps (image list isn't really a control; it supports lists used by other controls)
List	CListCtrl	window that displays a list of text with icons
Month	CMonthCalCtrl	control that displays date information calender
Progress	CProgressCtrl	window that indicates progress of a long operation
Rebar	CRebarCtrl	tool bar that can contain additional child window in the form of controls
rich edit	CRichEditCtrl	window in which user can edit with character and paragraph formatting (see Classes Related to Rich Edit Controls)
Slider	CSliderCtrl	window containing a slider control with optional tick marks
Spin button	CSpinButtonCtrl	pair of arrow buttons user can click to increment or decrement a value

Table 10.1 *Common Controls, continued*

Control	MFC Class	Description
Status bar	CStatusBarCtrl	window for displaying status information, similar to MFC class CStatusBar
Tab	CTabCtrl	analogous to the dividers in a notebook; used in "tab dialog boxes" or property sheets
Toolbar	CToolBarCtrl	window with command-generating button similar to MFC class CToolBar
Tool tip	CToolTipCtrl	small pop-up window that describes purpose of a toolbar button or other tool.
Tree	CTreeCtrl	window that displays a hierarchical list of items

With the introduction of the common controls we now have an increased choice. To complicate things slightly Microsoft has reimplemented the following (older) controls to take advantage of features of the newer controls:

- CStatusBar.
- CToolBar.
- Tool Tips.

CStatusBarCtrl and CToolBarCtrl are not integrated into the framework so using them requires additional effort on your part.

We will look at some of the above in later chapters.

Summary

All we have done in this chapter is introduce you briefly to the controls that are available.

There are two issues here:

- The first is to develop some idea of what is provided within the MFC library. As can be seen from Table 10.1 Microsoft have provided quite a wide range of controls for handling animation, graphics images, lists, progress indicators, dates and user interface features.
- The second is to use the on-line information provided to develop a better understanding of the capability and functionality of these classes including:
    - What classes are available.
    - The class hierarchy.
    - Constructors.
    - Member functions.

- Defaults
- What include files are required.

There is a lot of information available on-line and you need to develop a familiarity with this.

11

Controls: Toolbars

Overview

This chapter looks at toolbars which are a user interface feature that are frequently seen in windows applications..

Toolbars

MFC provides two classes to create toolbars:

- CToolBar

and

- CToolBarCtrl (which wraps the windows common control API).

CToolBar is the easier to use and requires less programming effort on your part.

The application

Toolbars require a little more effort than the resources we have seen so far. We have a number of steps:

- Decide which of the menu options we want to make available on the toolbar.
- Decide on the appearance of the buttons. We can use predefined buttons or create our own using a graphical editor.
- Add the extra code to the resource file.
- Add the extra code to the ID file.

- Add the extra code to the C++ source file.

We will look at each in turn.

Menu options

One very important design decision is to provide a standard interface to your program that fits in with the normal windows interface style. We will therefore add the following menu options as buttons:

- File new, open and save.
- Edit cut, copy and paste.
- Print.
- Help.

We will also add separators between the buttons.

We will use the example program from chapter five as our starting point. The complete source for this example is given in Appendix A.

Button appearance

It is important to provide the user of your program with visual clues as to what to do and how to use the program. Fortunately Microsoft provide a lot of predefined samples of bitmaps, icons and cursors. Browse around your computer to see what has been provided. With a standard Developer Studio installation you should find the samples under:

```
/Program Files/Microsoft Visual Studio/Common/Graphics
```

This example will use the bitmaps provided in:

```
/Bitmaps/OffCtlBr/Large/Color
```

under the first directory.

There are a number of windows programs that make browsing and manipulating graphical images very easy. You can use the resource editor with Developer Studio or Paint which is provided with Windows 95, 98 and NT.

You can use a third party program. One of these is Corel Photo Paint. Another is Paint Shop Pro.

Details of these products can be found at:

- http://www.corel.com

and

- http://www.jasc.com

respectively.

The resource file

We are going to use the example from chapter five as the basis for this example. We will omit details of the common code whenever possible. The complete file is given in Appendix A. This is the additional information that needs to be added to the resource file. After using the toolbar editor this file will be changed by Developer Studio to conform to the style used by Microsoft when using the various wizards.

```
DEFAULTMENU TOOLBAR DISCARDABLE   16,  15
{
    BUTTON          ID_MA_FILE_NEW
    BUTTON          ID_MA_FILE_OPEN
    BUTTON          ID_MA_FILE_SAVE
    SEPARATOR
        BUTTON          ID_MA_EDIT_CUT
        BUTTON          ID_MA_EDIT_COPY
        BUTTON          ID_MA_EDIT_PASTE
    SEPARATOR
        BUTTON          ID_MA_FILE_PRINT
    SEPARATOR
        BUTTON          ID_MA_APP_ABOUT
}
```

As you can see each button is linked with a menu option. We will need 8 buttons. We will use the resource editor to do this.

The ID file

We need to add additional IDs to the file. These are for the toolbar and the bitmap file associated with the toolbar. See Appendix A for a complete listing.

```
#define ID_TOOLBAR          50
#define ID_TOOLBAR_BMP      60
```

The C++ source file

We need to add a relatively small amount of code to add toolbars to our program:

- A couple of additional include files.
- A CToolBar variable.
- Code to create the toolbar.
- Code to load it.

The complete C++ source listing is in Appendix A.

```
#include <afxcmn.h>
#include <afxext.h>
```

The first include file contains the MFC COMCTL32 control classes. These include:

- CToolInfo, CImageList, CListBox, CDragListBox, CListCtrl, CTreeCtrl, CSpinButtonCtrl, CHeaderCtrl, CSliderCtrl, CProgressCtrl, CComboBox, CComboBoxEx, CHotKeyCtrl, CToolTipCtrl, CTabCtrl, CAnimateCtrl, CToolBarCtrl, CStatusBarCtrl, CRichEditCtrl, CIPAddressCtrl.

The second include file contains the MFC Advanced Extensions and Advanced Customizsable classes. These include:

- CBitmapButton, CControlBar, CStatusBar, CToolBar, CDialogBar, CReBar; CSplitterWnd.

```
CToolBar MyToolBar
```

This variable needs to be added to the CMainWindow class.

```
MyToolBar.CreateEx(this,
    TBSTYLE_FLAT,
    WS_CHILD |
    WS_VISIBLE |
    CBRS_TOP|
    CBRS_GRIPPER |
    CBRS_TOOLTIPS |
    CBRS_FLYBY |
    CBRS_SIZE_DYNAMIC);
```

This statement creates the toolbar. The function prototype is given below.

Function prototype CToolBar::CreateEx

```
BOOL CreateEx(CWnd* pParentWnd,
DWORD dwCtrlStyle = TBSTYLE_FLAT,
DWORD dwStyle = WS_CHILD | WS_VISIBLE | CBRS_ALIGN_TOP,
CRect rcBorders = CRect(0, 0, 0, 0),
UINT nID = AFX_IDW_TOOLBAR);
```

Function prototype return value

This is non zero if successful otherwise 0.

Function prototype parameters:

These are:

- pParentWnd: Pointer to the window that is the toolbar's parent.
- dwCtrlStyle: Additional styles for the creation of the embedded CToolBarCtrl object. By default, this value is set to TBSTYLE_FLAT. For a complete list of toolbar styles, see dwStyle.
- dwStyle: The toolbar style. See Toolbar Control and Button Styles in the Platform SDK for a list of appropriate styles.
- rcBorders: A CRect object that defines the widths of the toolbar window borders, and the defaults mean no borders.
- nID: The toolbar's child-window ID.

We call this function to create a Windows toolbar (a child window) and associate it with the CToolBar object. It also sets the toolbar height to a default value.

Use CreateEx, instead of Create, when certain styles need to be present during the creation of the embedded tool bar control. For example, set dwCtrlStyle to:

- TBSTYLE_FLAT | TBSTYLE_TRANSPARENT

to create a toolbar that resembles the Internet Explorer 4 toolbars.

```
MyToolBar.LoadToolBar("DEFAULTMENU");
```

This loads the toolbar. The function prototype and details are given below.

Function prototype CToolbar::LoadToolBar

There are two constructors:

- BOOL LoadToolBar(LPCTSTR lpszResourceName);
- BOOL LoadToolBar(UINT nIDResource);

Constructor return value:

This is non zero if successful otherwise 0.

Constructor parameters:

These are:

- lpszResourceName: Pointer to the resource name of the toolbar to be loaded.

- nIDResource: Resource ID of the toolbar to be loaded.

You call this member function to load the toolbar.

Running the program

Create a new project. Add the source and resource file to the project. Move to the resource view. Expand the accelerator, menu and toolbar resources. When you click on the Toolbar you will be prompted to create a bitmap for the toolbar. Choose yes.

You will now be presented with a default empty toolbar. We will now load the bitmaps from the:

```
Bitmaps\OffCtlBr\Large\Color
```

directory and open them one at a time and add them to the toolbar. You use the:

- **File | Open**

menu to open each one.
You use the:

- **Edit | Copy**

menu to copy each one in turn. When you have finished save the workspace. Then build your program and run it. You should see the following window:

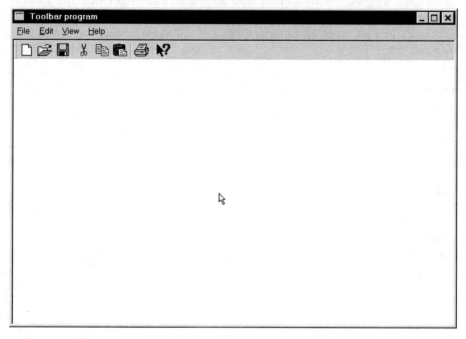

Figure 11.1 Toolbars.

Summary

Toolbars are a common feature of windows programs. Microsoft provide a good selection of samples that can be reused. It makes sense to use the ones Microsoft provide for the common functionality we see in many windows programs:

- File:
  - New.
  - Open.
  - Save.
- Edit:
  - Cut.
  - Copy.
  - Paste.
- Print.
- Help.

They help to give your program that distinctive look and feel that epitomises a windows application. This helps the user of your program to do the common tasks easily, because they are already familiar with them from using other windows applications.

You can also add your own toolbars and it is fun to experiment and create your own buttons.

12

Controls: Status Bar and Tooltips

Overview

This chapter covers some of the common controls that were introduced with Windows 95 – status bars and tooltips.

Status bars and tooltips

There are two additional user interface features that go with toolbars and these are status bars and tooltips. The tooltip is a small text prompt that appears when you move the cursor over the toolbar buttons. A more complete textual explanation normally appears on the status bar at the bottom of the window.

The application

We will use the example from the previous chapter as the basis for this example. All we are doing is enhancing this example.

The ID file

We can use the same ID file as in the previous example. The complete listing is in Appendix B.

The resource file

Here is the latest resource file segment. The complete listing is in Appendix B.

```
DEFAULTMENU TOOLBAR DISCARDABLE    24,23
BEGIN
    BUTTON          ID_MA_FILE_NEW
    BUTTON          ID_MA_FILE_OPEN
    BUTTON          ID_MA_FILE_SAVE
    SEPARATOR
    BUTTON          ID_MA_EDIT_CUT
    BUTTON          ID_MA_EDIT_COPY
    BUTTON          ID_MA_EDIT_PASTE
    SEPARATOR
    BUTTON          ID_MA_FILE_PRINT
    SEPARATOR
    BUTTON          ID_MA_APP_ABOUT
END
```

This sets up the toolbar.

```
DEFAULTMENU BITMAP   DISCARDABLE         "defaultm.bmp"
```

This is the bitmap for the toolbar.

```
STRINGTABLE DISCARDABLE
BEGIN
    ID_MA_FILE_NEW
"Create a new document\nNew"
    ID_MA_FILE_OPEN
"Open an existing document\nOpen"
    ID_MA_FILE_SAVE
"Save the active document\nSave"
    ID_MA_FILE_PRINT
"Print the active document\nPrint"
    ID_MA_APP_ABOUT
"Display program information, version number and copy-
right\nAbout"
    ID_MA_EDIT_COPY
"Copy the selection and put it on the Clipboard\nCopy"
    ID_MA_EDIT_CUT
"Cut the selection and put it on the Clipboard\nCut"
    ID_MA_EDIT_PASTE
"Insert Clipboard contents\nPaste"
END
```

These are the tool tips that will appear. There are two forms:

- Short text form that comprises the tooltip
- Long text form that appears on the status bar

Note that there are some layout problems with the STRINGTABLE due to the length of some of the lines.

The C++ source file

Here are the additional code segments. The complete listing is in Appendix B.

```
#include <afxwin.h>
#include <afxcmn.h>
#include <afxext.h>
```

These three headers need to be included to ensure that all of the necessary symbols are made available. When you have entered the program in Developer Studio right-click in the included files to see what these files make available.

```
static UINT indicators[]=
{
   ID_SEPARATOR,
   ID_INDICATOR_CAPS,
   ID_INDICATOR_NUM,
   ID_INDICATOR_SCRL,
};
```

Array of keyboard indicators that will appear on the bottom of the status bar. We add three indicators for:

- Caps lock.
- Num lock.
- Scroll lock.

The IDs are in the afxres.h file. We looked briefly at this file earlier.

```
class CMainWindow : public CFrameWnd
{
.
stuff deleted.
.
protected:

   CToolBar     MyToolBar;
```

Tool bar variable.

```
CStatusBar    MyStatusBar;
```

Status bar variable.

```
MyStatusBar.Create(this);
```

Create the status bar.

```
MyStatusBar.SetIndicators(indicators,sizeof(indica-
tors)/sizeof(UINT));
```

Set up the indicators.

Running the program

Run the program. You should see a window similar to that below:

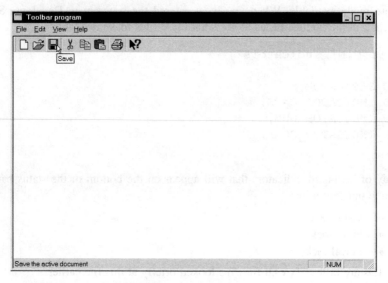

Figure 12.1 Status bar and tooltips.

Experiment by moving the mouse around to see what messages appear over the toolbars and on the status line.

Summary

Status bars and tooltips are easy to add to your program. They provide the user with simple visual clues about how to use your program.

13

Icons

Overview

This chapter introduces another user interface feature – icons. One of the most common uses for an icon is to identify your application.

Icons

An icon is a picture that is used to identify an application, file, or other object. It consists of a bit image combined with a mask. An application's icon always appears on the taskbar while the application is running, and it can be used to go to the application's main window when another window has the foreground.

The application

Every application should register both 16-by-16-pixel and 32-by-32-pixel icons for its main executable file and the types of files it stores in the file system.

Icons are like images, and you edit them in the same way. When you create a new icon the graphics editor first creates an image for VGA. The image is initially filled with the "screen" (transparent) colour.

By default, the graphics editor supports the creation of images for the devices shown in the following table.

Table 13.1 Supported formats

Devices	Colours	Width Pixels	Height Pixels
Monochrome	2	32	32
Small	16	16	16
Normal	16	32	32
Large	256	64	64

Graphics editor

The graphics editor has an extensive set of tools for drawing images, as well as features to support the creation of toolbar bitmaps. In addition to creating and editing images in bitmap format, you can edit images in GIF or JPEG format. You can also convert images in GIF or JPEG format to bitmap format.

Microsoft provided icons

On one system I work with the icons could be found in the following directory:

```
D:\Program Files\Microsoft Visual Studio\Common\
Graphics\Icons>
```

The exact directory will depend on how you did the Developer Studio install. The icons are arranged in the following categories: Arrows, Comm, Computer, Dragdrop, Elements, Flags, Industry, Mail, Misc, Office, Traffic, Writing, Win95.

Function prototype CWinApp::LoadIcon

There are two forms:

- HICON LoadIcon(LPCTSTR lpszResourceName) const.
- HICON LoadIcon(UINT nIDResource) const.

Function prototype return value

The function returns a handle to an icon if successful otherwise NULL.

Function prototype parameters

These are:
- lpszResourceName: Points to a null-terminated string that contains the name of the icon resource. You can also use a CString for this argument.
- nIDResource: ID number of the icon resource.

The menu ID file

This is given in Appendix C.

The resource file

The complete source is given in Appendix C. The important new statement is given below:

```
MyICON                    ICON     "earth.ico"
```

MyICON is the name used in the C++ source, and earth.ico is the external file name.

The C++ source file

The complete source is given in Appendix C.

```
BOOL CMyApplication::InitInstance()
{
    CBrush background;

    background.CreateStockObject(WHITE_BRUSH);

    LPCSTR classname = AfxRegisterWndClass(
        0,
        0,
        background,
        LoadIcon("MyICON"));

    m_pMainWnd = new CMainWindow(classname);

    m_pMainWnd->ShowWindow(m_nCmdShow);
    m_pMainWnd->UpdateWindow();
```

```
return TRUE;
}
```

This is the override for InitInstance.

The CBrush class encapsulates a windows Graphics Device Interface (GDI) brush. To use a CBrush object we construct a CBrush object and pass it to the CDC member function that requires it. Brushes can be solid, hatched, or patterned.

There are four constructors. The constructor with no arguments constructs an uninitialized CBrush object that must be initialised before it can be used.

The brush can be initialised by a number of functions including: CreateSolidBrush, CreateHatchBrush, CreateBrushIndirect, CreatePatternBrush, CreateDIBPatternBrush, CreateStockObject.

The constructor with no arguments always succeeds.

We initialise the brush with:

```
background.CreateStockObject(WHITE_BRUSH);
```

and use one of the predefined colours. There are a number of brush macros that we can use including:

- BLACK_BRUSH – black.
- DKGRAY_BRUSH – dark grey.
- HOLLOW_BRUSH – see through.
- LTGRAY_BRUSH – light grey.
- WHITE_BRUSH – white.

We use the last in this example. We can also use COLORREF to do this. The COLORREF value is a 32-bit value used to specify an RGB colour. When specifying an explicit RGB colour, the COLORREF value has the following hexadecimal form:

- 0x00bbggrr

The low-order byte contains a value for the relative intensity of red; the second byte contains a value for green; and the third byte contains a value for blue. The high-order byte must be zero. The maximum value for a single byte is 0xFF.

For simplicity we use one of the built-in macros to specify the colour.

The default brush when creating a window is white when we use the MFC default window class.

We can then use this brush as the HBRUSH parameter in the AfxRegisterWndClass, as the CBrush class defines a conversion from CBrush to HBRUSH.

Function prototype AfxRegisterWndClass

LPCTSTR AFXAPI AfxRegisterWndClass(

```
UINT nClassStyle,
HCURSOR hCursor = 0,
HBRUSH hbrBackground = 0,
HICON hIcon = 0 )
```

Function prototype return value

A null-terminated string containing the class name. You pass this class name to the Create member function in CWnd or other CWnd-derived classes to create a window. The name is generated by the MFC library.

The return value is a pointer to a static buffer. To save this string, assign it to a CString variable.

Function prototype parameters

These are:

- NClassStyle – Specifies the windows class style or combination of styles, created by using the bitwise-OR (|) operator, for the window class. For a list of class styles, see theWNDCLASS structure in the Win32 SDK documentation. If NULL, the defaults will be set as follows:

  - Sets the mouse style to CS_DBLCLKS, which sends double-click messages to the window procedure when the user double-clicks the mouse.
  - Sets the arrow cursor style to the windows standard IDC_ARROW.
  - Sets the background brush to NULL, so the window will not erase its background.
  - Sets the icon to the standard, waving-flag windows logo icon.

- hCursor – Specifies a handle to the cursor resource to be installed in each window created from the window class. If you use the default of 0, you will get the standard IDC_ARROW cursor.
- hbrBackground – Specifies a handle to the brush resource to be installed in each window created from the window class. If you use the default of 0, you will have a NULL background brush, and your window will, by default, not erase its background while processing WM_ERASEBKGND.
- hIcon – Specifies a handle to the icon resource to be installed in each window created from the window class. If you use the default of 0, you will get the standard, waving-flag Windows logo icon.

The MFC library automatically registers several standard window classes for you. We call this function to register our own window classes.

Running the application

Follow the normal steps to run the program You should end up with a window as shown below:

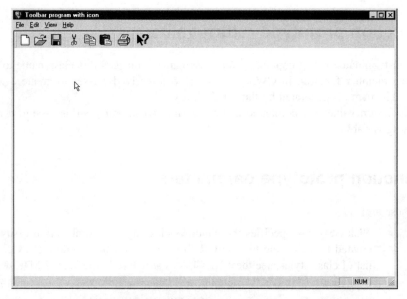

Figure 13.1 Simple icon example.

Summary

This example has shown how to add our own icon to our application. In this example we have used one of the predefined ones provided by Microsoft. You can of course design your own using the tools provided to personalise your application.

14

Text i/o Using Device Contexts

Overview

This chapter looks at text i/o. We also look at device contexts. A device context is a structure that defines a set of graphic objects and their associated attributes, and the graphic modes that affect output. The graphic objects include:

- A pen for line drawing.
- A brush for painting and filling.
- A bitmap for copying or scrolling parts of the screen.
- A palette for defining the set of available colours.
- A region for clipping and other operations.
- A path for painting and drawing operations.

Text i/o using device contexts

All but one of the examples so far have looked at user interaction using the following:

- Menus.
- Dialog boxes.
- Radio buttons.
- Edit boxes.
- List boxes.

It was only in the chapter on message passing we looked at the client window. In this chapter we will look at text handling and the client window in a little more depth.

Overview

Microsoft provide a very extensive set of functions to control text output. We will only look at a small subset of the functionality available. The key class is the CDC class. This class defines a class of device-context objects. A device context is a Windows data structure containing information about the drawing attributes of a device such as a display or a printer. All drawing calls are made through a device-context object, which encapsulates the windows APIs for drawing lines, shapes, and text. Device contexts allow device-independent drawing in windows. Device contexts can be used to draw to the screen, to the printer, or to a metafile. The graphic objects include:

- A pen for line drawing.
- A brush for painting and filling.
- A bitmap for copying or scrolling parts of the screen.
- A palette for defining the set of available colours.
- A region for clipping and other operations.
- A path for painting and drawing operations.

The CDC object provides member functions for working with a device context, such as a display or printer, as well as members for working with a display context associated with the client area of a window.

We do all drawing through the member functions of a CDC object. The class provides member functions for:

- Device-context operations.
- Working with drawing tools.
- Type-safe graphics device interface (GDI) object selection.
- Colours and palettes.

It also provides member functions for:

- Getting and setting drawing attributes.
- Mapping.
- Working with the viewport.
- Working with the window extent, converting coordinates.
- working with regions;
- clipping;
- drawing lines;
- drawing simple shapes, ellipses, and polygons.

Member functions are also provided for:

- drawing text;
- working with fonts;
- using printer escapes;
- scrolling;
- playing metafiles.

To use a CDC object we construct it, and then call its member functions that parallel windows functions that use device contexts.

Device contexts

All drawing calls are made through a device-context object, which encapsulates the windows APIs for drawing lines, shapes, and text. Device contexts allow device-independent drawing in windows. Device contexts can be used to draw to:

- The screen.
- A printer.
- A metafile.

In the earlier example we used the CPaintDC class to do all of our text i/o and handle the display of button presses. This class encapsulated:

- Calling the BeginPaint function.
- Drawing in the device context.
- Calling the EndPaint function.

CClientDC objects encapsulate working with a device context that represents the client area of a window. The CClientDC constructor calls the GetDC function, and the destructor calls the ReleaseDC function.

CWindowDC objects encapsulate a device context that represents the whole window including its frame.

In this example we are going to use two device contexts. The first is the context that we do all output to. This is a virtual device context. We use GetSystemMetrics to get the screen size and PatBlt to create a bit pattern.

The second is the actual client area of a window. We copy the virtual device context to the client window using BitBlt.

Function prototype GetSystemMetrics

The GetSystemMetrics function retrieves various system metrics (widths and heights of display elements) and system configuration settings. All dimensions retrieved by GetSystemMetrics are in pixels. See the Developer help for a complete coverage.

Function prototype CDC::PatBlt

BOOL PatBlt(int x, int y, int nWidth, int nHeight, DWORDdwRop)

Function prototype return value

This is non zero if the function is successful otherwise 0.

Function prototype parameters

These are:
- x: Specifies the logical x-coordinate of the upper-left corner of the rectangle that is to receive the pattern.
- y: Specifies the logical y-coordinate of the upper-left corner of the rectangle that is to receive the pattern.
- nWidth: Specifies the width (in logical units) of the rectangle that is to receive the pattern.
- nHeight: Specifies the height (in logical units) of the rectangle that is to receive the pattern.
- dwRop: Specifies the raster-operation code. Raster-operation codes (ROPs) define how GDI combines colours in output operations that involve a current brush, a possible source bitmap, and a destination bitmap. This parameter can be one of the following values:
    - PATCOPY: Copies pattern to destination bitmap.
    - PATINVERT: Combines destination bitmap with pattern using the Boolean XOR operator.
    - DSTINVERT: Inverts the destination bitmap.
    - BLACKNESS: Turns all output black.
    - WHITENESS: Turns all output white.

This function creates a bit pattern on the device. The pattern is a combination of the selected brush and the pattern already on the device.

Function prototype CDC::BitBlt

BOOL BitBlt(int x, int y, int nWidth, int nHeight, CDC* pSrcDC, int xSrc,
int ySrc, DWORD dwRop)

Function prototype return value

This is non zero if the function is successful otherwise 0.

Function prototype parameters

These are:

- x: Specifies the logical x-coordinate of the upper-left corner of the destination rectangle.
- y: Specifies the logical y-coordinate of the upper-left corner of the destination rectangle.
- nWidth: Specifies the width (in logical units) of the destination rectangle and source bitmap.
- nHeight: Specifies the height (in logical units) of the destination rectangle and source bitmap.
- pSrcDC: Pointer to a CDC object that identifies the device context from which the bitmap will be copied. It must be NULL if dwRop specifies a raster operation that does not include a source.
- xSrc: Specifies the logical x-coordinate of the upper-left corner of the source bitmap.
- ySrc: Specifies the logical y-coordinate of the upper-left corner of the source bitmap.
- dwRop: Specifies the raster operation to be performed. Raster-operation codes define how the GDI combines colours in output operations that involve a current brush, a possible source bitmap, and a destination bitmap. The following lists raster-operation codes for dwRop and their descriptions:
    - SRCCOPY: Copies the source bitmap to the destination bitmap.

Copies a bitmap from the source device context to the current device context. See the Developer Studio help for more information.

Function prototype CDC::TextOut

There are two:

- virtual BOOL TextOut(int x, int y, LPCTSTR lpszString, int nCount)
- BOOL TextOut(int x, int y, const CString& str)

Function prototype return value

This is non zero if the function is successful otherwise 0.

Function prototype parameters

These are:

- x: Specifies the logical x-coordinate of the starting point of the text.
- y: Specifies the logical y-coordinate of the starting point of the text.
- lpszString: Points to the character string to be drawn.
- nCount: Specifies the number of bytes in the string.
- str: A CString object that contains the characters to be drawn.

This function writes a character string at the specified location using the currently selected font.

Character origins are at the upper-left corner of the character cell. By default, the current position is not used or updated by the function.

If an application needs to update the current position when it calls TextOut, the application can call the SetTextAlign member function with nFlags set to TA_UPDATECP. When this flag is set, windows ignores the x and y parameters on subsequent calls to TextOut, using the current position instead.

Drawing text

After an application selects the appropriate font, sets the required text-formatting options, and computes the necessary character width and height values for a string of text, it can begin drawing characters and symbols by calling any of the four text-output functions. Two of these functions:

- DrawText

and

- TabbedTextOut

are part of Window Manager and found in the library USER.DLL; the remaining two functions are part of GDI and found in the library GDI.DLL. When an application calls one of these functions, the operating system passes the call to the graphics engine, which in turn passes the call to the appropriate device driver. At the device driver level, all of these calls are supported by one or more calls to the driver's own ExtTextOut or TextOut function. An application will achieve the fastest execution by calling the ExtTextOut function, which is quickly converted into an ExtTextOut call for the device. However, there are instances when an application should call one of the other three functions; for example, to draw multiple lines of text within the borders of a specified rectangular region, it is more efficient to call the DrawText function. To create a multi-column table with justified columns of text, it is more efficient to call the TabbedTextOut function.

CFont

The CFont class encapsulates a windows GDI font and provides member functions for manipulating the font. To use a CFont object, construct a CFont object and attach a windows font to it with CreateFont, CreateFontIndirect, CreatePointFont, or CreatePointFontIndirect, and then use the object's member functions to manipulate the font.

The CreatePointFont and CreatePointFontIndirect functions are often easier to use than CreateFont or CreateFontIndirect since they do the conversion for the height of the font from a point size to logical units automatically.

For more information on CFont, see Graphic Objects in Visual C++ Programmer's Guide.

Flicker and the repaint problem

A common problem in graphics programming is so called flicker. By this we mean the display flickering as i/o is done. We have avoided this by the use of a virtual window that is copied to the screen when a WM_PAINT message is received.

Example 1: Simple text i/o

There are two examples in this chapter. The first looks at simple character i/o using device contexts, and the second looks at altering the font attributes.

The example is based on the earlier one in chapter four.

The C++ source file

The complete source is given below. Comments have been included.

```
#include <afxwin.h>
#include <string.h>

char line[80];
char textline[80];
int  charcount=0;
int  mx=0,my=0;
int  wx=1,wy=1;
```

```cpp
class CMainWindow : public CFrameWnd
{
public :

   CDC          my_memDC;
   CBitmap      my_bitmap;
   CBrush       my_brush;
//
// The device context, bitmap and brush variables
// required in this example.
//
   CMainWindow();

   afx_msg void OnChar(UINT ch, UINT count, UINT flags);
   afx_msg void OnPaint();

   DECLARE_MESSAGE_MAP()
};

CMainWindow::CMainWindow()
{
   Create(
   NULL ,
   " Simple text i/o using virtual device context");

   CClientDC dc(this);

// The client device context required for this example.

   mx=GetSystemMetrics(SM_CXSCREEN);

   my=GetSystemMetrics(SM_CYSCREEN);
//
// pick up the x and y size.
//
   my_memDC.CreateCompatibleDC(&dc);
   my_bitmap.CreateCompatibleBitmap(&dc,mx,my);
   my_memDC.SelectObject(&my_bitmap);
//
// link up the two device contexts
//
   my_brush.CreateStockObject(WHITE_BRUSH);
   my_memDC.SelectObject(&my_brush);
```

```
    my_memDC.PatBlt(0,0,mx,my,PATCOPY);
//
// generate a white background
//
}

class CMyApplication : public CWinApp
{
public :
    BOOL InitInstance();
};

BOOL CMyApplication::InitInstance()
{
    m_pMainWnd = new CMainWindow;
    m_pMainWnd->ShowWindow(m_nCmdShow);
    m_pMainWnd->UpdateWindow();

    return TRUE;
}

BEGIN_MESSAGE_MAP(CMainWindow,CFrameWnd)
    ON_WM_CHAR()
    ON_WM_PAINT()
END_MESSAGE_MAP()

afx_msg void CMainWindow::OnChar(UINT ch, UINT count,
UINT flags)
{
    textline[charcount]=char(ch);
    charcount++;
    wx=1;
    wy=1;
    strcpy(line,textline);
    my_memDC.TextOut(wx,wy,line,strlen(line));
    InvalidateRect(NULL);
    if (charcount==79) charcount=0;
    return;
}

afx_msg void CMainWindow::OnPaint()
{
    CPaintDC dc(this);

    dc.BitBlt(0,0,mx,my,&my_memDC,0,0,SRCCOPY);
```

```
//
// Copies a bitmap from the source
// device context to the
// current device context.
//
   return;
}

CMyApplication Application;
```

Running the program

We follow the normal process of compiling and building.

The example is very similar to the earlier one in chapter four. You should see something like that shown below:

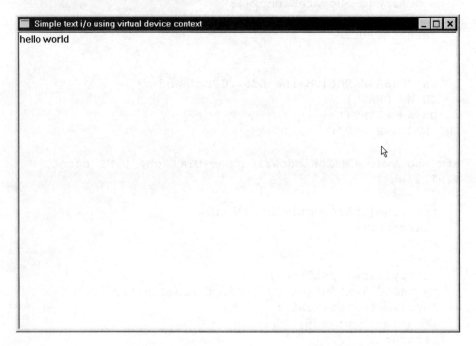

Figure 14.1 Text i/o using device contexts.

Example 2: Altering the font

In this example we are going to alter the font. Windows 3.1 provided three kinds of fonts. These can be categorised by how the font is rendered for screen and printer:

- raster fonts : which are stored as bitmaps and which cannot be scaled or rotated;
- vector fonts: which are rendered from a mathematical model and which can be scaled to any size or aspect ratio;
- TrueType fonts: outline fonts which were a new technology that was introduced with that release of windows. They can be scaled and rotated.

TrueType fonts are now an integral part of windows. Fonts have a number of attributes and three of the most important are the name, style and size.

Type face name

Type faces have names, often copyrighted.

There are a number of fonts supplied with windows. The following screenshot shows what happens within Wordpad:

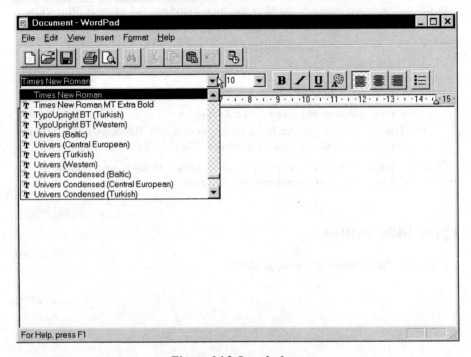

Figure 14.2 Sample fonts.

If you install a printer or another application then it is possible that additional fonts will be installed for you to use.

You can also use the Control Panel to see what fonts are installed.

There is one other type of font that we will look at and these are Adobe Postscript fonts. Adobe PostScript is a computer language that describes the appearance of a page, including elements such as text, graphics, and scanned images, to a printer or other output device. It was introduced in 1985 and is now in its third version. Adobe PostScript technology is used in a wide range of output devices, including black-and-white printers, colour printers, imagesetters, platesetters, screen displays, and direct digital presses. For more information visit the Adobe home page:

```
http://www.adobe.com/
```

On one system there were nearly 200 installed. Quite a bewildering choice!

Two important categories of fonts are:

- Serif – characters with twiddly bits.

and

- San serif – plain characters.

This line of text is shown in a serif font: Times Roman.

This line of text is shown in a san serif font: Helvetica.

Serif fonts are easier to read. San serif fonts catch the eye more.

Style

Three common styles are:

- normal
- **bold**
- *italic*

Size

The size of a font can be expressed in a variety of ways. We will use the one used in typography and this is in terms of points. One point is one seventy second of an inch.

We are going to alter the point size in response to a mouse click. The left button will increase the point size and the right-hand button will decrease the point size.

The C++ program source

The complete listing is in Appendix D. We just look at the additional statements here.

```
int    pointsize=100;
```

Variable used to hold the pointsize. Windows does this internally scaled by a factor of 10.

```
class CMainWindow : public CFrameWnd
{
public :

    CDC         my_memDC;
    CBitmap     my_bitmap;
    CBrush      my_brush;
    Cfont       my_font;
```

Memory context, bitmap, brush and font variables.

```
    afx_msg void OnLButtonDown(UINT flags, CPoint loc);
    afx_msg void OnRButtonDown(UINT flags, CPoint loc);
```

Additional handlers. The left-button will increase the point size and the right-button will decrease the point size.

```
BEGIN_MESSAGE_MAP(CMainWindow,CFrameWnd)
    ON_WM_CHAR()
    ON_WM_PAINT()
    ON_WM_LBUTTONDOWN()
    ON_WM_RBUTTONDOWN()
END_MESSAGE_MAP()
```

Additional handlers in the message map.

```
afx_msg void CMainWindow::OnChar(UINT ch, UINT count,
UINT flags)
{
    textline[charcount]=char(ch);
    charcount++;
    wx=1;
    wy=1;
    strcpy(line,textline);

    CFont tfont;
```

Temporary font variable.

```
    CDC* pdc;
```

Pointer to a device context.

```
    pdc=&my_memDC;
```

Set to the memory context.

```
    tfont.CreatePointFont(pointsize,"Arial",pdc);
```

Create the new font (Arial) for the device context at a particular point size.

```
    CFont* poldfont = (CFont*) pdc->SelectObject(&tfont);
```

Save the old font and set the new font into the device context.

```
    my_memDC.TextOut(wx,wy,line,strlen(line));
```

Do the text output.

```
    pdc->SelectObject(poldfont);
```

Reset the old font.

```
InvalidateRect(NULL);
```

Cause a repaint.

```
if (charcount==79) charcount=0;
return;
}
```

Reset character count if necessary.

```
afx_msg void
CMainWindow::OnLButtonDown(UINT flags, CPoint loc)
{
    pointsize+=20;
    InvalidateRect(NULL);
    return;
}
```

Respond to left mouse button. Note again the scale factor used internally by windows.

```
afx_msg void
CMainWindow::OnRButtonDown(UINT flags, CPoint loc)
{
    pointsize-=20;
    InvalidateRect(NULL);
    return;
}
```

Respond to right mouse button.

Running the program

Follow the normal steps to run the program. You should end up with a window something like this:

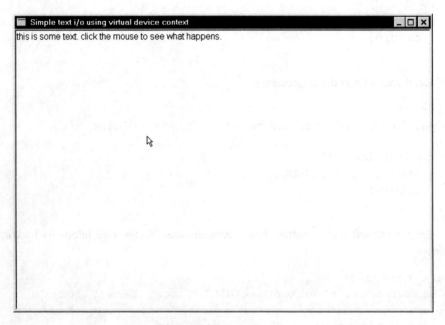

Figure 14.3 Sample text.

You should experiment with clicking the mouse buttons and see what happens to the text as the point size increases and decreases.

Summary

The examples in this chapter have looked at text i/o in terms of device contexts. We have also touched briefly on fonts. TrueType fonts render very well on the screen and on printers. The highest quality printing devices use Postscript fonts. Resolutions of 2,540 dots per inch are not uncommon.

15

Graphics Using Device Contexts

Overview

This chapter looks at simple graphics. There is a coverage of:

- Device contexts.
- Bitmaps.
- Brushes.
- Pens.
- Colour.
- Coordinate systems.

Graphics using device contexts

This chapter looks at simple graph plotting using the MFC library.

Graphic objects

Windows provides a variety of drawing tools to use in device contexts. We have already seen how to use brushes to fill interiors and fonts to draw text. In this chapter we will use pens to draw lines. MFC provides graphic-object classes equivalent to the drawing tools in windows. The table below shows the available classes and the equivalent windows GDI handle types.

Classes for windows GDI objects

Table 15.1 GDI objects and classes

Class	Windows handle type
CPen	HPEN
Cbrush	HBRUSH
CFont	HFONT
CBitmap	HBITMAP
Cpalette	HPALETTE
CRgn	HRGN

Each graphic-object class in the class library has a constructor that allows you to create graphic objects of that class, which you must then initialise with the appropriate function.

The field of graphics is quite extensive. I would recommend the following as a good place to start. There are several versions available.

Computer Graphics: Principles and Practice, Foley, van Dam, Feiner, Hughes, Addison Wesley.

Process of creating a graphic object in a device context

The following four steps are typically used when you need a graphic object for a drawing operation:

- Define a graphic object on the stack frame. Construct and initialise the object in two separate stages. The constructor creates the object and an initialization function initialises it. Two-stage construction is preferred to one stage as it is safer.
- Select the object into the current device context, saving the old graphic object that was selected before.
- When done with the current graphic object, select the old graphic object back into the device context to restore its state.
- Allow the frame-allocated graphic object to be deleted automatically when the scope is exited.

Obviously if you use an object repeatedly, you can allocate it once and select it into a device context each time it is needed. Be sure to delete such an object when you no longer need it.

Function prototype MoveToEx

The MoveToEx function updates the current position to the specified point and optionally returns the previous position.
The function prototype is:

- BOOL MoveToEx(HDC hdc, int X,int Y, LPPOINT lpPoint)

Function prototype return values

This is non zero if successful, fail is zero.

Parameters

These are:

- hdc: handle to a device context.
- X: specifies the x-coordinate of the new position, in logical units.
- Y: specifies the y-coordinate of the new position, in logical units.
- lpPoint: pointer to a POINT structure in which the previous current position is stored. If this parameter is a NULL pointer, the previous position is not returned.

The MoveToEx function affects all drawing functions

Function prototype CDC::LineTo

These are:

- BOOL LineTo(int x, int y);
- BOOL LineTo(POINT point);

Function prototype return values

As usual success is non zero.

Function prototype parameters

These are:

- x: specifies the logical x-coordinate of the endpoint for the line.

- y: specifies the logical y-coordinate of the endpoint for the line.
- point: specifies the endpoint for the line. You can pass either a POINT structure or a CPoint object for this parameter.

Draws a line from the current position up to, but not including, the point specified by x and y (or point). The line is drawn with the selected pen. The current position is set to x,y or to point.

Example 1

```
#include <afxwin.h>
#include <math.h>

int mx;
int my;

class CMainWindow : public CFrameWnd
{
public :

    CDC        my_memDC;
    CBitmap    my_bitmap;
    CBrush     my_brush;
    CFont      my_font;

    CPen       my_redpen;
    CPen       my_bluepen;
    CPen       my_blackpen;

    CMainWindow();

    afx_msg void OnPaint();

    void DrawGraph();

    DECLARE_MESSAGE_MAP()
};

CMainWindow::CMainWindow()
{
    Create(NULL , " Simple graphics output using virtual
device context");

    CClientDC dc(this);
```

```
      mx=GetSystemMetrics(SM_CXSCREEN);
      my=GetSystemMetrics(SM_CYSCREEN);

      my_memDC.CreateCompatibleDC(&dc);
      my_bitmap.CreateCompatibleBitmap(&dc,mx,my);
      my_memDC.SelectObject(&my_bitmap);

      my_brush.CreateStockObject(WHITE_BRUSH);
      my_memDC.SelectObject(&my_brush);

      my_memDC.PatBlt(0,0,mx,my,PATCOPY);

      my_redpen.CreatePen(  PS_SOLID,2,RGB(255,   0,   0));
      my_bluepen.CreatePen( PS_SOLID,2,RGB(  0,   0,255));
      my_blackpen.CreatePen(PS_SOLID,2,BLACK_PEN);

}

class CMyApplication : public CWinApp
{
public :
BOOL InitInstance();
};

BOOL CMyApplication::InitInstance()
{

    m_pMainWnd = new CMainWindow;
    m_pMainWnd->ShowWindow(m_nCmdShow);
    m_pMainWnd->UpdateWindow();

    return TRUE;
}

BEGIN_MESSAGE_MAP(CMainWindow,CFrameWnd)
    ON_WM_PAINT()
END_MESSAGE_MAP()

afx_msg void CMainWindow::OnPaint()
{
    DrawGraph();

    CPaintDC dc(this);
```

```
    dc.BitBlt(0,0,mx,my,&my_memDC,0,0,SRCCOPY);

    return;
}

void CMainWindow::DrawGraph()
{

    int    angled;
    double angler;
    double y=180;
    int sine=180;
    int cosine=360;
    const double pi=4*atan(1.0);

    my_memDC.SelectObject(&my_redpen);

    for (angled=0;angled<361;++angled)
    {
       my_memDC.MoveTo(angled,sine);
       angler = angled*2*pi/360;
       y         = sin(angler);
       sine      = 180 + int(180*y);
       my_memDC.LineTo(angled,sine);
    }

    my_memDC.SelectObject(&my_bluepen);

    for (angled=0;angled<361;++angled)
    {
       my_memDC.MoveTo(angled,cosine);
       angler = angled*2*pi/360;
       y         = cos(angler);
       cosine = 180 + int(180*y);
       my_memDC.LineTo(angled,cosine);
    }

    my_memDC.SelectObject(&my_blackpen);

    my_memDC.MoveTo(0,180);

    my_memDC.LineTo(360,180);

}
```

```
CMyApplication  Application;
```

Running the program

Follow the normal steps to compile and run the program. You should see something like:

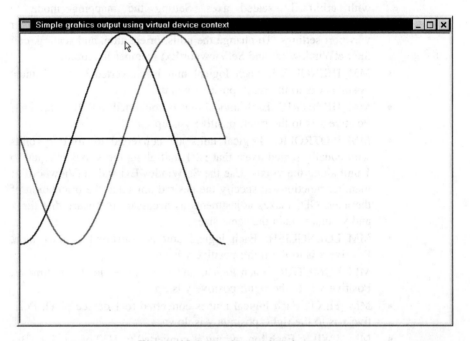

Figure 15.1 *Simple graphical output.*

The lines are coloured red and blue. We will ignore the mathematical meaning of the plots for the time being.

Additional features

We will now look at some of the functionality provided by Visual C++ in the graphics area.

Function prototype CDC::SetMapMode

virtual int SetMapMode(int nMapMode)

Function prototype parameter

This is:

- NMapMode: Specifies the new mapping mode. It can be any one of the following values:

    - MM_ANISOTROPIC: Logical units are converted to arbitrary units with arbitrarily scaled axes. Setting the mapping mode to MM_ANISOTROPIC does not change the current window or viewport settings. To change the units, orientation, and scaling, call the SetWindowExt and SetViewportExt member functions.
    - MM_HIENGLISH: Each logical unit is converted to 0.001 inch. Positive x is to the right; positive y is up.
    - MM_HIMETRIC: Each logical unit is converted to 0.01 millimeter. Positive x is to the right; positive y is up.
    - MM_ISOTROPIC: Logical units are converted to arbitrary units with equally scaled axes; that is, 1 unit along the x-axis is equal to 1 unit along the y-axis. Use the SetWindowExt and SetViewportExt member functions to specify the desired units and the orientation of the axes. GDI makes adjustments as necessary to ensure that the x and y units remain the same size.
    - MM_LOENGLISH: Each logical unit is converted to 0.01 inch. Positive x is to the right; positive y is up.
    - MM_LOMETRIC: Each logical unit is converted to 0.1 millimeter. Positive x is to the right; positive y is up.
    - MM_TEXT: Each logical unit is converted to 1 device pixel. Positive x is to the right; positive y is down.
    - MM_TWIPS: Each logical unit is converted to 1/20 of a point. (Because a point is 1/72 inch, a twip is 1/1440 inch.) Positive x is to the right; positive y is up.

Sets the mapping mode. The mapping mode defines the unit of measure used to convert logical units to device units; it also defines the orientation of the device's x- and y-axes. GDI uses the mapping mode to convert logical coordinates into the appropriate device coordinates. The MM_TEXT mode allows applications to work in device pixels, where 1 unit is equal to 1 pixel. The physical size of a pixel varies from device to device. The:

- MM_HIENGLISH
- MM_HIMETRIC
- MM_LOENGLISH
- MM_LOMETRIC
- MM_TWIPS

modes are useful for applications that must draw in physically meaningful units (such as inches or millimeters). The MM_ISOTROPIC mode ensures a 1:1 aspect ratio, which is useful when it is important to preserve the exact shape of an image. The MM_ANISOTROPIC mode allows the x- and y-coordinates to be adjusted independently.

Function prototype CDC::SetViewportExt

The function prototype are:

- virtual CSize SetViewportExt(int cx, int cy)
- virtual CSize SetViewportExt(SIZE size)

Function prototype return value

The previous extents of the viewport as a CSize object. When an error occurs, the x- and y-coordinates of the returned CSize object are both set to 0.

Function prototype parameters

These are:

- cx: Specifies the x-extent of the viewport (in device units).
- cy: Specifies the y-extent of the viewport (in device units).
- size: Specifies the x- and y-extents of the viewport (in device units).

Sets the x- and y-extents of the viewport of the device context. The viewport, along with the device-context window, defines how GDI maps points in the logical coordinate system to points in the coordinate system of the actual device. In other words, they define how GDI converts logical coordinates into device coordinates.

When the following mapping modes are set, calls to SetWindowExt and SetViewportExt are ignored:

- MM_HIENGLISH MM_LOMETRIC
- MM_HIMETRIC MM_TEXT
- MM_LOENGLISH MM_TWIPS

When MM_ISOTROPIC mode is set, an application must call the SetWindowExt member function before it calls SetViewportExt.

Function prototype CDC::SetViewportOrg

These are:

- virtual CPoint SetViewportOrg(int x, int y)
- virtual CPoint SetViewportOrg(POINT point)

Function prototype return value

The previous origin of the viewport (in device coordinates) as a CPoint object.

Function prototype parameters

These are:

- x: Specifies the x-coordinate (in device units) of the origin of the viewport. The value must be within the range of the device coordinate system.
- y: Specifies the y-coordinate (in device units) of the origin of the viewport. The value must be within the range of the device coordinate system.
- point: Specifies the origin of the viewport. The values must be within the range of the device coordinate system. You can pass either a POINT structure or a CPoint object for this parameter.

Sets the viewport origin of the device context. The viewport, along with the de-vice-context window, defines how GDI maps points in the logical coordinate system to points in the coordinate system of the actual device. In other words, they define how GDI converts logical coordinates into device coordinates.

The viewport origin marks the point in the device coordinate system to which GDI maps the window origin, a point in the logical coordinate system specified by the SetWindowOrg member function. GDI maps all other points by following the same process required to map the window origin to the viewport origin. For example, all points in a circle around the point at the window origin will be in a circle around the point at the viewport origin. Similarly, all points in a line that passes through the window origin will be in a line that passes through the viewport origin.

Example 2

We have added a small amount of additional code. The complete source is in Ap-pendix E. We will set a map-mode, window-extent , view-port and view-port origin. There is also an additional function - tangent.

Running the program

You should see something that shown below:

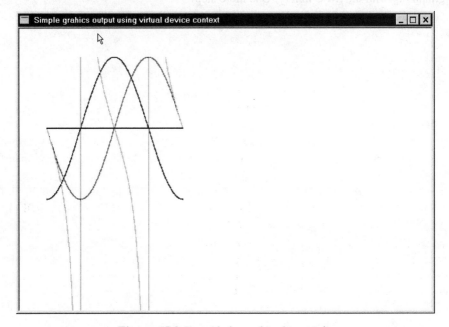

Figure 15.2 Extended graphical example.

The additional code is:

```
dc.SetMapMode(MM_ISOTROPIC);
dc.SetWindowExt(720,720);
dc.SetViewportExt(500,500);
dc.SetViewportOrg(50,50);
```

Summary

There has been a coverage of:

- Device contexts.
- Bitmaps.
- Brushes.
- Pens.
- Colour.
- Coordinate systems.

And it is necessary to develop an understanding of each of the above to make effective use of the MFC for graphics programming.

We have now covered all but one of the essential components of windows programming with the MFC library. One more step!

16

Bitmaps Using Device Contexts

Overview

This chapter looks at bitmaps. Two types **are** supported by windows, and these are:

- bmp.
- DIB with a control, e.g. dialog box.

Bitmaps using device contexts

A bitmap is a graphics image and there are two kinds of bitmaps:

- Device dependent.
- Device independent.

We will concentrate on the first in this chapter.

Device-dependent bitmaps -- DDB

These were the first to be supported by windows and can be created by a number of programs. The file format is supported by a wide variety of applications including:

- Paint – the default file format for this application.
- Word.
- Paint Shop Pro.
- Corel Photo-Paint.

to name just a few. Their appearance will vary with the device being used.

Device-independent bitmaps – DIB

The DIB file format was designed to ensure that bitmapped graphics created using one application can be loaded and displayed in another application, retaining the same appearance as the original. Achieving this is not as straightforward as it might first appear. The most obvious problem is between a screen image and a printed image. Here there is the problem of transmitted versus reflected light, and the differences in resolutions.

Colour

It is necessary to look at the concept of colour to understand some of the problems that can occur with bitmaps. As Foley et al say *Color is an immensely complex subject, one that draws on concepts and results from physics, physiology, psychology, art and graphic design.* You are strongly recommend getting hold of their book if you want to develop a better understanding of the whole computer graphics field. Details are given at the end of this chapter.

Each pixel has a number of bits associated with it that provide colour information and the following table summarises this.

Table 16.1 Colour availability.

Number of bits	Number of Colours
1	2
2	4
4	16
8	256
16	65536
24	16777216

Windows works with the Red Green Blue or RGB colour model. This is one of a number of colour models in existence, e.g.

- HSV – Hue, Saturation and Value
- CMY – Cyan, Magenta and Yellow
- YIQ – used in U.S. commercial colour televison broadcasting

Each component of the RGB model can take on 256 values. This means 24 bit colour and is sometimes called true colour.

Screen resolution, graphics memory and colours displayed

There is obviously going to be a link between the screen resolution, the amount of graphics memory in your graphics and the number of colours that can be displayed.

A 2Mb graphics card can therefore provide 16 bit colour at 1024*768. This same card could provide 24 bit colour at 800*600. Modern 8Mb graphics cards support 24 bit colour at 1024*768.

Creating a bitmap

There are a number of options here, and the choice is yours. Paint is probably the obvious one as this program is installed with windows. You can use the resource editor within Developer Studio too.

You can also browse your computer to see what samples can be found. One place to look is:

```
Program Files\Microsoft Visual Studio\Common\
Graphics\Bitmaps
```

and there are a couple of directories to look in.

These bitmaps have both a small number of pixels and a low numbers of bits for colour information.

Two other options include scanned images and using a digital camera. The bitmap in this example started out as a colour photograph. The bitmap is 522*791 pixels in 24 bit colour mode.

CBitmap

The CBitmap class encapsulates a windows graphics device interface (GDI) bitmap and provides member functions to manipulate the bitmap. To use a CBitmap object we:

- Construct the object.
- Attach a bitmap handle to it.
- Call the object's member functions.

Function prototype CBitmap::LoadBitmap

This member function loads the bitmap resource named by lpszResourceName, or identified by the ID number in nIDResource, from the application's executable file. The loaded bitmap is attached to the CBitmap object. The function prototypes are:

- BOOL LoadBitmap (LPCTSTR lpszResourceName);
- BOOL LoadBitmap (UINT nIDResource);

The two stage process involves therefore:

- Construction: CBitmap – Constructs a CBitmap object.
- Initialisation: LoadBitmap -- Initialises the object by loading a named bitmap resource from the application's executable file and attaching the bitmap to the object.

The resource file

```
jenny   bitmap  jenny.bmp
```

The bitmap name within the C++ source file is jenny and the file exists externally with the name jenny.bmp.

The C++ source file

This is given below.

```
#include <afxwin.h>
#include <math.h>

int mx;
int my;

class CMainWindow : public CFrameWnd
{
public :

    CDC         my_memDC;
    CBitmap     my_bitmap;
    CBrush      my_brush;

    CBitmap     my_photo_bitmap;

    CMainWindow();
```

```
    afx_msg void OnPaint();

    DECLARE_MESSAGE_MAP()
};

CMainWindow::CMainWindow()
{
    Create(NULL ,
" Simple graphics output using virtual device context");

    CClientDC dc(this);

    mx=GetSystemMetrics(SM_CXSCREEN);
    my=GetSystemMetrics(SM_CYSCREEN);

    my_memDC.CreateCompatibleDC(&dc);
    my_bitmap.CreateCompatibleBitmap(&dc,mx,my);
    my_memDC.SelectObject(&my_bitmap);

    my_brush.CreateStockObject(WHITE_BRUSH);
    my_memDC.SelectObject(&my_brush);

    my_memDC.PatBlt(0,0,mx,my,PATCOPY);

    my_photo_bitmap.LoadBitmap("jenny");
    my_memDC.SelectObject(&my_photo_bitmap);

}

class CMyApplication : public CWinApp
{
public :
BOOL InitInstance();
};

BOOL CMyApplication::InitInstance()
{

    m_pMainWnd = new CMainWindow;
    m_pMainWnd->ShowWindow(m_nCmdShow);
    m_pMainWnd->UpdateWindow();

    return TRUE;
}
```

```
BEGIN_MESSAGE_MAP(CMainWindow,CFrameWnd)
   ON_WM_PAINT()
END_MESSAGE_MAP()


afx_msg void CMainWindow::OnPaint()
{
   CPaintDC dc(this);

   dc.BitBlt(0,0,mx,my,&my_memDC,0,0,SRCCOPY);

   return;
}


CMyApplication Application;
```

The two additional statements in this example are:

```
my_photo_bitmap.LoadBitmap("jenny");
my_memDC.SelectObject(&my_photo_bitmap);
```

The first loads the bitmap from the external file. The second selects the object into the device context.

Running the program

Compile and run the program in the normal way. You should end up with a window similar to the one below:

Figure 16.1 Simple bitmap.

Well not exactly like the one above. This started off as a photograph, scanned on an Apple Mac, FTP'ed to another system as the scanned image was too big for a floppy disk. FTP'ed to a pc and then converted to bmp format.

DIB

Bitmaps that contain a colour table are device-independent. A colour table describes how pixel values correspond to RGB color values. RGB is a model for describing colours that are produced by emitting light. A DIB contains the following information:

- The colour format of the device on which the image was created.
- The resolution of the device on which the image was created.
- The palette for the device on which the image was created.
- An array of bits that maps red, green, blue (RGB) triplets to pixels in the rectangular image. A data-compression identifier that indicates the data compression scheme (if any) used to reduce the size of the array of bits.

The colour and dimension information is stored in a BITMAPINFO structure.

More information can be found in the on-line help. Some additional sources are given in the bibliography.

Summary

This example has shown how to use bitmaps within our windows programs. The process is quite straightforward.

Bibliography

Foley, van Dam, Feiner, Hughes, *Computer Graphics: Principles and Practice*, Addison Wesley

Essential reading if you are going to get involved in graphics programming. This looks at graphics programming generally.

17

Where Next?

Overview

Simple really – where do we go next?

Where next?

We have now covered the essentials of windows programming using the MFC library. This includes:

- The two key Windows classes:
  - CFameWnd and CWinApp.
- Message maps and message handling.
- User interface features using controls:
  - Menus, dialog boxes, list boxes, check boxes, edit boxes, radio buttons.
- Graphical output using device contexts:
  - Text i/o, simple graphics i/o and bitmaps.

However there is no such thing as a free lunch. You should have seen by now that learning about windows and the MFC library requires some real effort on your part. You have taken the first step down the road.

Inheritance is a major component of successful MFC programming. You need to have a knowledge of the class hierarchy and refine your understanding over time.

On-line help

The on-line help – essential. When you have a problem you need to persevere until you find the information that you require to sort things out. The information that you need turns up in some strange places at times.

MSDN CDs

If you don't have a version of Developer Studio with these CDs you are missing out on a very valuable source of information. Take a look in your local bookshop and see what these CDs replace in terms of printed documentation.

This information is also made available at the following url:

```
http://msdn.microsoft.com/library/default.htm
```

As was stated earlier, if you have internet access then this is a very valuable resource.

On-line examples

The on-line examples provide another very useful source of information. They show how Microsoft expect applications to be developed.

Wizards

The wizards can be used to generate skeleton code that can be tailored to your specific needs.

Books

Have a look at:

- Zaratian B., *Visual C++ Programmer's Guide*, Microsoft Press.
- Kruglinski David J., Shepherd George, Wingo Scot, *Programming Microsoft Visual C++ 6, Fifth Edition,* Microsoft Press..
- Prosise J., *Programming Windows 95 with MFC,* Microsoft Press.
- Eugene Kain, *The MFC Answer Book*, Addison Wesley.

Also have a look for books by Mike Blaszczak. He is one of the major architects behind MFC. Two to consider are:

- Blaszczak M., *Professional MFC With Visual C++ 6*, Wrox Press.

- Blaszczak M., *The Revolutionary Guide to Win32 Programming Using Visual C++*, WROX Press.

Here is some of his background taken from the Amazon website.

"Mike Blaszczak ... he took a position in Microsoft's Consulting Services in March of 1992. In November of 1993, Mike joined the development team, working on the Microsoft Foundation Classes in Redmond, Washington. Mike accepted a promotion (which is Latin for 'lateral move') to Program Manager and was, for a time, responsible for managing the development, documentation and delivery of the Microsoft Foundation Classes and the C Run-time Libraries. Mike decided that playing with cards was much more fun than playing with schedules, so he laterally removed himself back to the development team. ... Mike does presentations wherever they'll invite him back. He likes referring to himself in third-person. Mike is currently responsible for telling all of his friends about the rules in ice hockey, saving up money to buy another vowel for his last name, getting nicer strings for his bass guitar and completing a variety of design and development tasks relating to MFC. You can write to Mike at 76360,157 on CompuServe. He also answers Internet mail at mikeblas@msn.com. Mail sent care of The Goose Pub and Eatery may be answered but is not guaranteed to reach the author."

Another place to look is on-line at Amazon to see what is currently available. They provide details of what is selling. A crude indicator, but better than none.

Try

```
http://www.amazon.com/
```

or

```
http://www.amazon.co.uk/
```

Depends where you live.

Web resources

The obvious one is:

```
http://www.microsoft.com/
```

They provide a massive amount of information.
More specific urls include:

```
http://msdn.microsoft.com/default.asp
```

and

```
http://msdn.microsoft.com/vstudio/
```

and

`http://msdn.microsoft.com/library/default.htm`

There are patches to Developer Studio and the last time I looked this was Service Pack 3. This was approximately 120 Mb. It is also available to registered users on CD.

Summary

Be patient. Rome wasn't built in a day. Getting on top of Visual C++ and the MFC library will take time.

Appendix A: Toolbar Example

Menu ID file

```
#define ID_MA_FILE_NEW          10
#define ID_MA_FILE_OPEN         11
#define ID_MA_FILE_SAVE         12
#define ID_MA_FILE_SAVE_AS      13
#define ID_MA_FILE_PAGE_SETUP   14
#define ID_MA_FILE_PRINT        15
#define ID_MA_APP_EXIT          16

#define ID_MA_EDIT_UNDO         20
#define ID_MA_EDIT_CUT          21
#define ID_MA_EDIT_COPY         22
#define ID_MA_EDIT_PASTE        23
#define ID_MA_EDIT_DELETE       24

#define ID_MA_VIEW_NORMAL       30
#define ID_MA_VIEW_ZOOM         31

#define ID_MA_APP_HELP          40
#define ID_MA_APP_ABOUT         41

#define ID_TOOLBAR              50

#define ID_TOOLBAR_BMP          60
```

Resource file

```
#include "resource.h"
#include "menuids.h"

DEFAULTMENU MENU DISCARDABLE
BEGIN
    POPUP "&File"
    BEGIN
        MENUITEM "&New\tCntl+N",ID_MA_FILE_NEW
        MENUITEM "&Open\tCntl+O",ID_MA_FILE_OPEN
        MENUITEM "&Save\tCntl+S",ID_MA_FILE_SAVE
        MENUITEM "Save &as",ID_MA_FILE_SAVE_AS
        MENUITEM SEPARATOR
        MENUITEM "Page Set&up",ID_MA_FILE_PAGE_SETUP
        MENUITEM "&Print\tCntl+P",ID_MA_FILE_PRINT
        MENUITEM SEPARATOR
        MENUITEM "&Exit",ID_MA_APP_EXIT
    END
    POPUP "&Edit"
    BEGIN
        MENUITEM "&Undo\tCntl+Z",ID_MA_EDIT_UNDO
        MENUITEM "Cu&t\tCntl+X",ID_MA_EDIT_CUT
        MENUITEM "&Copy\tCntl+C",ID_MA_EDIT_COPY
        MENUITEM "&Paste\tCntl+V",ID_MA_EDIT_PASTE
        MENUITEM "&Delete",ID_MA_EDIT_DELETE
    END
    POPUP "&View"
    BEGIN
        MENUITEM "&Normal",ID_MA_VIEW_NORMAL
        MENUITEM "&Zoom",ID_MA_VIEW_ZOOM
    END
    POPUP "&Help"
    BEGIN
        MENUITEM "&Help",ID_MA_APP_HELP
        MENUITEM "&About",ID_MA_APP_ABOUT
    END
END


DEFAULTMENU ACCELERATORS MOVEABLE PURE
BEGIN
    "N",ID_MA_FILE_NEW,VIRTKEY, CONTROL
    "O",ID_MA_FILE_OPEN,VIRTKEY, CONTROL
```

```
          "S",ID_MA_FILE_SAVE,VIRTKEY,  CONTROL
          "P",ID_MA_FILE_PRINT,VIRTKEY,  CONTROL
          "Z",ID_MA_EDIT_UNDO,VIRTKEY,  CONTROL
          "X",ID_MA_EDIT_CUT,VIRTKEY,  CONTROL
          "C",ID_MA_EDIT_COPY,VIRTKEY,  CONTROL
          "V",ID_MA_EDIT_PASTE,VIRTKEY,  CONTROL
END

DEFAULTMENU TOOLBAR DISCARDABLE   24,23
BEGIN
     BUTTON          ID_MA_FILE_NEW
     BUTTON          ID_MA_FILE_OPEN
     BUTTON          ID_MA_FILE_SAVE
     SEPARATOR
     BUTTON          ID_MA_EDIT_CUT
     BUTTON          ID_MA_EDIT_COPY
     BUTTON          ID_MA_EDIT_PASTE
     SEPARATOR
     BUTTON          ID_MA_FILE_PRINT
     SEPARATOR
     BUTTON          ID_MA_APP_ABOUT
END

DEFAULTMENU BITMAP DISCARDABLE "defaultm.bmp"
```

C++ source file

```cpp
#include <afxwin.h>
#include <afxcmn.h>
#include <afxext.h>
#include "menuids.h"

class CMainWindow : public CFrameWnd
{

public :
   CMainWindow();

   afx_msg void OnNew();
   afx_msg void OnOpen();
   afx_msg void OnSave();
   afx_msg void OnSaveas();
   afx_msg void OnPageSetup();
   afx_msg void OnPrint();
```

```cpp
    afx_msg void OnExit();

    afx_msg void OnUndo();
    afx_msg void OnCut();
    afx_msg void OnCopy();
    afx_msg void OnPaste();
    afx_msg void OnDelete();

    afx_msg void OnNormal();
    afx_msg void OnZoom();

    afx_msg void OnHelp();
    afx_msg void OnAbout();

protected:

    CToolBar      MyToolBar;

    DECLARE_MESSAGE_MAP()
};

CMainWindow::CMainWindow()
{
    Create(NULL ,
               " Toolbar program " ,
               WS_OVERLAPPEDWINDOW ,
               rectDefault ,
               NULL ,
               "DEFAULTMENU");
    LoadAccelTable("DEFAULTMENU");

    MyToolBar.CreateEx(this, TBSTYLE_FLAT, WS_CHILD |
WS_VISIBLE | CBRS_TOP
        | CBRS_GRIPPER | CBRS_TOOLTIPS | CBRS_FLYBY |
CBRS_SIZE_DYNAMIC);

    MyToolBar.LoadToolBar("DEFAULTMENU");
}


class CMyApplication : public CWinApp
{
public :
    BOOL InitInstance();
};
```

```
BOOL CMyApplication::InitInstance()
{
    m_pMainWnd = new CMainWindow;
    m_pMainWnd->ShowWindow(m_nCmdShow);
    m_pMainWnd->UpdateWindow();

    return TRUE;
}

BEGIN_MESSAGE_MAP(CMainWindow,CFrameWnd)

    ON_COMMAND( ID_MA_FILE_NEW,OnNew )
    ON_COMMAND( ID_MA_FILE_OPEN,OnOpen)
    ON_COMMAND( ID_MA_FILE_SAVE,OnSave)
    ON_COMMAND( ID_MA_FILE_SAVE_AS,OnSaveas)
    ON_COMMAND( ID_MA_FILE_PAGE_SETUP,OnPageSetup)
    ON_COMMAND( ID_MA_FILE_PRINT,OnPrint)
    ON_COMMAND( ID_MA_APP_EXIT,OnExit)

    ON_COMMAND(  ID_MA_EDIT_UNDO,OnUndo)
    ON_COMMAND(  ID_MA_EDIT_CUT,OnCut)
    ON_COMMAND(  ID_MA_EDIT_COPY,OnCopy)
    ON_COMMAND(  ID_MA_EDIT_PASTE,OnPaste)
    ON_COMMAND(  ID_MA_EDIT_DELETE,OnDelete)

    ON_COMMAND(  ID_MA_VIEW_NORMAL,OnNormal)
    ON_COMMAND(ID_MA_VIEW_ZOOM,OnZoom)

    ON_COMMAND(ID_MA_APP_HELP,OnHelp)
    ON_COMMAND(ID_MA_APP_ABOUT,OnAbout)

END_MESSAGE_MAP()

afx_msg void CMainWindow::OnNew()
{ MessageBox("New","New");}

afx_msg void CMainWindow::OnOpen()
{ MessageBox("Open","Open");}

afx_msg void CMainWindow::OnSave()
{ MessageBox("Save","Save");}

afx_msg void CMainWindow::OnSaveas()
{ MessageBox("Saveas","Saveas");}
```

```
afx_msg void CMainWindow::OnPageSetup()
{ MessageBox("PageSetup","PageSetup"); }

afx_msg void CMainWindow::OnPrint()
{ MessageBox("Print","Print"); }

afx_msg void CMainWindow::OnExit()
{ MessageBox("Exit","Exit"); }

afx_msg void CMainWindow::OnUndo()
{ MessageBox("Undo","Undo"); }

afx_msg void CMainWindow::OnCut()
{ MessageBox("Cut","Cut"); }

afx_msg void CMainWindow::OnCopy()
{ MessageBox("Copy","Copy"); }

afx_msg void CMainWindow::OnPaste()
{ MessageBox("Paste","Paste"); }

afx_msg void CMainWindow::OnDelete()
{ MessageBox("Delete","Delete"); }

afx_msg void CMainWindow::OnNormal()
{ MessageBox("Normal","Normal"); }

afx_msg void CMainWindow::OnZoom()
{ MessageBox("Zoom","Zoom"); }

afx_msg void CMainWindow::OnHelp()
{ MessageBox("Help","Help"); }

afx_msg void CMainWindow::OnAbout()
{ MessageBox("About","About"); }

CMyApplication Application;
```

Appendix B:
Statusbar and
Tooltips Example

Menu ID file

```
#define  ID_MA_FILE_NEW         10
#define  ID_MA_FILE_OPEN        11
#define  ID_MA_FILE_SAVE        12
#define  ID_MA_FILE_SAVE_AS     13
#define  ID_MA_FILE_PAGE_SETUP  14
#define  ID_MA_FILE_PRINT       15
#define  ID_MA_APP_EXIT         16

#define  ID_MA_EDIT_UNDO        20
#define  ID_MA_EDIT_CUT         21
#define  ID_MA_EDIT_COPY        22
#define  ID_MA_EDIT_PASTE       23
#define  ID_MA_EDIT_DELETE      24

#define  ID_MA_VIEW_NORMAL      30
#define  ID_MA_VIEW_ZOOM        31

#define  ID_MA_APP_HELP         40
#define  ID_MA_APP_ABOUT        41

#define  ID_TOOLBAR             50

#define  ID_TOOLBAR_BMP         60
#define  NBUTTONS                8
```

Resource file

```
#include "resource.h"
#include "menuids.h"

DEFAULTMENU MENU DISCARDABLE
BEGIN
    POPUP "&File"
    BEGIN
        MENUITEM "&New\tCntl+N",ID_MA_FILE_NEW
        MENUITEM "&Open\tCntl+O",ID_MA_FILE_OPEN
        MENUITEM "&Save\tCntl+S",ID_MA_FILE_SAVE
        MENUITEM "Save &as",ID_MA_FILE_SAVE_AS
        MENUITEM SEPARATOR
        MENUITEM "Page Set&up",ID_MA_FILE_PAGE_SETUP
        MENUITEM "&Print\tCntl+P",ID_MA_FILE_PRINT
        MENUITEM SEPARATOR
        MENUITEM "&Exit",ID_MA_APP_EXIT
    END
    POPUP "&Edit"
    BEGIN
        MENUITEM "&Undo\tCntl+Z",ID_MA_EDIT_UNDO
        MENUITEM "Cu&t\tCntl+X",ID_MA_EDIT_CUT
        MENUITEM "&Copy\tCntl+C",ID_MA_EDIT_COPY
        MENUITEM "&Paste\tCntl+V",ID_MA_EDIT_PASTE
        MENUITEM "&Delete",ID_MA_EDIT_DELETE
    END
    POPUP "&View"
    BEGIN
        MENUITEM "&Normal",ID_MA_VIEW_NORMAL
        MENUITEM "&Zoom",ID_MA_VIEW_ZOOM
    END
    POPUP "&Help"
    BEGIN
        MENUITEM "&Help",ID_MA_APP_HELP
        MENUITEM "&About",ID_MA_APP_ABOUT
    END
END
DEFAULTMENU ACCELERATORS MOVEABLE PURE
BEGIN
    "N",ID_MA_FILE_NEW,VIRTKEY, CONTROL
    "O",ID_MA_FILE_OPEN,VIRTKEY, CONTROL
    "S",ID_MA_FILE_SAVE,VIRTKEY, CONTROL
    "P",ID_MA_FILE_PRINT,VIRTKEY, CONTROL
```

```
        "Z",ID_MA_EDIT_UNDO,VIRTKEY, CONTROL
        "X",ID_MA_EDIT_CUT,VIRTKEY, CONTROL
        "C",ID_MA_EDIT_COPY,VIRTKEY, CONTROL
        "V",ID_MA_EDIT_PASTE,VIRTKEY, CONTROL
END


DEFAULTMENU TOOLBAR DISCARDABLE   24,23
BEGIN
        BUTTON          ID_MA_FILE_NEW
        BUTTON          ID_MA_FILE_OPEN
        BUTTON          ID_MA_FILE_SAVE
        SEPARATOR
        BUTTON          ID_MA_EDIT_CUT
        BUTTON          ID_MA_EDIT_COPY
        BUTTON          ID_MA_EDIT_PASTE
        SEPARATOR
        BUTTON          ID_MA_FILE_PRINT
        SEPARATOR
        BUTTON          ID_MA_APP_ABOUT
END


DEFAULTMENU BITMAP DISCARDABLE "defaultm.bmp"
STRINGTABLE DISCARDABLE
BEGIN
    ID_MA_FILE_NEW "Create a new document\nNew"
    ID_MA_FILE_OPEN "Open an existing document\nOpen"
    ID_MA_FILE_SAVE "Save the active document\nSave"
    ID_MA_FILE_PRINT "Print the active document\nPrint"
    ID_MA_APP_ABOUT
"Display program information, version number and copyright\nAbout"
    ID_MA_EDIT_COPY
"Copy the selection and put it on the Clipboard\nCopy"
    ID_MA_EDIT_CUT
"Cut the selection and put it on the Clipboard\nCut"
    ID_MA_EDIT_PASTE "Insert Clipboard contents\nPaste"
END
```

C++ source file

```cpp
#include <afxwin.h>
#include <afxcmn.h>
#include <afxext.h>
#include "menuids.h"

static UINT indicators[]=
{
   ID_SEPARATOR,
   ID_INDICATOR_CAPS,
   ID_INDICATOR_NUM,
   ID_INDICATOR_SCRL,
};

class CMainWindow : public CFrameWnd
{

public :
   CMainWindow();

   afx_msg void OnNew();
   afx_msg void OnOpen();
   afx_msg void OnSave();
   afx_msg void OnSaveas();
   afx_msg void OnPageSetup();
   afx_msg void OnPrint();
   afx_msg void OnExit();

   afx_msg void OnUndo();
   afx_msg void OnCut();
   afx_msg void OnCopy();
   afx_msg void OnPaste();
   afx_msg void OnDelete();

   afx_msg void OnNormal();
   afx_msg void OnZoom();

   afx_msg void OnHelp();
   afx_msg void OnAbout();
```

```
protected:

    CToolBar      MyToolBar;
    CStatusBar    MyStatusBar;

    DECLARE_MESSAGE_MAP()
};


CMainWindow::CMainWindow()
{
    Create(NULL ,
            " Toolbar program " ,
            WS_OVERLAPPEDWINDOW ,
            rectDefault ,
            NULL ,
            "DEFAULTMENU");

    LoadAccelTable("DEFAULTMENU");


    MyToolBar.CreateEx(this, TBSTYLE_FLAT, WS_CHILD |
WS_VISIBLE | CBRS_TOP
        | CBRS_GRIPPER | CBRS_TOOLTIPS | CBRS_FLYBY |
CBRS_SIZE_DYNAMIC);


    MyToolBar.LoadToolBar("DEFAULTMENU");

        MyStatusBar.Create(this);

        MyStatusBar.SetIndicators(indicators,sizeof(indica-
tors)/sizeof(UINT));

}
```

```cpp
class CMyApplication : public CWinApp
{
public :
   BOOL InitInstance();
};


BOOL CMyApplication::InitInstance()
{

   m_pMainWnd = new CMainWindow;
   m_pMainWnd->ShowWindow(m_nCmdShow);
   m_pMainWnd->UpdateWindow();

   return TRUE;
}
BEGIN_MESSAGE_MAP(CMainWindow,CFrameWnd)


    ON_COMMAND(ID_MA_FILE_NEW,OnNew)
    ON_COMMAND(ID_MA_FILE_OPEN,OnOpen)
    ON_COMMAND(ID_MA_FILE_SAVE,OnSave)
    ON_COMMAND(ID_MA_FILE_SAVE_AS,OnSaveas)
    ON_COMMAND(ID_MA_FILE_PAGE_SETUP,OnPageSetup)
    ON_COMMAND(ID_MA_FILE_PRINT,OnPrint)
    ON_COMMAND(ID_MA_APP_EXIT,OnExit)


    ON_COMMAND(ID_MA_EDIT_UNDO,OnUndo)
    ON_COMMAND(ID_MA_EDIT_CUT,OnCut)
    ON_COMMAND(ID_MA_EDIT_COPY,OnCopy)
    ON_COMMAND(ID_MA_EDIT_PASTE,OnPaste)
    ON_COMMAND(ID_MA_EDIT_DELETE,OnDelete)


    ON_COMMAND(ID_MA_VIEW_NORMAL,OnNormal)
    ON_COMMAND(ID_MA_VIEW_ZOOM,OnZoom)


    ON_COMMAND(ID_MA_APP_HELP,OnHelp)
    ON_COMMAND(ID_MA_APP_ABOUT,OnAbou)

END_MESSAGE_MAP()
```

```
afx_msg void CMainWindow::OnNew()
{ MessageBox("New","New"); }

afx_msg void CMainWindow::OnOpen()
{ MessageBox("Open","Open"); }

afx_msg void CMainWindow::OnSave()
{ MessageBox("Save","Save"); }

afx_msg void CMainWindow::OnSaveas()
{ MessageBox("Saveas","Saveas"); }


afx_msg void CMainWindow::OnPageSetup()
{ MessageBox("PageSetup","PageSetup"); }

afx_msg void CMainWindow::OnPrint()
{ MessageBox("Print","Print"); }


afx_msg void CMainWindow::OnExit()
{ MessageBox("Exit","Exit"); }


afx_msg void CMainWindow::OnUndo()
{ MessageBox("Undo","Undo"); }

afx_msg void CMainWindow::OnCut()
{ MessageBox("Cut","Cut"); }

afx_msg void CMainWindow::OnCopy()
{ MessageBox("Copy","Copy"); }

afx_msg void CMainWindow::OnPaste()
{ MessageBox("Paste","Paste"); }

afx_msg void CMainWindow::OnDelete()
{ MessageBox("Delete","Delete"); }

afx_msg void CMainWindow::OnNormal()
{ MessageBox("Normal","Normal"); }

afx_msg void CMainWindow::OnZoom()
{ MessageBox("Zoom","Zoom"); }
```

```
afx_msg void CMainWindow::OnHelp()
{ MessageBox("Help","Help"); }

afx_msg void CMainWindow::OnAbout()
{ MessageBox("About","About"); }

CMyApplication Application;
```

Appendix C: Icon example

Menu ID file

```
#define  ID_MA_FILE_NEW          10
#define  ID_MA_FILE_OPEN         11
#define  ID_MA_FILE_SAVE         12
#define  ID_MA_FILE_SAVE_AS      13
#define  ID_MA_FILE_PAGE_SETUP   14
#define  ID_MA_FILE_PRINT        15
#define  ID_MA_APP_EXIT          16

#define  ID_MA_EDIT_UNDO         20
#define  ID_MA_EDIT_CUT          21
#define  ID_MA_EDIT_COPY         22
#define  ID_MA_EDIT_PASTE        23
#define  ID_MA_EDIT_DELETE       24

#define  ID_MA_VIEW_NORMAL       30
#define  ID_MA_VIEW_ZOOM         31

#define  ID_MA_APP_HELP          40
#define  ID_MA_APP_ABOUT         41

#define  ID_TOOLBAR              50

#define  ID_TOOLBAR_BMP          60
```

Resource File

```
#include "resource.h"
#include "menuids.h"

DEFAULTMENU MENU DISCARDABLE
BEGIN
     POPUP "&File"
     BEGIN
          MENUITEM "&New\tCntl+N",ID_MA_FILE_NEW
          MENUITEM "&Open\tCntl+O",ID_MA_FILE_OPEN
          MENUITEM "&Save\tCntl+S",ID_MA_FILE_SAVE
          MENUITEM "Save &as",ID_MA_FILE_SAVE_AS
          MENUITEM SEPARATOR
          MENUITEM "Page Set&up",ID_MA_FILE_PAGE_SETUP
          MENUITEM "&Print\tCntl+P",ID_MA_FILE_PRINT
          MENUITEM SEPARATOR
          MENUITEM "&Exit",
ID_MA_APP_EXIT
     END
     POPUP "&Edit"
     BEGIN
          MENUITEM "&Undo\tCntl+Z",ID_MA_EDIT_UNDO
          MENUITEM "Cu&t\tCntl+X",ID_MA_EDIT_CUT
          MENUITEM "&Copy\tCntl+C",ID_MA_EDIT_COPY
          MENUITEM "&Paste\tCntl+V",ID_MA_EDIT_PASTE
          MENUITEM "&Delete",
ID_MA_EDIT_DELETE
     END
     POPUP "&View"
     BEGIN
          MENUITEM "&Normal",ID_MA_VIEW_NORMAL
          MENUITEM "&Zoom",ID_MA_VIEW_ZOOM
     END
     POPUP "&Help"
     BEGIN
          MENUITEM "&Help",ID_MA_APP_HELP
          MENUITEM "&About",ID_MA_APP_ABOUT
     END
END

DEFAULTMENU ACCELERATORS MOVEABLE PURE
BEGIN
     "N", ID_MA_FILE_NEW,VIRTKEY, CONTROL
```

```
        "O",  ID_MA_FILE_OPEN,VIRTKEY,  CONTROL
        "S",  ID_MA_FILE_SAVE,VIRTKEY,  CONTROL
        "P",  ID_MA_FILE_PRINT,VIRTKEY, CONTROL
        "Z",  ID_MA_EDIT_UNDO,VIRTKEY,  CONTROL
        "X",  ID_MA_EDIT_CUT,VIRTKEY,   CONTROL
        "C",  ID_MA_EDIT_COPY,VIRTKEY,  CONTROL
        "V",  ID_MA_EDIT_PASTE,VIRTKEY, CONTROL
END


DEFAULTMENU TOOLBAR DISCARDABLE   24,23
BEGIN
        BUTTON          ID_MA_FILE_NEW
        BUTTON          ID_MA_FILE_OPEN
        BUTTON          ID_MA_FILE_SAVE
        SEPARATOR
        BUTTON          ID_MA_EDIT_CUT
        BUTTON          ID_MA_EDIT_COPY
        BUTTON          ID_MA_EDIT_PASTE
        SEPARATOR
        BUTTON          ID_MA_FILE_PRINT
        SEPARATOR
        BUTTON          ID_MA_APP_ABOUT
END


STRINGTABLE DISCARDABLE
BEGIN
    ID_MA_FILE_NEW  "Create a new document\nNew"
    ID_MA_FILE_OPEN "Open an existing document\nOpen"
    ID_MA_FILE_SAVE "Save the active document\nSave"
    ID_MA_FILE_PRINT "Print the active document\nPrint"
    ID_MA_APP_ABOUT
"Display program information, version number and copyright\nAbout"
    ID_MA_EDIT_COPY
"Copy the selection and put it on the Clipboard\nCopy"
    ID_MA_EDIT_CUT
"Cut the selection and put it on the Clipboard\nCut"
    ID_MA_EDIT_PASTE "Insert Clipboard contents\nPaste"
END


DEFAULTMENU BITMAP  DISCARDABLE "defaultm.bmp"

MyICON                          ICON      "earth.ico"
```

C++ Source File

```cpp
#include <afxwin.h>
#include <afxcmn.h>
#include <afxext.h>
#include "menuids.h"

static UINT indicators[]=
{
    ID_SEPARATOR,
    ID_INDICATOR_CAPS,
    ID_INDICATOR_NUM,
    ID_INDICATOR_SCRL,
};

class CMainWindow : public CFrameWnd
{

public :
    CMainWindow();

    afx_msg void OnNew();
    afx_msg void OnOpen();
    afx_msg void OnSave();
    afx_msg void OnSaveas();
    afx_msg void OnPageSetup();
    afx_msg void OnPrint();
    afx_msg void OnExit();

    afx_msg void OnUndo();
    afx_msg void OnCut();
    afx_msg void OnCopy();
    afx_msg void OnPaste();
    afx_msg void OnDelete();

    afx_msg void OnNormal();
    afx_msg void OnZoom();

    afx_msg void OnHelp();
    afx_msg void OnAbout();

protected:
    CToolBar      MyToolBar;
    CStatusBar    MyStatusBar;
```

```
public:

    CMainWindow(LPCSTR ClassName);

    DECLARE_MESSAGE_MAP()
};

CMainWindow::CMainWindow(LPCSTR ClassName)
{
    Create(ClassName ,
                " Toolbar program with icon " ,
                WS_OVERLAPPEDWINDOW ,
                rectDefault ,
                NULL ,
                "DEFAULTMENU");

    LoadAccelTable("DEFAULTMENU");

    MyToolBar.CreateEx(this, TBSTYLE_FLAT, WS_CHILD |
WS_VISIBLE | CBRS_TOP
        | CBRS_GRIPPER | CBRS_TOOLTIPS | CBRS_FLYBY |
CBRS_SIZE_DYNAMIC);

    MyToolBar.LoadToolBar("DEFAULTMENU");

    MyStatusBar.Create(this);

    MyStatusBar.SetIndicators(indicators,sizeof(indica-
tors)/sizeof(UINT));

}

class CMyApplication : public CWinApp
{
public :
    BOOL InitInstance();
};

BOOL CMyApplication::InitInstance()
{
    CBrush background;

    background.CreateStockObject(WHITE_BRUSH);
```

```
    LPCSTR classname = AfxRegisterWndClass(
        0,
        0,
        background,
        LoadIcon("MyICON"));

    m_pMainWnd = new CMainWindow(classname);

    m_pMainWnd->ShowWindow(m_nCmdShow);
    m_pMainWnd->UpdateWindow();

    return TRUE;
}

BEGIN_MESSAGE_MAP(CMainWindow,CFrameWnd)

    ON_COMMAND(ID_MA_FILE_NEW, OnNew)
    ON_COMMAND(ID_MA_FILE_OPEN, OnOpen)
    ON_COMMAND(ID_MA_FILE_SAVE, OnSave)
    ON_COMMAND(ID_MA_FILE_SAVE_AS, OnSaveas)
    ON_COMMAND(ID_MA_FILE_PAGE_SETUP, OnPageSetup)
    ON_COMMAND(ID_MA_FILE_PRINT, OnPrint)
    ON_COMMAND(ID_MA_APP_EXIT, OnExit)

    ON_COMMAND(ID_MA_EDIT_UNDO, OnUndo)
    ON_COMMAND(ID_MA_EDIT_CUT, OnCut)
    ON_COMMAND(ID_MA_EDIT_COPY, OnCopy)
    ON_COMMAND(ID_MA_EDIT_PASTE, OnPaste)
    ON_COMMAND(ID_MA_EDIT_DELETE, OnDelete)

    ON_COMMAND(ID_MA_VIEW_NORMAL, OnNormal)
    ON_COMMAND(ID_MA_VIEW_ZOOM, OnZoom)

    ON_COMMAND(ID_MA_APP_HELP, OnHelp)
    ON_COMMAND(ID_MA_APP_ABOUT, OnAbout)

END_MESSAGE_MAP()

afx_msg void CMainWindow::OnNew()

{ MessageBox("New","New"); }

afx_msg void CMainWindow::OnOpen()

{ MessageBox("Open","Open"); }
```

```
afx_msg void CMainWindow::OnSave()

{ MessageBox("Save","Save");}

afx_msg void CMainWindow::OnSaveas()

{MessageBox("Saveas","Saveas");}

afx_msg void CMainWindow::OnPageSetup()

{ MessageBox("PageSetup","PageSetup");}

afx_msg void CMainWindow::OnPrint()

{ MessageBox("Print","Print");}

afx_msg void CMainWindow::OnExit()

{ MessageBox("Exit","Exit");}

afx_msg void CMainWindow::OnUndo()

{ MessageBox("Undo","Undo");}

afx_msg void CMainWindow::OnCut()

{ MessageBox("Cut","Cut");}

afx_msg void CMainWindow::OnCopy()

{ MessageBox("Copy","Copy");}

afx_msg void CMainWindow::OnPaste()

{ MessageBox("Paste","Paste");}

afx_msg void CMainWindow::OnDelete()

{ MessageBox("Delete","Delete");}

afx_msg void CMainWindow::OnNormal()

{ MessageBox("Normal","Normal");}
```

```
afx_msg void CMainWindow::OnZoom()

{ MessageBox("Zoom","Zoom"); }

afx_msg void CMainWindow::OnHelp()

{ MessageBox("Help","Help"); }

afx_msg void CMainWindow::OnAbout()

{ MessageBox("About","About"); }


CMyApplication Application;
```

Appendix D: Second text i/o example

C++ source file

```cpp
#include <afxwin.h>
#include <string.h>


char line[80];
char textline[80];
int  charcount=0;
int  mx=0,my=0;
int  wx=1,wy=1;
int  pointsize=100;


class CMainWindow : public CFrameWnd
{

public :

        CDC         my_memDC;
        CBitmap     my_bitmap;
        CBrush      my_brush;
        CFont       my_font;

    CMainWindow();

    afx_msg void OnChar(UINT ch, UINT count, UINT flags);
    afx_msg void OnPaint();
    afx_msg void OnLButtonDown(UINT flags, CPoint loc);
    afx_msg void OnRButtonDown(UINT flags, CPoint loc);
```

```
    DECLARE_MESSAGE_MAP()

};


CMainWindow::CMainWindow()
{

    Create(
    NULL ,
    " Simple text i/o using virtual device context");

        CClientDC dc(this);

        mx=GetSystemMetrics(SM_CXSCREEN);
        my=GetSystemMetrics(SM_CYSCREEN);

        my_memDC.CreateCompatibleDC(&dc);
      my_bitmap.CreateCompatibleBitmap(&dc,mx,my);
        my_memDC.SelectObject(&my_bitmap);

        my_brush.CreateStockObject(WHITE_BRUSH);
        my_memDC.SelectObject(&my_brush);

        my_memDC.PatBlt(0,0,mx,my,PATCOPY);


}


class CMyApplication : public CWinApp
{

public :
    BOOL InitInstance();

};

BOOL CMyApplication::InitInstance()
{

    m_pMainWnd = new CMainWindow;
    m_pMainWnd->ShowWindow(m_nCmdShow);
    m_pMainWnd->UpdateWindow();
```

```
      return TRUE;

}

BEGIN_MESSAGE_MAP(CMainWindow,CFrameWnd)
   ON_WM_CHAR()
   ON_WM_PAINT()
   ON_WM_LBUTTONDOWN()
   ON_WM_RBUTTONDOWN()
END_MESSAGE_MAP()

afx_msg void CMainWindow::OnChar(UINT ch, UINT count,
UINT flags)
{
    textline[charcount]=char(ch);
    charcount++;
    wx=1;
    wy=1;
    strcpy(line,textline);

    CFont tfont;

    CDC* pdc;

    pdc=&my_memDC;

    tfont.CreatePointFont(pointsize,"Arial",pdc);

    CFont* poldfont = (CFont*) pdc->SelectObject(&tfont);

      my_memDC.TextOut(wx,wy,line,strlen(line));

    pdc->SelectObject(poldfont);

    InvalidateRect(NULL);
    if (charcount==79) charcount=0;
    return;
}

afx_msg void CMainWindow::OnPaint()
{
      CPaintDC dc(this);

      dc.BitBlt(0,0,mx,my,&my_memDC,0,0,SRCCOPY);
```

```
    return;
}

afx_msg void CMainWindow::OnLButtonDown(UINT flags,
CPoint loc)
{
    pointsize+=20;
    InvalidateRect(NULL);
    return;
}
afx_msg void CMainWindow::OnRButtonDown(UINT flags,
CPoint loc)
{
    pointsize-=20;
    InvalidateRect(NULL);
    return;
}

CMyApplication Application;
```

Appendix E: Second graphics i/o example

C++ source file

```cpp
#include <afxwin.h>
#include <math.h>

int mx;
int my;

class CMainWindow : public CFrameWnd
{
public :

    CDC         my_memDC;
    CBitmap     my_bitmap;
    CBrush      my_brush;
    CFont       my_font;

    CPen        my_redpen;
    CPen        my_bluepen;
    CPen        my_greenpen;
    CPen        my_blackpen;

    CMainWindow();

    afx_msg void OnPaint();

    void DrawGraph();

    DECLARE_MESSAGE_MAP()
};

CMainWindow::CMainWindow()
```

```
{

   Create(
   NULL ,
" Simple graphics output using virtual device context"
   );

   CClientDC dc(this);

   mx=GetSystemMetrics(SM_CXSCREEN);
   my=GetSystemMetrics(SM_CYSCREEN);

   my_memDC.CreateCompatibleDC(&dc);
   my_bitmap.CreateCompatibleBitmap(&dc,mx,my);
   my_memDC.SelectObject(&my_bitmap);

   my_brush.CreateStockObject(WHITE_BRUSH);
   my_memDC.SelectObject(&my_brush);

   my_memDC.PatBlt(0,0,mx,my,PATCOPY);

   my_redpen.CreatePen(  PS_SOLID,2,RGB(255,  0,  0));
   my_bluepen.CreatePen( PS_SOLID,2,RGB(  0,  0,255));
   my_greenpen.CreatePen(PS_SOLID,2,RGB(  0,255,  0));
   my_blackpen.CreatePen(PS_SOLID,2,BLACK_PEN);

}

class CMyApplication : public CWinApp
{
public :
BOOL InitInstance();
};

BOOL CMyApplication::InitInstance()
{

   m_pMainWnd = new CMainWindow;
   m_pMainWnd->ShowWindow(m_nCmdShow);
   m_pMainWnd->UpdateWindow();

   return TRUE;
}

BEGIN_MESSAGE_MAP(CMainWindow,CFrameWnd)
   ON_WM_PAINT()
```

```
END_MESSAGE_MAP()


afx_msg void CMainWindow::OnPaint()
{
    DrawGraph();

    CPaintDC dc(this);

        dc.SetMapMode(MM_ISOTROPIC);
        dc.SetWindowExt(720,720);
        dc.SetViewportExt(500,500);
        dc.SetViewportOrg(50,50);


    dc.BitBlt(0,0,mx,my,&my_memDC,0,0,SRCCOPY);

    return;
}

void CMainWindow::DrawGraph()
{

    int     angled;
    double  angler;
    double  y;
    int  sine=180;
    int  cosine=360;
    int  tangent=180;
    const double pi=4*atan(1.0);

    my_memDC.SelectObject(&my_redpen);

    for (angled=0;angled<361;++angled)
    {
        my_memDC.MoveTo(angled,sine);
        angler = angled*2*pi/360;
        y       = sin(angler);
        sine    = 180 + int(180*y);
        my_memDC.LineTo(angled,sine);
    }

    my_memDC.SelectObject(&my_bluepen);

    for (angled=0;angled<361;++angled)
```

```
    {
        my_memDC.MoveTo(angled,cosine);
        angler  = angled*2*pi/360;
        y         = cos(angler);
        cosine = 180 + int(180*y);
        my_memDC.LineTo(angled,cosine);
    }

    my_memDC.SelectObject(&my_greenpen);

    for (angled=0;angled<361;++angled)
    {
        my_memDC.MoveTo(angled,tangent);
        angler   = angled*2*pi/360;
        y          = tan(angler);
        tangent = 180 + int(180*y);
        my_memDC.LineTo(angled,tangent);
    }

    my_memDC.SelectObject(&my_blackpen);

    my_memDC.MoveTo(0,180);

    my_memDC.LineTo(360,180);

}

CMyApplication Application;
```

Index

Too → BTL 12/18

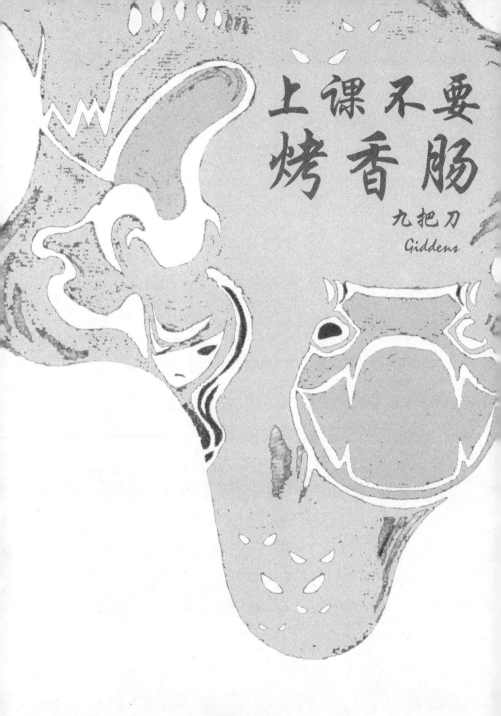

上课不要
烤香肠

九把刀

Giddens

中国出版集团

现代出版社

上课不要烤香肠

序
十二年来奇书之首

创作有很多型态，尤其十二年来我写了六十四本书，偶尔也想不受控制地暴走，毫无顾忌，很过瘾。于是这本书充满了乱七八糟的幽默、各式各样没营养的笑点以及通篇不负责任的鬼扯——然而，在出版此书的此时此刻，我意外发现了凌驾在我之上的幽默感。

是故，我要认真感谢现代出版社编辑部为了让此书顺利出版，不仅小幅改写了我的拙劣用词，更改动了部分故事情节，试图以此作品对社会产生正面影响。

感激涕零之余，我更发现此举背后的高深幽默，身为一个懂得感恩的创作者，我当然要热烈拥抱这一个美丽的共笔合写，特别以另种字体标示编辑部的用心，纪念我个人出版史上前所未有的奇书之诞生。

这本书绝对值得收藏！

九把刀

第一章_
常去钓虾场的外星人

1

大家好，我是王大明。

虽然这是一个很不起眼的名字，我也是一个很不起眼的人，但，我的老板可是一个很超级的作家。是的，他是九把刀，一个除了很色、很自大、很践、头发卷得很丑、很自我感觉良好、很无视员工安危、网志只回正妹的留言之外，其实也没什么大缺点的好老板。

如果你有买我帮九把刀代笔的上一本书，就会知道我是如何成为九把刀的助手，又如何为他出卖我的灵魂上天下海帮他搜集创作灵感。

为了避免让有买上一本《上课不要看小说》的读者觉得我靠回忆在灌水，所以之前发生过什么惊涛骇浪的大冒险我就不再赘述了，自己去买来看，贡献一下版税，我老板才能按时付我薪水。

此时此刻，我正在帮九把刀整理《哈棒传奇》的续集稿子。

据他自己说，这篇内容充满"打手枪"的恶烂小说其实在 2005 年就已经开始写了，还写了一半，只是当时遇到一些让九把刀不爽的烂事，逼得坚持要以快乐心情写哈棒的他暂停哈棒二的稿子，另外写别的小说搪塞出版社。真是抗压力超低的草莓族。

话说九把刀最近拍完了电影《那些年，我们一起追的女孩》，心情 high 了，又开始续写哈棒二，我仔细看了一下稿子，写得真是糟糕透顶，那种智障又下流的内容居然可以编成一本书，出版社未免也太瞧不起读者了吧？！

"写得怎样？"

九把刀拉起皮衣拉链，脚边放着红色行李箱。

"写得太棒了，从打手枪这一件人人都会做的事写到心理层面、社会层面乃至人类演化层面，真的是写作史上的一大突破，我该怎么说呢？根本就是炉火纯青了吧？"我毫不费力就挤出灿烂的笑容。

"我是天才吧哈哈哈哈哈哈！"开始爽起来的九把刀拿起桌上的车钥匙。

"岂止天才，根本就是天才中的天才啊老板！"我只能如此赞叹。

九把刀一边说，一边绑鞋带。

"等一下你走的时候记得下楼倒垃圾啊，还有别忘了把干尸踢到阳台再拴好，对了对了，还有这张水电费去便利商店缴一下，千万别忘了啊！"

"是的，老板。"

在我印象里的九把刀行事历中，他今天似乎要飞去香港谢谢观众那么爱看他的初恋电影，顺便吃美食吃冰火菠萝油喝好立克加麦片吃许留山逛街买皮衣牛仔裤住五星级饭店在顶楼游泳池肆无忌惮看穿比基尼的大奶洋妞，身为他的灵感助理却一点份也没有，只能留在台湾帮他无止尽地校稿挑错字。

说到校稿挑错字，我发现九把刀有一个恶癖，就是明知错字还硬要用。

比如说，浏海的"浏"，明明应该写成"刘"才是正解，但九把刀明知如此却还是硬写成"浏"，理由是大家都习惯写成"浏海"而不是"刘海"，他觉得语言要有约定俗成的延展性，"积非成是"本是语言的特性之一。

又比如说"蛮"跟"满"，正确的用法是："他满高兴的"。而不是"他蛮高兴的"。但九把刀老是用"他蛮高兴的"，理由也是一样。虽然有时候编辑会偷偷把"蛮"改成"满"。

最夸张莫过于"不明就里"这个成语，九把刀老是爱用"不明究理"这四个字取代正确的用法，编辑问他干吗故意更动成语，他却说："我比较喜欢不明究理。"真是直接了当的混蛋王八蛋——说到直接了当，有时候九把刀会用"直截了当"，也时候也会用"直接了当"，真的是一个当王八蛋也当得毫无原则的王、八、蛋！

离题了。

就在王八蛋九把刀站在玄关准备出门的时候，他突然回过头来。

这种突然的回头，总让我不寒而栗。

"王大强，你相信这个世界上有外星人吗？"九把刀眯起眼。

"老板，是这个样子的……嗯，我叫王大明。"我忍住卷袖子的冲动。

"咦？我刚刚就是叫你王大明啊？"九把刀一脸困惑。

"是的老板。"我点头，老板个屁。

"反正！最近有一个读者每天都写信给我，跟我说他最近被外星人抓去做实验，详细他想见了面再跟我说，感觉很酷，但我没空，我要去香港答谢电影观众的嘛！总之大强，你去帮我听一听。"

"因为他是男的吧？"

"你去跟读者见面，某个程度就代表了我，一定要给读者亲切的印象，有礼貌，鼻毛要剪干净，打扮要超潮，绝对不能语带脏话，更不能油腔滑调，总之就是要有型。"

"因为他是男的吧？"

"如果读者任何的行为带给你困扰，也不能露出一点点不耐烦的表情，要竭尽所能地用微笑来敷衍他，说一些谢谢指教、或是的我会改进之类无关痛痒的话，总之就是要假得有诚意。"

"因为他是男的吧？"

"但是注意了，这种非得见了面才肯把故事说给我听的读者，百分之九十九都有偏执狂，如果用猎人的念能力体系来比喻的话，就是庞姆那类的强化系，总之你自己小心一点了。"

"因为他是男的吧？"

"记得，虽然你自己要小心一点，但你身为一个专业的灵感搜集专家，一定要有专业的灵敏度，遇到生命有危险的情况时，就表示什么？"

"……就表示什么？"

"就表示这是一个非常有价值的灵感情报，基于你是一个专业的灵感搜集专家，你一定要有即使牺牲自己性命也要把情报交给我之后才断气的觉悟，尊重生命，尊重专业。"九把刀语重心长地拍拍我的肩膀，"了解吗？大强？"

"是的老板，我非常了解。"我非常了解我老板是一条大便。

九把刀将那一个网友的联络方式留给我之后，就出门前往机场了。

2

对付潜在的偏执狂，最好约在公众场所，我对对方也只有提出这个要求。

所以我们约在一间平凡无奇的钓虾场。

"为什么约我在钓虾场？"我狐疑，手里拿着一根钓竿。

"因为外星人就是在这间钓虾场抓我去实验的。"那个老伯东张西望，看起来有点神经兮兮，"而且……"

我屏气："而且什么？"

老伯慎重地说："而且我想钓虾。"

嗯，没错，这就是偏执狂的典型。

明明觉得钓虾场很危险，还执意要来钓虾场受访，看样子不好应付了今天。

"说到外星人，你在写给九把刀的 email 里提到你被外星人抓去做实验，那是怎么一回事？"我假装很有兴趣，就当作是同情。

　　"我说出这个故事，有没有钱可以拿啊？"老伯打量着我。

　　"钱？"

　　"采访费啊，我说我自己的故事给你老板听，要收钱的。"

　　"真的很抱歉，我老板九把刀是一个非常小气的人，我出来帮他访问提供情报的读者，从来没有给过钱，关于这点实在无法破例。"我反而松了一口气，"所以我觉得今天就算了吧，大家一起钓个虾交个朋友就好了。"

　　"这不大对啊，九先生拿我的故事写成书，读者再付钱买他的书，那他付我钱，不就是天经地义吗？啊？给我钱不就是天经地义吗？啊？给我钱不就是天经地义吗？啊？给我钱不就……"

　　"我当然知道是天经地义，BUT！"我打断老伯歇斯底里的叠字废话，"人生最无解的就是这个BUT！BUT我就是没有经费可以给你，所以你也不必讲故事，OK老伯，这种事本来就是你情我愿。"

　　"但我需要钱，连外星人把我的奶头拿走都有给钱了，为什么……九先生给我钱不也是天经地义吗？啊？给我钱不就是……"

　　"关于钱的问题我实在帮不上忙，反正我们今天就

17

快快乐乐钓虾。"我再度打断老伯的废话，"你不必讲故事，我也不必听故事，大家都 happy。"

于是对话不愉快地中断。

虽然气氛有点尴尬，但我既然来了钓虾场，也想钓一下下再走。

我一边钓，一边偷偷观察这个老伯。

这个口口声声号称被外星人抓去实验的老伯，年约六十多岁，长得很普通，身高很普通，口条很普通，想拿钱的想法也很普通，手里的钓竿在半个小时内丝毫没有动静，可见钓虾的技术也是普普通通。

问题是，这位老伯既然特地写了封很时尚的 email，肯定不会就此罢休。

不知道晃了多久，我钓到了五只虾子，老伯钓了个屁。

我听见一声好长的叹气。

"其实……我也可以不拿钱。"叹气的当然是老伯，表情像是下定决心。

"别太勉强啊老伯。"我根本不在意，看着水面上的钓鱼线。

"听好了，我可以推荐你老板九先生一起去给外星人做实验，只要九先生把外星人给他的实验费给我，我就跟你讲那些外星人是怎么在我身上做实验的，毕竟我讲故事给九先生去写书，收九先生钱是天经地义，但九先生不给我讲故事的钱，就要给我实验费当补贴，这也是天经地义啊！"

哇靠，这种事还可以推荐啊？

"谢谢你老伯，那请问什么时候上飞碟呢？"我忍住笑意。

"他们做实验不在飞碟的，是在……啊！"老伯突然大惊，"我说得太多了，那种事都是收钱才能说给你听的，毕竟……"

"毕竟你说故事给我听，我给钱也是天经地义的，我了解我知道。"我被迫打断老伯的废话连篇，"但我说了没钱给你，老伯你真的可以专心钓虾或早点回家睡觉。"

"我没办法睡觉，因为那些外星人把我的脑袋割掉一部分，所以我很久都没有睡过觉了……啊！其实这种事我也不能免费说给你听的，毕竟……"

"好好好，我知道，如果我真的被你推荐去给外星人做实验，只要他们给我钱，我就把钱通通给你，这样行了吧？"既然不可能发生，我也就完全不在意。

"不不不不不，不是这样的，是你老板九先生要去被外星人做实验，不是你。"

虽然我老板九把刀根本来不及同意（我想也不可能同意），但老伯已经开始无法克制地说起了那些乱七八糟的实验故事，我也只好一边钓虾一边听着。

3

　　一年前，这个老伯在这间钓虾场钓虾的时候，外星人来了。

　　起先外星人很有礼貌地发名片，问在场有没有人愿意配合实验，结果没有人感兴趣，于是生气翻脸的外星人就用奇怪的高科技带了几个人走，包括老伯。

　　老伯被带到一间外表普通、内部也很普通的位于汐止的一栋顶楼加盖公寓，跟他一起被绑走的人大概有五六个，有男有女，经过简单的基本资料访谈后，第一个登场的实验就是交换手。

　　所谓的交换手，顾名思义，就是交换手。

　　外星人将大家的手通通切下来，然后随机移植给彼此。

　　手术结束后，大家被关在公寓里限制行动，外星人煞有其事地记录大家的手术反应，或许是看看有没有人不适应新手、有无过敏反应、会不会不高兴被换手之类的吧，这段时间外星人无限供应鸡排跟珍珠奶茶以及蔬果 579，维持所有人基本的营养。

不像电影，外星人都会消除对方的记忆才放人类回家，那些外星人只是将他们送回钓虾场就走了，所以老伯一直对自己曾经被外星人切手换手的经历耿耿于怀。

后来老伯凭着记忆回到汐止那间顶楼加盖的公寓，那间公寓竟然没有像科幻小说形容的"凭空消失"，只有一户寻常人家住在里面，老伯问那一家人关于外星人的事，那一家人只说他们刚搬来不久，什么外星人的根本没听说，最后还叫警察把失控叫器的老伯带走。

然后……

"等一等。"我阻止老伯继续讲下去。

以上短短一段超精简的叙述，至少有七处可疑……或者说愚蠢的地方。

1. 外星人来了？外星人大刺刺走到钓虾场的画面，已经令我晕眩。

2. 外星人发名片？短短六个字就知道所有叙述都是唬烂。

3. 没有飞碟，而是公寓顶楼加盖，超不科幻的烂设定。

4. 交换手是什么烂实验？

5. 鸡排跟珍珠奶茶也就算了，什么蔬果 579 根本就
是置入性行销。

6. 为什么外星人不消除大家的记忆？

7. 鬼话连篇。

我看了一下老伯的手，完全不见手术的痕迹，一滴
疤都没有。

"你的手看起来没什么改变嘛！"我冷笑。

"我的运气很好，虽然是随机挑选，但我竟然还是
幸运地接回我自己的手，完全没有感觉到曾经被手术过，
非常神奇，外星人的科技很高，既然可以穿梭宇宙来到
地球，一个简单的切手又接手的手术做得如此完美，果
然是天经地义啊！"老伯有些得意地展示自己完全没有
手术痕迹的双手。

"但这个实验有什么目的吗老伯？"我勉强自己发
问。

"刚刚不是说了吗？外星人想知道交换手的感觉
嘛！"老伯没好气。

"请问这种实验有、什、么、意、义、吗、老、伯？"

"就外星人想知道交换手的感觉啊！"老伯难以置

信地看着我。

那种眼神，好像在看一个低能儿。

"名片呢？我要看外星人的名片。"我压抑着白白被浪费时间的微怒。

"早就丢了，那种不值钱的东西我才不要咧。"老伯嗤之以鼻。

老伯继续说着看扁所有读者智商的故事。

后来外星人持续来钓虾场发名片抓人去做实验，由于老伯常常来钓虾场，所以他一直重复地被抓去做实验，也是非常合理的一件事。而每一次外星人都会在不同的顶楼加盖的公寓里进行怪手术，老伯猜测是方便飞碟起落的关系……尽管他从未看过飞碟。

第二次被抓去，外星人用奇怪的科技将老伯其中一个奶头给消掉。

第三次被抓去，老伯参加的实验主题是吃萝卜比赛。干那是三小！

第四次被抓去，老伯的脑袋被切掉一部分，从此再也不需要睡觉也根本睡不着。终于有一点高科技实验的样子了，但有没有睡觉谁说了算？

第五次被抓去，老伯泡在奇怪的液体里睡了几个小时，醒来时外表已严重老化。

"所以不要再叫我老伯了，我今年只有二十一岁，说不定比你还年轻。"老伯语重心长地说。

"但你看起来实在是不像……二十一岁啊老伯。"我渐渐提不起劲。

瞧我不信，老伯表情神秘地从口袋里拿出一张皱皱的身份证。

身份证上面的资料表示，这个老伯叫张柏圣，1991年生，户籍在新店，完全可以证明这个叫张柏圣的人今年的确是21岁。

但问题是，我眼前这位老伯长得完全不像是那个叫张柏圣的年轻人的老年版！

他们根本就是两个人！

"怎么样，不由得你不信了吧？"老伯神气得很。

"真是不得不信了呢。"我随便附和，加重语气，"老、伯。"

捡到一张身份证就想唬烂我，会不会太瞧不起人了。

不过我很快就想到，刚刚老伯提及的那五个实验里，唯一可以证明外星人曾经在老伯身上动手过的项目，就是消掉奶头了吧？

虽然是个蠢不可及的实验，我还是压抑住我蠢蠢欲动的智商问道："老伯，不介意的话，我想看一下你的奶头。"

面对我单刀直入的问题，老伯显得有点害羞。

面对老伯装模作样的害羞，我觉得非常的火大。

我不想说话，老伯也没有说话，场面顿时有点尴尬。

"你先给我看奶头，我再给你看我的奶头。"老伯脸红。

"我不要。"我断然拒绝。

"你不要，那我也不要。"老伯咬牙。

"老伯，今天不是我想看你的奶头，而是我想确定你的故事是不是真的，所以即使我很不想看也不得不看。"我不由自主握紧拳头，真的是超气，"我想看你的奶头，完全出于非常正常且合理的动机，你想看我的奶头，却只是想看我的奶头，完全很无聊。"

"我给你看我的奶头，你也给我看你的奶头，这叫天经地义。"老伯的脸更红了，倒底是在红三小。

我气到失去理智，气到马上拉开衣服，把我的奶头秀给老伯看。

老伯也只好依照约定拉开他的衣服，把他被外星人弄消失的奶头秀还给我。

等等。

不是被外星人消掉奶头了吗？怎么我看到好端端的两个深枣色的大奶头呢？

"你有两个奶头。"我的表情一定很肃杀。

"没错。"

"你不应该有两个奶头。"

"如果你仔细看的话就会发现，我左右两边的奶头其实不是同一对奶头，我左边的奶头比较大，而且颜色有点偏紫，比起我右边的奶头小一点，颜色淡多了，还有几根金毛在边边，你看……靠近一点看……"

我拒绝了。

近距离凝视一个男人的奶头，不是我做人处事的风格。

"老伯，你不是说外星人把你的奶头消掉了吗？"

"没错，那是一种非常高科技的手术，首先他们把一种黏黏的药膏涂在我右边的奶头上，一开始有点凉凉的，再来我的奶头就开始发热，热到好像着火了，我一看，结果我的奶头真的在冒烟，我吓坏了，我心想这次的实验未免也太恐怖了吧？那些外星人开始拿像吸管一样的软软的东西压在我冒烟的奶头上，然后开始吸……"

"总之你右边的奶头就这样不见了。"

“是的。”

“但他妈的你的奶头好端端长在干你娘的胸部上啊老伯。”

“不要叫我老伯，我今年才二十一岁。”

“年轻人，我说你他妈的奶头好端端长在你的胸部上啊！”

“那是因为我还没有跟你提到我去做的第八次实验，那个实验很恐怖，外星人把他们搜集到的好几个人的奶头，移植到不同人的身上，我现在右边这个新奶头就是那个时候被移植过来的，我研究这个新奶头很久，我猜这个奶头以前的主人一定是一个洋鬼子，要不然奶头边边这几根毛怎么会是金色的？说不定还是一个女白人的奶头！”

“原来如此。”我恍然大悟。

我已经百分之一亿确定，今天晚上的对话通通都是——废话！

有了这一层果断的认知之后，我心中的怒气反而一扫而空。

相信这个世界上有外星人容易，还是相信你旁边有一个神经病容易？

答案不言而喻。

既然是神经病，就不用太计较，我开始呵欠连连。

话匣子打开，老伯继续他诡异的实验叙述，关于第六次第七次第八次第九次第十次的种种莫名其妙的外星人手术，其实验内容之无聊透顶，比如"把包皮与眼皮交换看看，看会怎样"跟"人类可以在一个小时之内生吞几只蜗牛"之类，显示外星人是一群千里迢迢跑来地球的智障。

"所以这位有为的年轻人，这么晚了还不回家睡觉啊？"我又打了个呵欠。

"因为我不用睡觉啊！"老伯压低声音，指着绝对没有手术痕迹的脑袋。

"嗯啊，那很好啊。"我真是白问了，是我的错。

"后来我太常被外星人抓去实验，久了，大家也有点熟了，我干脆建议他们至少付个钱，大家的配合意愿会比较高，他们觉得我的建议很好，所以从第六次实验起他们就开始付我钱，有时候他们想要特定品质的人类让他们实验，他们还会请我帮忙推荐，除了被推荐的人可以拿实验费之外，我也可以拿推荐费。"

"嗯啊，那很好啊。"

我发现池面上的钓鱼线微微晃动，一拉，果然又钓到一条肥嫩嫩的泰国虾。

"我拿推荐费本来就是天经地义，但你老板九先生不能免费听我的故事，所以外星人给九先生的实验费，我也要拿，这也是天经地义。"

"嗯啊，那很好啊。"

我将钓到的泰国虾放进脚边的水桶里。

"每次外星人抓人去做实验，都有不同的主题。"老伯兀自唠唠叨叨个不停，"他们说，之后有一个实验主题需要几个智商特别高的人，要针对智商超高的人做针对性的实验，他们希望我推荐一些很聪明的人配合一下。"

"喔我了解了，所以你觉得九把刀智商很高是吧？"

我慢条斯理将肉块重新挂上钓钩，抛线入池。

"没错，我觉得九把刀可以一直乱写书催眠读者，一定很聪明吧？所以我就把他列入推荐名单中，希望他可以配合一下，就当作是促进地球的宇宙外交，而且还可以当小说题材写，这也是天经地义是吧？"

"九把刀是不是智商高我不那么确定，但如果外星人要找道德低落的人实验的话，我一定亲手把九把刀送上飞碟……喔不，是公寓。"

"反正你已经答应我了，务必请你老板跟我去一趟实验。"老伯认真起来。

"拜托不必那么麻烦，促进地球宇宙外交这种事我也很有兴趣，我来就可以了，别看我一副帅气的外表就以为我没有内涵，其实我可以担任九把刀的灵感助理，就是因为我有超凡入圣的高智商，如果老伯你不介意的话，下次外星人找你做实验，别忘了带高智商的我去飞碟……喔不，是公寓，去见识见识。"

老伯沉默了片刻，这才搭腔："这样也行，只要你通过外星人的智商测试、证明你的确是一个高智商的人以后，你就可以代替你老板去做实验。"

"一言为定。"我又打了个呵欠。

"如果你通不过智商测试，你老板还是得亲自去实验。"

"就一言为定了啊。"

"但如果是你去，你还是要把实验费通通给我。"老伯不忘这点。

"知道了……"我还是打了一个呵欠，"这是天经地义嘛！"

那天晚上，常常去钓虾的老伯没有钓到一只虾子，我则钓到了十七只。

我在一旁烤虾子的时候，大方地分了这位年轻有为的老伯一起吃。

　　本以为这只是一场莫名其妙的外星人之夜，但很遗憾，这个世界对我并没有那么好。

　　当然那又是另一个故事了。

第二章_
红山大旅舍

1

上一篇莫名其妙的读者访谈记录里，我提过我叫王大明。

但我忘了跟大家复习一下我为什么成为作家九把刀的专职助理。

是的，虽然帮九把刀有钱赚，但我有更崇高的理想，我是为了寻找我爸爸被不明液体溶解之谜，才决定委屈自己帮九把刀上天下海寻找写小说的种种灵感，我觉得可以用九把刀给我的经费增广见闻之余，一定可以搜集更多关于我爸爸神秘死因的情报，也因为如此，我历经了许多人十辈子也难以想象的奇异旅程。

然而，真正的男子汉是不能老是遥想过去的丰功伟业自慰，我们要活在当下！

当下，我正与我的老友阿祥愉快地赶路。

话说，由于我老板的网志人气很高，常常有读者到九把刀的网志上要求东要求西的，比如恳求九把刀发文请网友点一下美少女票选的某号码，比如要九把刀找一下他家走失的狗狗，比如要九把刀帮忙宣传一下他们系上举办的有礼貌运动，比如要九把刀代贴一下他为了要写论文不得不设计的问卷让读者填写回送等等，一大堆的要求。但我老板大概只会帮忙找狗，其他都假装没看见。

但是啊，前几天有一个初中生读者写信给九把刀，说他的老家在花莲深山，那里有一个部落即将举办一个拥有几百年传统的神秘大蛇祭，那个读者希望九把刀发挥影响力，在网志上帮忙召募志愿献给大蛇的网友，还热情邀请九把刀去当观礼的嘉宾，并保证一定会安排最好的位置给他。

九把刀就纳闷啦，回覆问道："什么叫献给大蛇？跟大蛇丸有什么关系？"

由于我老板很少回覆不是正妹的留言，那读者就high啦，迅速又留言："当然是让大蛇活活吃掉啊！保证血腥，恐怖绝伦啊！请刀大一定要来赏脸！"

九把刀火速回覆："喔，但是你没有写大蛇祭在什么时候，我去个屁？"

那读者毕恭毕敬："刀大您有所不知，大蛇祭就好像过年围炉，当然要等人都到齐了才动筷子，大蛇祭当然也是要等献祭的人都到齐了，大蛇才会开动啊。所以一切就等愿意献身的网友聚集到部落的时间决定啦！"

"真的很酷吗？"惨了，九把刀开始感兴趣了。

"真的真的！如果刀大愿意过来，我们全村一定会拜托大蛇吞慢一点，让刀大看得一清二楚！"这个留言的读者简直乐坏了。

这种一看就是超白烂的留言，九把刀倒是看得津津有味。

他转头跟我说："王大明，这件事明显跟你爸爸当年被溶解的原因有关。"

我大惊："哪可能有关！"

九把刀坚定不移地说："就算只有千分之一可能有关，你还是得去看一下，毕竟这是你身为儿子调查真相的责任。就算只有万分之一可能有关，你还是要去看一下，因为你拿我的钱，叫我老板。"

好吧，最后那一句话说服了我。

反正交通费、住宿费、餐饮费甚至还有特别行动金，所有旅费通通都是九把刀那白痴出的，我倒是不介意拿他的钱去花莲玩一趟，就算完全没有搜集什么题材也不能怪我，这可是他自己的决定。

"好吧，我会想办法带回厉害的题材。"我敷衍道。

"记得要把大蛇吃人的画面拍得很有魄力喔！"九把刀用力拍我的肩，狂笑，"哈哈哈哈哈哈哈哈！可不要弄到自己也被吃了啊！哈哈哈哈哈……"

笑个屁。

当我开始收拾行李时，九把刀拿了三个红色小锦囊给我。

"这些是保命用的紧急锦囊，除非万不得已，否则不能打开。"九把刀面色凝重地说，"切记，切记。"

"啊？那里面装了什么？"虽然是好一，但我不禁好奇起来。

"装的当然是很厉害的东西，平常绝对不能打开来看，一打开，就会用掉一次救命的威力。"九把刀的表情很严肃，"记得随时带在身边，就算是睡觉也得放在枕头边，记住了吗？"

"嗯啊。"

"如果没用到，记得拿回来还我。"

"到底是什么厉害的东西啊？"

我咕哝，但还是把那三个红色锦囊放进背包里。

2

好不容易去一趟花莲，我立刻联络我的大学的社团同学阿祥。

说起阿祥，他跟我都是桥牌社的社员，原本我们当然都是抱着学桥牌的心态进去的，可是桥牌社仅有的四个学长都不会打桥牌，让我们大吃一惊。

那四个学长说，桥牌社不会打桥牌就是我们桥牌社重要的传统，万万不可以断在我们手上，所以他们坚持不教我们打桥牌，也不准我们自己私下学，有一次我偷偷看桥牌规则还给狠狠揍了一顿，于是我们只好开始玩象棋打发社团活动时间。

但有一次我们在社窝玩象棋被学长看到了，他们很生气，一边用棋盘打我们一边大叫："尊重两个字会不会写啊！要玩象棋不会去象棋社玩喔？搞清楚！这里是桥牌社！桥！牌！社！"然后就拉着我们一起玩大富翁。

学长说，虽然我们是桥牌社，但玩大富翁是桥牌社重要的传统，绝对不可以断在我们的手里，于是我们就被迫玩了整整一年的大富翁。

所以啰，等到我们当了学长，当然也尝试打了学弟很多次，好将桥牌社重要的精神传承下去——但我们失败了，学弟实在太强壮了，反过来还被他们痛扁，于是桥牌社的传统就改成学弟们非常着迷的扯铃。

我杂七杂八讲了这么久，就是在说阿祥跟我的革命情感。

阿祥老家就在花莲。

平时他在台北的光华商场卖笔记本电脑打工，但爱乡爱家的他每两个月就会回去一次。那唬烂至极的大蛇祭他听都没听过，不过他倒是很有兴趣顺便跟我去一趟。

"你不觉得超蠢吗？"我忍不住问，虽然阿祥要陪我我很高兴。

"是很蠢啊，不过你刚刚说那个部落靠近哪里？"

"地图是说，在红叶的更里面。"

"是了啊！红叶那边很漂亮耶，往里面再走一点一定更美。"阿祥兴高采烈拿出他新买的数码单眼相机，把玩着说，"我还特地带了新相机去，这个时节一定可以拍到很多枫叶火红的山景，真希望那个部落越神秘越好，我一定要拍到别人都没拍到的风景！"

嗯嗯这样也好，阿祥有他自己的旅行目的，如果根本没有什么大蛇祭，甚至根本没有那一个神秘的部落，我就不用费事跟他道歉了。

3

我们一起坐"太鲁阁"号舒舒服服来到花莲，再搭公车往红叶的山区前进。

下了公车，我们在附近的老旧温泉旅舍泡了一个畅快的温泉，暖暖身子，把搭车的疲惫感都洗去后，继续我们的小跋涉。

接下来就没有正常的路可以走，必须徒步穿越一个车子无法通过的区域，当然我手上拿着这一位读者传给九把刀的手绘地图翻拍照，才能勉强辨识前进。

不得不说这位读者用心良苦，为了白痴的九把刀，也为了根本不存在的献身志愿者，他在许多大树上都绑着显眼的红色旗布，每隔约三百米就有一棵被标记的大树让我们确认目前的进度是对的，所以没有什么害怕迷路的感觉。

只是地图上没有标明"所需时间"，我们又没什么登山经验，无从估计起到达神秘部落还要多久，于是我们只能继续前进，越走越深。

一下子听见潺潺溪水声，一下子水声又慢慢远去。然后又忽然听得很清楚。

一下子听见好像有熊在叫，一下子又听见蜂群隐隐在邻近处盘旋。

老实说，还真有点怕怕的。

幸好一路崎岖，但我们走的路不算难走。虽然没有好好地铺上人行石阶，还是可以感觉到脚底下的路偶而会有人走过的痕迹，并非原始的兽径，有时候还可以看到经过的树、树皮上还刻有某某情侣到此一游的留念。

虽然没公德心，但看了竟然有种安心的感觉。

"真棒，久久回一次花莲，每次都觉得山里的空气让我身心舒畅呢！"阿祥倒是乐在其中，沿途不停地按快门。

"是喔，我是希望快一点到啦。"我敷衍道，一直走走走，脚实在是累了。

天色渐渐昏暗起来，还看不到所谓的部落。唯一的安慰就是偶而可以看到绑着红布的大树，证明我们还走在正确的路上。

"阿祥，你觉得还要走多久啊？"我观察天色。

"我怎么知道？"阿祥自顾自拍照。

"总之，看样子天黑前是走不到了。"我叹气。

"你累了的话，就找个地方休息吧。"阿祥正在拍蝴蝶，真有闲情逸致。

"不是累而已，我听说登山晚上绝对不要赶路，容易迷失方向，而且晚上本来就应该好好休息，白天才有力气冲冲冲啊。"我没好气。

"好啊，所以我们要立刻扎营吗？"阿祥天真无邪地看着我。

"……我没有带帐篷。"我眉头一皱，发现问题并不单纯。

"我也没有耶。"阿祥停下脚步。

"我没有带睡袋。"我倒抽了一口凉气。

"我也没有。"阿祥瞪大眼睛，终于感觉到事态严重了。

这下可好，我们实在是太天真了，完全没有准备要在野外过夜的两个人，是一男一女也就算了，还可以用力抱着一起睡觉，冷到睡不着还可以一起做一些交换体温的运动，但两个男的怎么睡？刚刚一路上甚至没有看到凉亭，睡在地上肯定会睡到感冒。

唯一的希望就是，我手上的网友地图底下标明了"红山大旅舍"五个字，后面还附注一行小字：山友旅途的良友，深夜避寒的好去处。

感觉是个很可靠的地方。

"红山大旅舍？"阿祥探过头来看，咦了一声，"还有多远啊？"

"不知道，不过既然是大旅舍，应该一眼就可以远远看到了吧。"我张望着远方，满怀期待地说，"如果即时赶到的话，真想洗个热水澡啊！"

这个不晓得到底存在不存在的旅舍算是个目标吧，有目标走起路来就像重新加了马达一样，让人精神为之一振。

"你觉得那个旅舍有可能开在这种荒郊野外吗？"阿祥又拿起相机拍鸟。

"地图上面既然写了，就应该有吧？"我随口说，"民宿也常常盖在奇怪的深山或海边啊，这样才有特殊的风格吧。"

"对耶，真希望那间旅舍有温泉。"阿祥怀念起几个小时前的那一泡。

"说不定有喔，红山听起来就像一间老式旅馆，以前的旅馆常常都有温泉。"

"尤其在山里，更应该有温泉吧？"阿祥的逻辑有点自以为是。

"有温泉是很好啦，但现在只有普通的热水澡，我就谢天谢地了。"

我们一边走一边抬杠，起先还有点接话的兴致，可随着疲倦感渐渐有一搭没一搭地没了劲，阿祥拿起相机按下快门的次数也越来越少。实在是太累了。

当我们带来的水喝剩一口的时候，太阳已完全沉进我看不见的山谷底。

"会不会那间红什么的……旅舍倒掉啦？"阿祥气喘吁吁。

"就算倒掉，也还是有个建筑物在吧？"我也累得发晕，"睡在废弃的旅舍里面，也比睡在大树下好吧？"

再走一个小时，我们只能干吞口水解渴，天色已昏暗到没有打开手电筒就完全看不清楚前方的程度。

但我们没有打开手电筒——因为我们根本没有手电筒！

"唉，用手机照明吧？"我说，拿起手机。

"也只能这样了。"阿祥的声音充满疲惫，也拿起手机。

就在我们拿起手机，用发亮的萤幕往前一照的时候……

"红山大旅舍！"阿祥兴奋大叫。

"什么？"我傻眼。

"哈哈踏破铁鞋无觅处，柳暗花明又一村！"阿祥往前快跑，跑得飞快。

虽然这上下联组得怪怪的，但我还是跟着阿祥往前快跑。

"等等！跑慢一点啊，小心跌倒啊！"我跑得很心惊。

这么暗，阿祥却跑得超级快，甚至还没有拿起手机用荧幕照射前方的路。

"哪里暗？旅舍招牌的灯刺得我都快瞎啦！"阿祥非常兴奋。

"哪来的旅舍？"我觉得莫名其妙。

"你在说什么啊？就在那里啊！"阿祥简直欢呼起来，"到啦！"

正当我跑得心惊肉跳几乎要跌倒之际，恍恍惚惚中，一栋充满复古风情的小旅舍赫然出现在面前……

红山大旅舍，红色的五个大字刻在白色的招牌上。

"虽然开在深山里的旅舍一定很贵，但也没办法啦，是不是？"阿祥很开心。

"也是啦，难得有客人来，住宿一定不便宜。"我笑着附和，"不过我们累炸了，当然要给人家赚一下啦！"

我们加快脚步。

瞧外观，这栋位居深山郊道旁的小旅馆倒也不算小，有三层楼，旧旧的，感觉像是至少半个世纪以前的小温泉旅舍，走的是日式风格。在这疲倦困顿中即时赶到，让我们整个人都充满了精神。

门当然不是自动门，但门上的玻璃擦得挺干净，门上写着地图上的那两行字："山友旅途的良友，深夜避寒的好去处。"喔喔，果然一点没错。

一打开门也没有预期中的霉味，反而有一股淡淡的清香。

光线不是很明亮，只有一根日光灯管嵌在天花板上，发出冷冷的淡青色光。但整体来说感觉不坏，至少还有灯泡，而不是点白蜡烛的恐怖气氛。

我们走向柜台，柜台后只有一个上了年纪的老婆婆戴着老花眼镜在看书。

"老板娘，我们要住宿。"我打招呼。

虽然大概不需要，但我还是将身份证放在柜台桌上。

"……请问要住几天？"老婆婆笑咪咪看着我，果然没有要登记资料的意思。

"住一个晚上。"

"啊？才……"老婆婆的脸色一黯，语气失望，"才一个晚上啊。"

虽然我理解老婆婆难得遇到客人想多赚点钱的想法，但无论如何，我们明天就得启程前往那个可笑的神秘部落，无法久待，实在抱歉。

"哈哈放心啦老板娘，我们很可能会在回程时顺道在这里再过一晚上啦，毕竟这附近只有一间旅馆啊。"一直在大厅东张西望的阿祥，抓着头走过来说："对了老板娘，这里有温泉可以洗吗？"

"有。"老婆婆微一鞠躬。

"真不错耶！"阿祥惊喜，我也抖擞了一下。

"请问住一个晚上多少钱啊？"我赶紧拿起钱包。

"一个人，一百块钱。"老婆婆伸出一根手指。

天啊！才一百块钱！

还有温泉！

这里不只是山友的救星，价格还比公道价破盘再破盘！

"那……老婆婆，虽然我们只住一天，但我给你一个礼拜的住宿费吧。"我豪气十足地说，"反正是花我老板的钱，你不用客气真的。"

我立刻掏出七张百元钞票放在桌上。

"对啊，而且你在这里开旅舍很不容易耶，让我们赞助你一下！"阿祥也爽朗地拿起钱包，抽出钞票放在桌上，"我也给你一个礼拜的住宿费，哈哈，希望你努力把它经营下去啊！"

"你们人真好。"

老婆婆笑咪咪地收下我们的钱，向我们深深一鞠躬。

"好人会有好报的，就让我好好地招待你们吧。"

4

　　我们的房间是双人房，各自一张单人床，素素的没什么装潢，床头灯是老式的黄色灯泡，衣柜陈旧，床板很硬，被单有点薄，这些本在意料之中。

　　但房间着实打扫得蛮干净，棉被叠得很整齐，衣柜打开来一点霉味也没有，可以知道老婆婆平日的用心，真不愧是我们给足了七天住宿费的好地方。

　　"真想不到，这种穷乡僻壤的地方竟然会有这么棒的旅舍，我们真是太幸运啦。"阿祥将行李一股脑扔在地板上，大字型躺在床上，"哈哈哈哈哈……"

　　"穷乡僻壤？"我同样大字型摔在床上，不以为然地说，"这里根本就是荒郊野外啊。"

　　"对了，房间好像没浴室？"阿祥环顾一下小到根本不需要环顾的小房间，单手拿着数码相机便乱拍了几张。

　　"刚刚老板娘不是说了吗，这里有温泉。"我打了个哈欠，"温泉一定是在楼下的大澡堂啦，老式的日本旅舍都是这样，大家一起洗，热闹又有气氛。"

一想到暖呼呼的温泉，不管再怎么累我们还是硬爬了起来。

没有带帐篷与睡袋的我们，当然也不可能带毛巾，所幸这间小旅舍贴心地提供我们老式的橘黄色大毛巾让我们擦身体，还分文不取，根本就是行侠仗义等级的不可思议旅馆嘛！

"老板娘，其实做生意要赚钱，首先就是趁火打劫。"我叹了一口气，忍不住说道，"我们没有带毛巾，你可以租给我们，就算租金要一百块钱也很合理，毕竟这里是深山嘛。"

"对啊对啊，老板娘你太老实了啦。"阿祥也猛摇头。

"没关系，只是毛巾而已，不必那么客气。来，跟我走。"老婆婆佝偻着身，慢慢地走在前头带路，"有点儿暗，我们慢慢走。"

穿过狭窄的走廊，旅舍后面竟别有洞天，飘着蒸蒸热气的大澡堂正等着他们。

一个不规则形状的露天大池子就躺在澡堂中央，旁边还有大自然的树林环绕，古色古香。

"哇。"我赞叹，鼻子里都是硫磺温泉的气味。

"真不赖耶。"阿祥咧开了嘴。

"泡完温泉后，不嫌弃的话，让我招待你们一些粗茶淡饭吧。"

年迈的老板娘笑咪咪的，挽起袖子一副正要去厨房大显身手的模样。

"那就麻烦老板娘了，我们都超饿的呢。"我笑道，其实现在就想吃了。

"天啊我们真的是太幸运了。"阿祥笑得可灿烂了。

老婆婆走后，我们迫不及待跳进有点白浊的硫磺泉池子里，热呼呼的舒服极了。

无暇抬杠，我们忙着舀起泉水从头顶浇下，一路跋涉的疲惫感登时烟消云散。自古以来历史上的伟人都是这样的，先苦后甘，历经千辛万苦最后终于泡到人生终点站之胜利的温泉，肯定就是我们现在的境界。

不久，我们的皮肤都给烫红了。

"或许是太久没有招待客人了，老板娘显得很开心呢。"阿祥下巴浸在温泉里。

"嗯，等一下不管那个老婆婆做的菜有多难吃，我们都要全部吃光光，好回应她的热情。"我虽是这么说，但此时此刻简单炒个野菜就是人间美味了。

"我想吃温泉蛋。"阿祥的想法很古板,"加在泡面里就很好吃了。"

"我想吃炒高山高丽菜苗。"我认真许愿。

最后泡到肚子都咕噜咕噜叫了,我们这才依依不舍地裹着大毛巾离开温泉。

回到楼上房里要换干净衣服的时候,我将背包拉链打开的那一瞬间,登时有一种强烈的异样感冲击着我。

那种异样感是说不上的古怪。

"……"我感到有点晕眩,手臂上的皮肤都起鸡皮疙瘩了。

"怎么了?"阿祥问。

"没事。"我好像有点站不起来,"有点晕。"

"喔,我知道了,刚泡完温泉有时候都会这样,再加上肚子饿得血糖过低,头就晕啦。"阿祥喃喃,用力把我拉起来,"快下楼吃东西就对了。"

有道理,但这只能解释我为什么头晕,却无法解释我为什么会狂起鸡皮疙瘩。

我的眼睛瞥见背包里的……九把刀留给我的三个锦囊,我迅速想起来,刚刚那股异样感就是从我打开背包,看见那三个锦囊之后才开始起鸡皮疙瘩的。

不,不是刚刚,就连现在我手臂上的鸡皮疙瘩都还没退。

我下意识地将其中一个锦囊拿起，竟有一种全身触电的感觉，令我寒毛直竖。

"怎么房间有点臭臭的？"我嗅嗅，是霉味，还有很重很重的泥土味。

"哪有？什么味道都没有啊。"阿祥跟着嗅来嗅去。

"就是刚刚下过雨的时候经过公园，平常闻不到的泥土味就会乘以十，那种程度的泥土味啊。"我抽动鼻子，自己纠正自己，"啊，也像是草的味道，总之都差不多。"

不，不只是泥土味或草味啊……

我慢慢站了起来。

这个房间还是刚刚的房间，但是总觉得有哪里不一样。

衣柜还是衣柜，还是那一个衣柜，但总觉得有哪里悄悄变了。

床头灯还是刚刚那一个床头灯，但绝对有哪里不对劲。

还有，那一股发霉的气味几乎粘在我的鼻腔里，不管我怎么抽动鼻子都还是闻得到。

错不了的，不只这房间里的空气百分之百不一样，其他的摆设也一定有某些地方不一样了，只是我暂时还不知道是哪里不一样。这一种很想觉得一切都没问题、但心里却一直认定"一定有什么不对劲"的感觉，一旦开始了就该死地停不下来。

"喂？你别吓我。"阿祥皱眉。

"我……我没有吓你，我真的觉得这里很奇怪。"我抓抓头，想做一个故作轻松的表情却很勉强，"不过……到底是哪里奇怪，我暂时说不上来。"

"不管了，先下去吃饭吧！"阿祥翻白眼，"我快饿死了。"

"……好吧。"我同意，不管怎样我肚子都饿扁了。

而我的手，已不自觉顺势将那一个锦囊放进我的口袋里。

想想，不管再怎么不安，这一间旅舍可以恐怖到哪里去？不过就是鬼嘛！

"哼。"

我冷笑，什么场面我没看过！

5

下楼时，老婆婆已经堆满笑脸，在大厅摆了一桌等着我们开饭。

"洗过温泉，身子暖了吧。"老板娘很客气地微微鞠躬，"那么请愉快用餐吧，小小野店，招呼不周，招呼不周……"

咦？

这个老婆婆的的确确就是刚刚那一个老板娘，眼睛一样，鼻子一样，嘴巴一样，皱纹感觉也……一样，但是不久前才见过的老婆婆，有那么老态龙钟吗？到底是哪里变老了呢？

正当我感到迷惑的时候，阿祥忽然惊呼起来。

"哇！吃这么丰盛！"阿祥的眼睛闪闪发亮，"简直是满桌子的山珍海味嘛！"

"啊？"我倒是大大地吓了一跳。

哪来的山珍海味？

满桌子乱七八糟的东西！

一大盆的蚕茧，一大盘的活蚯蚓，一大碗公的死青
蛙，断了一碟子的蜥蜴尾巴，一小盘莫名其妙黏稠的虫
卵糊，一锅子搅了树叶树根与不知名野草的泥巴汤……
差点没叫我呕吐出来。

忽然，正在发呕的我从老婆婆的眼中感觉到一股强
烈的寒意。

那一瞬间，我看见老婆婆的屁股后面，摇着一条像
是尾巴一样的……尾巴！

也就在同一关键的瞬间，我之所以能够成为白痴王
九把刀的灵感助手的最佳理由，闪电般蹿进我的危机意
识里——那就是，天塌下来也处变不惊的无敌状态！

清醒了。

我的心灵小宇宙已经完全清醒了。

"没事没事，我只是有点感冒不舒服。"我面不改色
地拉椅子坐下。

"……"老婆婆打量着我，摇着她的尾巴，脸色颇
为阴沉，"真的没事吗？"

"一起吃吧老板娘，这么多菜，我们怎么吃得完呢？"阿祥也坐下，兴奋地拿起筷子。

"……也好。"老婆婆慢慢坐下，眼角余光似乎正观察着我。

那眼神叫我不寒而栗。

"谢谢老板娘的盛情款待，感激不尽！"我满脸堆欢，率先夹了一条活蹦乱跳的蚯蚓进碗里。

"那就不客气啦！谢谢老板娘！"阿祥一筷子夹起了半只被从中间撕裂的青蛙尸体，大口嚼下，"哇！这山鸡肉真是超好吃的！"

瞧阿祥那一副狼吞虎咽的模样，我已经明白今晚的局势了。

干天干地干你娘，恐怖的不幸已经降临……

百分之一亿，我们遇到了传说中的"魔神仔"。

以前我在网络上的鬼故事板看过许多关于"魔神仔"的传说，迅速将眼前所见与那些穿凿附会的传言结合在一起。

所谓的魔神仔，就是在深山里迷惑旅人的精怪，不是鬼，当然也不是神，好像也不算是妖，而是一种无法被归类的……不知道是什么东西，所以被取了一个"魔神仔"的专属称号。

魔神仔迷惑旅人做什么？

原因不清楚，但那些旅人被寻获的时候正在做什么却毫无疑问……他们会两眼无神坐在地上，满嘴的泥沙与昆虫，笨笨地傻笑说不出话，这种失智失神的情况偶而会持续好几天、甚至是好几个礼拜，最后才慢慢醒转。

醒来后问他们，到底他们在山里迷路的那几天都在做什么，那些旅人不是完全丧失记忆，就是信誓旦旦说他们那几天都住在非常豪华的大饭店里、还被招待好几顿丰盛的大餐……

丰盛的大餐是吗？

我的碗里正躺着一条又肥又粗的活蚯蚓。

"吃啊！刚刚不是还喊肚子饿吗？"阿祥笑嘻嘻地夹起一条蜥蜴尾巴。

"哈哈哈哈……好啊好啊……"我在心里狂干阿祥为什么不去死一死。

不知道为什么，不只是满桌子的烂菜，此时此刻我的眼睛里的所见都慢慢地产生了改变。

这不是旅舍。

这是一处充满腐败气味的断垣残壁，张牙舞爪的老树枯枝，扑天盖地的藤蔓，满地的腐烂落叶，畸形隆起的巨大树根，蚊蝇飞来飞去，几只乌鸦在树枝上哑哑怪叫。

而我身上黏黏的气味不是温泉的琉璜味，而是不知所谓的酸臭味……天知道我们刚刚泡的是什么鬼东西！

最重要的是，看起来越来越老的老婆婆根本不是人，而是一个甩着尾巴的人形怪物。

而这个半人半兽的人形怪物正用非常凌厉的眼神打量着我，似乎正怀疑我为什么不吃掉碗里的那一条蚯蚓。

我不禁打了一个寒颤。

这可是性命交关的时刻。

如果我不假装自己也陷入了魔神仔的迷惑幻觉，势必会有生命危险。虽然吃了还是可能有生命危险，但如果不吃，我现在！马上！立刻就有生命危险！

这根本不是怎么办的问题，唯一的答案非常明显。

"哇赛！这野菜真的是太好吃啦！"阿祥也夹了几条蚯蚓在碗里，然后迅速吃光光，大呼，"好新鲜啊，连舌头都在跳舞了！"

"那是我自己在院子里种的。"老婆婆怪声怪气，眼角余光还在刺探我。

没办法了。

无计可施了。

"自己种的啊？那一定要尝尝看了啊！"我再无犹豫，夹起那一条大蚯蚓送进嘴里。

"呕！"我忍不住身躯一震，用上全身的力气紧闭嘴巴，没有真的吐出来。

"？"阿祥古怪地看着我。

"没事……"我含糊地说，"太饿了，一下子吃东西有点不舒服。"

"哪来这种奇怪的讲法啊？哈哈。"阿祥不以为意，大口地嚼着满嘴的肥蚯蚓。

一旁怪物老婆婆的眼神渐渐露出凶暴的样态，我赶紧笑着用力咬下去。

"好吃吗？"老婆婆的眼神扫了过来。

"嗯嗯嗯嗯嗯……"

我猛点头，镇定地一阵乱七八糟的咀嚼，还装出十分好吃的扭曲表情。

我用尽全身的力气，将那一大口乱七八糟的蚯蚓尸液给吞了下去，大叫："妈啦！超好吃的！真不愧是自己种的！"

"好吃就多吃一点。"老婆婆像是松了一口气似的笑了起来，帮我夹蚯蚓到碗里："来来来，不要跟婆婆客气……"

客气个屁啦!

"好耶!"

我一阵狼吞虎咽,将那一大碗蚯蚓给通通扒进了嘴里,想一次解决。

可我几乎只嚼了一口,强烈的反胃感就从胃里逆扑至喉咙,让我几乎要吐了出来。

这种事没人会习惯的!不可能有人习惯!

吃一百条蚯蚓就是痛苦一百次,没有吃到第十条就突然感觉很爽口那种事!

"怎么啦?"阿祥疑惑地看着我,嘴里也塞满了蚯蚓。

"……"我张开眼睛,暴吼,"太!好!吃!啦!"

"来!这个更好吃!"阿祥用筷子猛指那一大碗公的死青蛙。

阿祥,我要杀了你。

"真的吗?该不会是骗我的吧?"我哈哈笑。

"骗你做什么?这块炒三杯鸡超好吃的啊!"阿祥

竖起大拇指。

阿祥，我一定要杀了你。

"不是吧？讲得那么好听。"我笑呵呵地看着那碗公的死青蛙。

"这种事有什么好骗的？"阿祥困惑地看着我。

"来来来，多吃一点，这老母鸡也是我在院子养的。"妖气十足的老婆婆温馨地笑道。

我顺着她的眼睛看像所谓的院子。

那不过是一个烂池塘，上面有几只白目不知死活的青蛙在呱呱叫。

"哈哈，好啊好啊。"我笑容满面，干在心里。

正当我的筷子瞄准碗公里最小的一只死青蛙时，老婆婆立刻帮我夹起里面最大最肥的一只死青蛙放进我的碗里，说道："年轻人多吃一点，别跟婆婆客气。"

客气个屁！

"那我就不客气啰！"我夹起那一只痴肥的大青蛙。

我看着筷子上的浑然大物，它生前一定吃了很多苍蝇蚊子蜻蜓蝴蝶，肥得要命。

可悲的是，这种体积绝对没有办法一口吃掉。

那怎办？

逆来顺受是我的强项，逆境就是我的力量，逆境——

就是我的天命啊!

"自己养的啊……那一定得好好品尝一下了。"我闭住气,张大嘴。

我嘴巴用力一咬,肥鼓鼓的蛙肚就爆破了,流出一堆乱七八糟的内脏与肠子。

"……"老婆婆看着我微笑。

我看着阿祥,他正愉快地吃着一只大青蛙,蛮不在乎地将它的脑袋给咬碎。

……真幸福啊阿祥,白白痴痴地吃着那种烂东西,你爸妈知道了一定很伤心。

"我要吃啰。"我大声说,说给自己听。

然后一口将青蛙的下半身连同那一堆乱七八糟内脏给咬进嘴巴里。

当那一团冰冷的蛙内脏躺在我的嘴巴里的时候,我不禁有一个巨大的困惑……

为什么人类要有味觉呢?

为什么为什么为什么为什么为什么为什么为什么为什么为什么为什么为什么为什么为什么为什么为

什么为什么为什么为什么为什么为什么为什么为什么为
什么为什么为什么为什么 为什么为什么为什么为什么为
什么为什么为什么为什么为什么为什么为什么为什么为
什么为什么为什么为什么为什么为什么为什么为什么为
什么为什么为什么为什么为什么为什么为什么为什么为
什么为什么为什么为什么为什么为什么为什么为什么为
什么为什么为什么为什么为什么为什么为什么为什么为
什么为什么为什么为什么为什么为什么为什么为什么为
什么为什么 为什么为什么为什么为什么为什么为什么为
什么为什么为什么为什么为什么为什么为什么为什么为
什么为什么为什么为什么为什么为什么为什么

好端端的为什么要有味觉！

小孩子会挑食都是因为多余的味觉，没有味觉的话
人类就营养均衡了不是吗！

为什么为什么为什么为什么为什么为什么为什么为
什么为什么为什么为什么为什么为什么为什么为什么为
什么为什么为什么为什么为什么为什么为什么为什么为
什么为什么为什么为什么 为什么为什么为什么为什么为
什么为什么为什么为什么为什么为什么为什么为什么为

什么为什么为什么为什么为什么为什么为什么为什么为
什么为什么为什么为什么为什么为什么为什么为什么为
什么为什么为什么为什么为什么为什么为什么为什么为
什么为什么为什么为什么为什么为什么为什么为什么为
什么为什么为什么为什么为什么为什么为什么为什么为
什么为什么 为什么为什么为什么为什么为什么为什么为
什么为什么为什么为什么为什么为什么为什么为什么为
什么为什么为什么为什么为什么为什么为什么为什么为
什么为什么为什么为什么为什么为什么为什么为什么为
什么为什么为什么为什么为什么为什么为什么为什么为
什么为什么为什么为什么为什么为什么为什么为什么为
什么

　　咕噜。

　　我没有咬，就整个唏哩呼噜地吞下去，黏腻的感觉
比生蚝还要像生蚝，比痰还更像痰。

　　咕噜。

　　"是不是！是不是超棒！"阿祥大赞，自己又夹了
一只死青蛙送进嘴里。

阿祥，我一定要杀了你。

然后再杀你第二次。

我看着那青蛙的上半身，那死不瞑目的灰白双眼。

你死得轻松，但我活得痛苦。

"的确是超棒！"我怒极反笑，大口吞掉那半只青蛙上身。

难吃！

为什么我要特地从台北跑来花莲深山吃这种鬼东西！

"你们觉得好吃，婆婆就很欣慰了。"老婆婆笑得可灿烂了……那个该死的老妖怪。

接着，老婆婆诉说起自从她老公过世后，孩子也离家到大城市工作，这里就留她独自一个人经营偌大的旅舍，一个人打扫，一个人做菜，一个人养鸡，一个人等待着遥遥无期的客人上门。自始至终老婆婆舍不得离开，就是因为这间旅舍是她与老公一起打拼的所有回忆……

唬烂！

大唬烂不打草稿的老魔神仔!

"哇,好感动喔。"阿祥猛点头,"一个人经营旅舍真的很不容易,这里说小不小,每天光打扫就很花工夫了吧?"

"对啊,老板娘真是情深意重。"我胡乱附和。

阿祥继续白痴至极地大吃大喝,而我则渐渐进入了少年格斗漫画里常见的"无"的状态。

我嬉皮笑脸扒着活蚯蚓,吞死青蛙,吃着蜥蜴尾巴,用汤匙挖起奇怪颜色的虫卵糊,将蚕茧当作药丸一颗一颗吞下,竭尽所能凌虐我的胃,脸上还不忘挂着僵硬的微笑。

老婆婆也是一起吃,在我不被迷惑的眼中,她露出满嘴尖尖的黑牙,眼睛里飘荡着一股深邃的丑陋黑暗。

但我真正恐惧的还没登场。

"吃得好饱,这辈子吃最好的就这一餐啦!"阿祥打了一个有够臭的嗝。

"真的真的,我真的没办法再吃任何一点东西啦。"我笑笑摸摸被害惨了的肚子。

"吃饱了,也喝着汤暖暖胃吧。"老婆婆殷勤地帮我们盛汤，一个人一大碗。

——砂石杂草混泥汤！

"来来来，不要浪费了，这锅汤很补的，是用人参、当归、川芎、冬虫夏草下去熬，还用野山猪排骨肉提味，慢火细炖十几个小时。"老婆婆笑吟吟地说，"年轻人吃饱喝足，再睡一个好觉，才有力气继续赶路喔。"

阿祥大喝了一汤匙，满脸赞不绝口："我！的！天！感觉好营养喔！"

"……"我瞪着汤匙里的泥巴，脑中一阵晕眩。

青蛙可以吃，只是很难吃。

蚯蚓可以吃，只是爆难吃。

蚕茧蜥蜴尾巴虫卵通通都可以吃，只是无敌难吃。

但我的碗里都是土！都是泥巴！都是小石头！都是杂草！

我已经不想抱怨了，我战战兢兢地舀起一大汤匙，送进我的嘴巴里，我想省略充满屈辱的咀嚼过程直接吞下，却发现根本没有办法。因为砂石充满了粗糙感，全都卡在喉咙里，难以下咽。

如果说蚯蚓充满了土味，那么，直接吃土的话又是什么味道呢？

就是土！

身为忍耐界的英雄，身为耻辱国的王者，我还是花了整整半个小时，才将这一碗毫无人性的汤给吞进肚子里。

"你哭了？"阿祥讶异地看着我。

"……"我拭去眼角迸出的泪水，"我太感动了，仿佛一天的疲劳都是为了晚上这一顿。"

"那最后这一只鸡腿给你吃吧，不好意思跟你抢啦。"阿祥帮我夹了最后一只蚯蚓到碗里。

我泪眼汪汪地看着我的挚友阿祥。

阿祥，我诅咒你。

我诅咒你等一下拉肚子的时候拉出一堆烂泥巴。

"客气什么啦，快吃吧，我饱到想睡觉啦。"阿祥满足地说。

"干你……嗯，谢谢。"

我像吸面条一样将那只蚯蚓给吸进嘴里，总算结束了这一顿悲惨的晚餐。

老婆婆慢吞吞收拾着碗筷，诡异的尾巴摇来摇去。

"好累好饱喔，那我们去睡觉啰。"我赶紧说，免得还有瞎扯烂的餐后点心要吃。

"谢谢老板娘，你的手艺真是超好的。"阿祥感激地说。

"好久没遇到客人啰，你们开心，婆婆就开心。"老婆婆笑的表情有够诡异。

我想阿祥跟我看到的老婆婆的表情，一定大不一样。

"老板娘晚安啦！"我从后面用力推着阿祥，"睡觉睡觉睡觉睡觉……"

"明天不用叫我们，我们会睡到自然醒。"阿祥看着我，"是吧？大明？"

"对啊对啊，我们醒来了自己会走。"我用拳头催促着阿祥，"睡觉了啦！"

阿祥走上楼。

由于我的眼睛里已看不到这虚幻的旅舍，只得亦步亦趋跟着阿祥上楼。

我们踩在破破烂烂的楼梯阶上，往二楼前进。

我想这里在很久以前，很可能真是一间日式旅舍，毕竟那一张从网络上列印出来的地图上的确有"红山大旅舍"的字样。但不管怎样，现在看起来这栋房子只不过是一间爬满树藤的鬼屋。

　　不过没关系，我已熬过最艰难的一部分了，接下来只要整晚不睡睁着眼睛看到日出，这虚幻的一切都将烟消云散，而无法看到真相的白痴阿祥也将清醒过来。

6

回到我们的房间里。

"我要睡了喔。"阿祥幸福地大字型摊着。

"晚安。"我冷冷地说，这个时候还不是跟阿祥解说我们遇到魔神仔的好时机。

躺在其实是冰冷石板的床上，我一点也不觉得温暖，还觉得肚子怪怪的。

不，肚子不是怪怪的，它只是正常反应了它的抗议。说真的，刚刚吃了那一些乱七八糟的烂东西之后就算我连续烙赛一个礼拜都不奇怪。

我看着爬满树藤的"天花板"，忍不住思考起这一切前因后果。

我想，之所以阿祥沉浸在美好的幻觉里，而我却能够回复清醒，这一定是跟我口袋里的九把刀锦囊有关——自从我将背包打开来看见那三枚锦囊以后，我就整个人哆嗦起来，紧接着我将锦囊放在口袋带下楼，一切幻影都归于现实。

这辈子我从来不曾感激过九把刀那一个大烂人，但这一次我的心里不禁涌起一股暖意。

或许是出于畅销作家可怕的灵感，九把刀这次真是神机妙算，不过……就算他神机妙算到我会在深山里遇到魔神仔，到底事先在锦囊里面装了什么趋吉避凶的法宝呢？

扣扣。

扣扣。

有人敲门。

阿祥与我迅速对看了一眼。

"等一下喔！来了来了！"无视我愤怒的眼神，阿祥迅速起身开门。

站在门外的当然是老板娘老婆婆。

"老板娘，有什么事？"阿祥很客气地问。

我暗暗祈祷不要专程送餐后小点心上楼，拜托拜托……

"年轻人，要叫小姐吗？"老婆婆轻声地问。

"啊？这种地方也可以……叫小姐？"阿祥讶异。

我震惊到无法说出任何一个字。

"顾客至上，只要你们想叫，老板娘自然就会帮你们叫到。"

"……不用了谢谢。"我嘴上笑笑，心中怕得要死。

"买一送一喔。"老婆婆笑得眼睛都眯成了一条线。

我在发抖。

我的老二……也在发抖！

7

"不，不要。"我断然拒绝，"我们走了一天的山路，很累了。"

"可是……"阿祥像是中邪似的看着我，吞吞吐吐，"我还不累耶。"

阿祥这个王八蛋绝对是精虫冲脑了。

"不要跟婆婆不好意思啦，婆婆是过来人啊。"老婆婆装出和蔼可亲的样子，笑道，"这鸡呢，是不叫白不叫，人生就是什么都要试一下，对不对？年轻人做一下再睡觉，会睡得更好喔。"

"大明！"阿祥转头对我大叫。

"冲三小！"我大惊。

阿祥压低声音，严肃地握起拳头："人生就是不停的……战斗！"

干战斗个屁事！

由于大便九把刀的读者有很多白痴初中生，所以接

下来发生的事，虽然是限制级中的限制级，但我尽量以
辅导级的角度报道出来，希望大家理解。

"呼……天啊这真的是太神奇了，我们两个的第一
次竟然是在这种深山里耶！"阿祥叽叽歪歪说个不停。

我握紧口袋里九把刀给我的锦囊。

此时有人咚咚咚敲门。

阿祥嘟囔着："好像没有一点力气了啊！"

我去开门。

门外站了两位……两位……

我差点昏了过去。

不过，电影跟电视剧里那种常常演出"被吓到就瞬
间昏过去"的桥段其实很难发生。话说，如果真的能昏
过去，也未尝不是一件好事。

进门的两只鸡，的的确确就是两只鸡。

——巨大的人形鸡。

明明就有鸡头、鸡屁股、鸡胸还有鸡翅，却离奇地
同样拥有人类的基本体态，认真说起来，就是货真价实
的鸡精了……不，是鸡妖！

"帅哥，等一下我们谁跟谁啊？"左边的那只鸡妖
开口了。

不晓得在阿祥的眼中这两只鸡到底是什么模样，只看得他两眼发直，一脸深受感动的样子。

"帅哥？帅哥！"门外的鸡妖喊了我好几声。

我一点反应都没有。

但妖怪们是自来熟的，她们自己一扭一扭走了房里来，开始往我和阿祥身上靠。

鸡妖望洋兴叹地看了一眼不争气的阿祥都向我身上靠过来。

我靠！

"姐姐，我有功能障碍啊！"

阿祥那个废物幸灾乐祸："哈哈哈，我早就知道你硬不起来！"

鸡妖矢志不渝："帅哥？你不喜欢我这一款的吗？"压在我身上的鸡妖发出一股浓浓的鸡腥味，在我耳边吐出的声音竟颇为失望。

不过，不管鸡妖怎么磨蹭我，我的老二始终比棉花糖还软，更重要的是，我也不打算硬，我甚至别过头来不想跟这只鸡妖的视线接触。

另一边的也不肯放过机会："那我怎么样呢？"

"呕！"我强自镇定，我真的快吐了，比晚餐吃的那堆蚯蚓和青蛙还恶心，显然我和阿祥的表现让鸡妖很生气，她们俩哼的一声扭着巨大的屁股摔门而去。

呼——

谢天谢地！

同时心里也开始愤愤不平。

为什么同样是遇妖，为什么《聊斋志异》里书生干的都是狐仙，我遇到的却是鸡呢？

为什么宁采臣碰上的是美若天仙的女鬼小倩，我碰上的却是鸡呢？

"哈哈哈……"阿祥依旧在笑。

这该死的阿祥！我一定要把他杀了沉尸到海底去。

阿祥挥之不去："哎，你真的是不行啊？"

"……不要跟我说话。"我无力地躺下，看着被黑藤爬满的破烂天花板。

"……"

罢了。

除了难堪的回忆，我想明天应该要尽快离开这里。

为了避免被妖怪破门突袭，我不敢睡，用力握着九把刀给我的锦囊，警戒地瞪着天花板。

听着阿祥那头传来充满幸福与安详的鼾声，在山里走了一天的我终究还是迷迷糊糊地睡着了……

8

一早醒来，什么也没变。

没有我预期的那种……迷途客一早醒来惊觉自己坐在荒山野岭之中，发现嘴里都是沙土杂草的画面。只是灿烂的阳光透进了这破败倾颓的旅舍，而阿祥早就醒来，慵懒地躺在床上玩相机。

"走吧，阿祥，我们快点赶路了！"我定了定神，从地上捞起背包就要走。

"走？外面下那么大的雨耶！"阿祥难以置信地看着我。

"下大雨？"我看着破碎的玻璃窗外，是无敌灿烂的大太阳啊。

阿祥的意识还在魔神仔的蒙蔽之下，没有随着一觉醒来就比较清醒。

"我刚刚醒来已经先去楼下吃过早餐了，那老板娘很亲切跟我抬杠啊，她说既然我们付足了一个礼拜的钱，就不急着走，等雨停了再赶路啊。"

"那……"我震惊不已。

"既然你说过，那个写信给九把刀的网友还是读者说，大蛇祭会等到九把刀到的时候才开始举行，所以我就跟老板娘说我们就住到雨停啰！"阿祥两手一摊。

"干……干！"我快暴气了。

"你快下楼吃早餐吧，吃完早餐我们再一起去泡温泉哈哈哈！悠闲的咧！"

现在是什么情况？

那个魔神仔打算继续困住我们吗？

我该不管三七二十一就硬拉阿祥走吗？

按照常理判断，比起晚上，大白天魔神仔的法力还是妖力应该没有那么厉害才对，是不是应该立刻马上right now拉着阿祥冲出这间妖气冲天的红山大旅舍？

正当我这么想的时候，我听到敲门的声音。

"年轻人，早啊！"

门打开，脸色青青的老婆婆走了进来，屁股还甩着我无法不注意的怪物尾巴，而她的手里还拿着一盘我拒绝叙述的烂鸟东西——毋庸置疑，是我的早餐。

"老板娘早。"我脸色铁青地接过她手中的盘子。

"外面雨那么大，我看今天还是别赶路了。"老婆婆笑得很诡异："多留一天，陪陪婆婆嘛。"

"嗯，我听阿祥说了。"我的脸色一定很难看。

"我说这雨那么大，一时半刻是停不了的，说不定明天还得继续下。"

"依老板娘看，这雨打算下几天？"我压抑自己不要失控。

"依照我在这里几十年的老经验，这雨劈哩啪啦的，恐怕还得再下个六天吧？"老婆婆悠悠说道。

"……"我倒抽一口凉气。

话中之意，是真的要囚禁我们整整七天就是了？

"不过你们别担心，在婆婆这里你们可以尽情休息，想睡就睡，饿了就吃东西，不饿就去泡温泉，到了晚上啊……婆婆再帮你们安排漂亮的小姐喔。"

"昨天的赞！"该死的阿祥明明没有做过，还逞强地在床上竖起大拇指。

那个白痴单细胞，完全不理会那些小姐怎么 call 来深山卖春如此可疑的点。

"那么婆婆今天晚上再叫更漂亮的小姐过来？"老婆婆得意地甩着尾巴。

　　"好啊好啊！"阿祥笑得合不拢嘴，看来他今晚打算大干一场。

　　我瞪着阿祥，瞪着手中那盘超不健康的烂货早餐，但不敢看老婆婆。

　　我很想握紧拳头偷偷宣泄我的愤怒，但我只是可耻地挤出僵硬的笑容。

　　虽然是阳光超大的大白天，但我还是没有当面跟魔神仔撕破脸的勇气，也没有办法真的丢下阿祥独自一个人逃走。

　　等老婆婆走后，再跟阿祥摊牌好好讨论？不，那个白痴完全被幻觉迷惑住了，不可能听进我的话，万一他跑去向魔神仔老婆婆告状的话我就死得不能再死。

　　于是我默默地吞掉了让我头晕目眩的那盘早餐，默默地跟阿祥去楼下的烂泥巴里洗澡，然后默默地去厕所拉肚子……那些大便的气味比我吃下去的那些烂东西还要正常得多。

　　接着呢？

　　当然是默默地吃午餐，默默地吃晚餐，默默地又泡了一次温泉。

　　到了睡前，又默默地接受了老婆婆安排的买一送一叫鸡服务。

喔不！

不好意思我说错了，不是叫鸡，今天晚上我们叫的是……

"帅哥，今晚我们谁跟谁啊？"

第二晚站在门外的，是两头用双脚站立的山猪……还是山猪。

请问我是在吉野家吗？为什么昨天加今天共来了鸡猪双宝呢？

"大明！今天我可不会像昨天那样啰。"阿祥色眯眯地说。

"……随便。"让那小子和山猪们去搞吧，活该他昨天那么对我。

我又把昨天对鸡妖说的那一套同样给山猪说了一通，好在妖怪们很单纯，并不会纠缠我。

倒是阿祥，果真是处男，可能太紧张，竟然在要脱山猪衣服的时候，就上交子弹了。

原来阿祥才是真正的"秒杀男"！他一直解释是失误失误，可我还是嘲笑了他一整晚。

第三天，据被鬼遮眼的阿祥说，外面还是倾盆大雨下个不停，于是我们又无可奈何地留在红山大旅舍一个晚上，接受魔神仔老婆婆的热情招待。

这天我怎么过的，复制上一段再贴上即可，完全没创意，只有无穷的忍耐力。

问题是，连续吃了三天又烂又腥的动物生尸，肠胃也是有自尊心的，它们完全没有打算适应那么烂的食物，我感觉到我的身体极为虚弱，一直都想吐，屁眼也因为一直拉肚子拉到快抽筋，产生灼热的刺痛感。

我心想，真的在这个鬼地方再待上四天，我很可能会因为营养不良提前挂掉，如果我不趁我还有一点体力逃出这里的话，就等于我刻意用拉肚子自杀。

正当我认真思索明天一早是否该把阿祥丢下时，我们叫的"小姐"又上门了。

这一次靠在门边搔首弄姿的，是两棵树。

树……

树……

我老板大便九把刀曾经大言不惭："我买过车子，买过房子，但这辈子我买过最贵的东西，是梦想。"

现在，我终于也有自己的名言："我哄过鸡，骗过猪，但这辈子我做过最荒唐的东西，是和树纠缠不清。"

我脑袋一片宇宙大的空白。

事到如今，船撞桥头，我不是不愿意干树，而是我完全不晓得要怎么干树，也完全无法想像我要如何发挥想象力的极限，去对树产生最低程度的淫欲！

"天啊，在这种深山里怎么有办法叫到高等级的小姐啊？"阿祥呆呆地看着那两棵树，又看了看我，"大明，今晚换你先选……"

此时，我笑了："然后交换。"

是的，你没看错，我竟然笑了。

我忽然明白，阿祥这种自始至终都被幻觉蒙蔽了的笨蛋，才是最幸福的人。

当我保持绝对的清醒去面对魔神仔布置的恶烂食物时，阿祥则傻呼呼地大快朵颐。

当我在烂泥巴里将皮肤抓得又红又肿时，阿祥笑嘻嘻地将大把烂泥淋在头上大呼畅快。

当我苦思冥想地如何对付鸡猪双宝时，阿祥却爽歪歪地在意淫他自以为的绝世美女。

当我为保持清醒感到庆幸时，阿祥才是真正因沉浸在美好幻境中，得到了百分之百的快乐。而我，则因为神智清醒体验到了百分之一百万的狼狈与痛苦。

我笑了。

原来坚持看到真相的人，才是最愚蠢的笨蛋。

"等等，两位小姐不好意思，我们准备一下。"我将
门关上。

"啊？你要准备什么？"阿祥不解，他已经全身都
硬了。

"就等等。"我转过头去。

接着，我迅速操起椅子，转身就把阿祥敲晕了。

想到门外面还有两棵树在等着我们，我赶紧将阿祥
拖到床上，扮成他在睡觉的样子，再打开门。

我决心再向她们撒个谎。但我不想再做阳痿男了。

"哦，那个，不好意思，其实，我和那个男的是一对。"
我指了指阿祥。他躺在那里睡得倒是舒服。

妖怪们互相看了眼后，就不怀好意地笑着离开了。

我总算松了一口气。

这一晚，我睡得格外好，呼呼大睡到了隔天早上。

醒来，旅馆外面是唏哩哗啦的大雨。

不知道阿祥是吃多了蚯蚓和死青蛙导致记忆力下
降，还是真被我一椅子砸傻了，竟然没有找我麻烦，反
而一个劲问昨晚后来发生了什么。

我瞎诌说那两个小姐嫌他难看，就主动离开了。阿祥居然还信了，并且还照了照镜子，说自己不丑啊！

我没管他，自己大步下楼，就像不知道真相一样的吃掉了蚯蚓跟青蛙组成的早餐，那又怎么样呢？

纵使知道泡的是搅和了枯叶与污水的烂泥巴，但幻觉里热热的温泉让我四肢百骸都舒畅了……这才是重点，而这个重点跟吃微波食物一样，明知道不健康还是照吃不误。

不过这也算是好事。

第四天过了。第五天过了。第六天过了。终于第七天也过了。

雨停了。

而就当我们要告别红山大旅舍的时候……

9

窗外一片风和日丽，是时候踏上未完的旅程了。

收拾好背包，愉快地吃完最后一顿用料不明的早餐，再一边打嗝一边泡了半小时的温泉后，阿祥跟我背起行囊走到柜台，向招待我们七天的老婆婆道别。

人的记忆力跟适应力是不相上下的奇怪，此时的我已几乎忘了，这一切只是妖怪搞出来的海市蜃楼，还笑嘻嘻地跟老婆婆鞠躬道谢。

"谢谢老板娘啊，这几天真是太愉快了！"阿祥笑得很开怀，"食物很美味，小姐们也很赞，不过……放心，下次有机会一定还会再来的！"

老婆婆笑笑地摸摸阿祥的头，慈祥地点点头。

"那我们就继续赶路了，谢谢老板娘这几天的招待。"我也笑得合不拢嘴，"下次经过一定还会再来叨扰。"

老婆婆看着我，眼睛却奇怪地眨了眨。

在我还在思考老婆婆意义不明的眨眼意思时，阿祥忽然坐倒在地，呼呼大睡起来，这个突变让我瞬间想起了自己的立场——我还没脱离这个魔神仔结界！

"你下次经过，真的还会来这里休息吗？"老婆婆怪声怪气地说，面孔模糊起来。

并不是我的眼睛花了，而是老婆婆的脸确实糊了开来，不仅五官难辨像一坨正在重塑的黏土，原本很矮小的身形更慢慢扭曲起来，以奇怪的骨骼重生方式喀喀喀拔高。

只一下子，老婆婆就不再是慈眉善目的老婆婆了。

一条不晓得该长在哪种动物身上的兽尾，从这个"魔神仔"的屁股上迸了出来，而魔神仔的脸并不是我所知道的任何动物的变形，四肢也只能说是野兽的形态，却讲不出是哪一种野兽，甚至四条腿长得都不大一样，好像是被奇特力量硬拼起来的无名怪兽，恐怖绝伦！

我大骇，吓得跌在地上，裤裆间热了起来。

?

"干……干三小！"我的后脑全麻了。

"我问你，你下次经过，真的还会来这里休息吗？"魔神仔的声音忽大忽小。

　　四周的景色，不知不觉从一间干净的老旧旅舍，变成了黏着在荒郊野外的断垣残壁，而我正坐在一条粗大的弯曲树根上，背脊顶着一只塞满了树叶的破马桶。

　　看样子，魔神仔终究是识破了我，到了翻脸摊牌的时候。

　　按照爬山系列的鬼故事最后的结局，只有两种。

　　第一种，就是某某旅者被搜救队发现的时候，旅者傻呼呼坐在地上吃土吃泥巴，被扛下山后抓去收惊，收了几天在山上迷了路的魂才回来。

　　第二种就超惨了……只有一句语气幽幽的经典结尾词："从此以后，再也没有人看见过他了……"

　　面对魔神仔的咄咄逼人，很显然糊里糊涂的阿祥就是第一种白痴结局的模范生，而我呢，恐怕就是第二种恐怖结局的范本了啊！

　　"我问你！你还会再来吗！"魔神仔的身形急速膨胀。

　　魔神仔的脸孔完全不是人的样子，一下子没有眼珠，等一下又进出七八只眼睛，嘴巴一下子开在头顶上，忽然又跑到脖子上张嘴，完全就是变形虫。

　　"不要！不要过来！"我大叫。

　　出于生猛的本能，我的左手直觉地插进背包拉链缝里，用最快的速度掏出……烂人九把刀交给我的第二个锦囊。虽然不知道锦囊里装了什么宝贝，我还是将锦囊紧紧握在手上，高举过额，不停大叫。

"……！！！"魔神仔瞬间停止恐怖的变形，还往后大退了好几步。

锦囊有效！

机不可失，我想丢下阿祥逃跑，但脚不听话，只好继续大吼大叫。

"不要过来！"

"！！！！！"

魔神仔没有继续逼近，我也没能逃跑，一妖一人就这么乱七八糟地对峙下去，慢慢的，奇形怪状的魔神仔又变回了老婆婆的模样，不过这次的变形没有完全，有时还会隐隐显露出非人的型态。

或许是感受到了魔神仔人形化的善意，我总算是回复了冷静。

"我又没对你怎样！你到底要干吗啦？"我很不爽，但两腿还是无力。

歪了歪头，甩了甩尾巴，魔神仔阴恻恻地说："我问你还会不会过来，就是跟给你这个锦囊的人有关，你告诉我，给你锦囊的人到底是谁？"

"干！你管我！"我拼命晃着锦囊。

"……"魔神仔老婆婆像是努力压抑住什么，瞪着我说，"那至少告诉我，锦囊里装的到底是什么？"

锦囊里装了什么？

我还真不知道九把刀给我的锦囊里装了什么，但为什么感觉像是惧怕锦囊的魔神仔，也不知道锦囊里装了什么东西呢？

"那……"我承认我很好奇，不过讨价还价也是基本，"那我打开来看，不过你要保证你不会对我怎样！"

"保证什么？"魔神仔老婆婆眯起眼睛，狠狠地说，"我大可以先吃了你，然后再打开锦囊看，不也一样？"

听起来很有道理，不过身经百战的我没有选择吓到拉屎，而是……灵光一现！

不。

不是这样。

"好啊！来啊！快啊！快来吃我啊！"我的双腿忽然充满了力量，霍然站起。

魔神仔老婆婆面容一白。

我握着那坨软软的锦囊，大步走向魔神仔老婆婆，边走边叫："来啊！"

魔神仔老婆婆吓得不断后退，身形越缩越小："别过来！别……别过来！"

情势大逆转，不知道为什么占上风的我气势更盛，到后来几乎将锦囊压在魔神仔的头上，而步步败退的魔神仔老婆婆最后缩到只剩下一个三岁小孩的身高，还给我吓到哭了出来。

"哭三小啦！"我太气了，真的是太气了，"刚刚给我大变身，最后还想吃我！现在给我哭！哭屁啊！"

"对不起……对不起……"魔神仔老婆婆哭得很崩溃，"请快点把那种东西拿走……不要吓我……不然我辛辛苦苦的修行会化为乌有的……"

"有没有想过我刚刚的感受啊！你是妖怪耶！我是人耶！到底是谁吓谁啊！"

"对不起，对不起……刚刚我也不是很想吃你，只是……"

"还哭！"

弄拧了就不妙了，见好就收也是我的强项，趁着占上风赶快收手，等一下万一——不留神屈居下风的时候还可以用嘴巴讨点人情回来。

我谨慎地后退一小步，将锦囊慢慢随着手放下。

面对魔神仔这种传说中的山间怪物，我的筹码只有区区一个我不知道装了什么的锦囊，现在占上风只是一时幸运，万万不可托大。为了避免等一下情势被逆转，我决定要好好调整一下自己的态度。

"好了好了，其实我们也无冤无仇，只要你不找我麻烦，我就不那个那个。"我想办法装大器，但面对魔神仔，声音还是有些发抖，"其实这个锦囊的主人大有来头，我会来这里，跟锦囊主人的命令脱不了关系。"这也是实话。

"……"缩小化了的魔神仔喘着气。

"从现在开始，我……我问你的每一个问题，你都要老老实实回答。"我晃晃捏在拳头里的锦囊，咬着牙说，"好好回答的话，我就不那个那个，知道吗？"

"知道。"魔神仔的表情惊疑不定。

"你是传说中的魔神仔，对吧？"我找了一块大石头坐下。

"……是。"

"那到底什么是魔神仔啊？！"

"魔神仔就是……我也不是很清楚。"

"三小不是很清楚？你刚刚不是承认了你就是魔神仔吗！怎么还会不清楚！"

"我也不晓得自己是什么东西……"

魔神仔感觉起来有点悲伤。

10

接下来就是取材赚钱的时间了。

原来所谓的魔神仔，是一种还真的不知道是什么东西的东西。

打从魔神仔发现自己已经存在这个世界上的时候，他，或她……或它，就有了稀薄如烟的思想，也具有了一些粗糙不明的形体。

魔神仔不是狐狸精，因为狐狸精是由狐狸所变。

魔神仔不是蛇精，因为蛇精是由蛇慢慢修炼千百年所变。

当然了，魔神仔也不是树妖，因为树妖是由千年古木修炼所化。

魔神仔并不是由原来就有固定形体的动物或植物所修炼成妖成仙，而是莫名其妙就有了形体，根据魔神仔本人的证词，它也许是由山间的灵气所变，这灵气混杂着雾气、流水、阳光、土肥、树香等等略具灵异的元素所构成，也许是其中之一，也许是通通都有，更有可能通通都不是，而是来自于一片虚无的混沌，反正不管什么东西放久了就会有灵，就连混沌也是吧？总之等到魔神仔忽然有了自己的意识时，它已具备了基本的神通，却猜不透自己所由何来。

不过魔神仔没有初级的形态，也就没有型态的局限，它能幻化的物事比其他精怪都要包罗万象，但没有型态，也意味着魔神仔对型态的渴望——渴望知道自己是什么，来自何物。知其源而不可得时，只好退而求其次，就是至少渴望变成个什么——而悲情的魔神仔到底想变成什么呢？

跟所有的精怪一样，魔神仔也是想变成地球上的终极型态，万物之灵，人。

"白痴。"我毫不客气，"变成人有什么好？"

"我也不知道，但这里的大家都想变成人，所以这个愿望肯定是不会错的。"魔神仔毫无困惑。

"大家吃屎你就吃屎啊？"

"大家吃屎，那么吃屎就一定不会有错。"魔神仔完全不像开玩笑，正经八百地说，"所以大家吃屎，我就吃屎，而且拼命吃屎。"

故事继续。

越是深山，就越产妖怪，不过越是深山，就代表越少人来。

既然深山里的精怪们都想修炼成人，所以就开始偷偷研究那些会到深山里来的人类，也就是登山客。一开始当然只是默默观察，观察久了就会模仿，有些神通高超的妖怪就想办法变成人形，装模作样地靠近真正的人，与人互动，学习关于人的一切，学久了，也就越来越像人。

不过像是一回事，终究还是非人。

所以有时候要采取一些霹雳手段，比如幻化成婀娜多姿的美女，诱惑登山客与其相干，登山客充满生命力的元气一射入妖怪的体内，就等于注入人气的顶级精华，大大裨益精怪的修行。

不过山里怪事多，登山客遇到美女争相求干，一定会提高警觉，逃之夭夭，所以幻化能力特别高强的魔神仔，就负责将废墟幻化成深藏山间的旅舍，戮力将一切合理化。而疲倦的登山客一旦中了幻术，就会傻呼呼地住进根本不可能存在于山里的旅舍，有房间，有温泉，有大餐，有床，当然了，晚上叫小姐也就勉勉强强有个粗糙的因果。

根据魔神仔单方面对其有利的证词所称，被魔神仔

迷惑，不见得是坏事。其实很多登山客都是迷路好几天
了，又累又倦，随时都会昏死过去，幸亏住进了魔神仔
搭建的虚幻旅舍，才得以补充营养，充分休息。

"吃那种蚯蚓死蛙泥巴汤，也叫营养？"我完全不
能认同。

"你想想，我们哪来真正的大餐可以招待旅人？没
有的东西无法无中生有。"魔神仔振振有词地说，"所以
我们只能将手边勉强能吃的东西，变成你们眼中的大餐，
让你们吃下肚，补充基本的营养。不然，直接把蚯蚓拿
给你吃，你真的会吃吗？"

"那倒是。"我涨红着脸，"谁要吃那种烂东西啊？"

"是啊，但为了让迷路的旅人活久一点，我们也只
能凡事尽量，给你们吃，让你们睡，还得让你们好好洗
澡。"魔神仔想之当然地说，"到了晚上轮到你们贡献一
点精气滋补一下我们，帮助我们早点修炼成人，是不是
也很应该？"

"……勉强说得过去。"我倒是无法辩驳，礼尚往来
嘛。

"如果撑得到让你们被其他的登山客或搜救队找到，
你们当然会是大梦初醒的感觉，但如果撑不到那个时候

你们就营养不良死掉，我们就会干脆把你们吃掉，反正死了也就是死了，不如贡献最后一股人气让我们修炼修炼，吃形补形，以形养形嘛。"

"你倒是说得轻松自然啊干。"

"我只是实话实说。"

原来山里常有人失踪，找也找不到尸体，真相就是被吃干抹净了。

生于天地，被吃于天地，也没什么大不了的其实。

"可是我们又没有迷路，没事干吗迷惑我们？"我不解。

"哎呀，就算旅人没有迷路，我们还是想搞修炼，年轻男子的精气实在是太补了，就连我都打算向你们采集呢，可惜你有功能障碍啊，还喜欢那个男的……"

干，我那是在解救自己啊！

"……"我又羞又怒，一时之间不知道该怎么接话。

"不过你们怎么会到这个山区？这里平常非常少人进来。"

"我有一份朋友给的地图，这地图上面还标了你们旅舍的位置。"

"你们拿着地图，专程造访我们旅舍？"

"不，不是那样啦。"我耸了耸肩，很自然地说出我

们此行的目的，"我们要去大蛇祭，这里只是好死不死
路过。"

"大蛇祭啊……"

"听过吗？"

"嗯啊……那蛇很大喔！"魔神仔睁大眼睛，"真的
很大喔！"

大？能有多大？

"反正不关你的事。"

"那……你可以打开锦囊，让我看看里面装了什么
东西吗？"魔神仔觊觎着我手中的锦囊，语气又怕又羡
慕。

"休想。"我摇摇头，坚定地说，"让你知道什么东
西克你克得死死的，说不定你就知道破解的方法，然后
我就会被你吃掉。哼，想都别想。"

"那，至少可以告诉我，锦囊的主人是一个什么样
的人吗？"魔神仔怯生生地说，那神态接近哀求。

"一个大烂人啦！"我极度不屑。

"……好希望他本人可以来我们旅舍一趟喔，我们
一定会热情招待他，一入了夜，他与众不同的人气一定
会带来很棒的滋补。"

"他超烂的，烂透了，滋补个大头鬼。"

"如果可能的话，下次你与他碰面，能邀他来我们的旅舍住几晚吗？"

"只要那个烂人一口气付我十年薪水，你要赏给他十年的幻觉、搜集他十年的臭精气，我都无所谓啦！"

就这样，在奇怪的对峙关系底下，我跟魔神仔又乱聊了好一阵子。

聊狐狸精，聊树妖，聊山里的种种传说……奇莱山神秘失踪事件啦、太极峡谷的经典灵异照片啦、大霸尖山的悲惨山难啦等等。

说起来真好笑，其实魔神仔——或者说我眼前的这一位魔神仔，经年累月只管着自己跟一帮友好妖怪的事，对许许多多山野怪谭并不知情。

也许那些传说只存在人类耳语之间，并没有真正发生过。

更也许，是山里的怪事真的太多太多，多到连妖怪自己也无法清楚所有的事。

没错，说到我们人，即使我们有报纸有电视有网路，也没办法了解发生在我们周遭的一切事，怎么能反过来期待妖怪就一定了解所有发生在妖怪世界里的一切事呢？说不定过了这一座山，又是另一座山的规矩，那里的魔神仔跟这里的魔神仔也有着不同的思想与做法。

"说得好有道理。"魔神仔频频点头,"难怪这里的大家都想变成人,人真的好聪明啊。"

"不是人聪明,是我。"我不忘强调,"是我聪明。"

最后我抓起背包要走,魔神仔还恋恋不舍地说,他从来没有这样跟人类开诚布公说话过,希望我以后能够常常来找他聊天,不然品尝过与人类聊天滋味的他,一定会很寂寞很寂寞。

我说,不要。

阿祥醒了,但他所见到的并不是魔神仔,而是又变成人形了的和蔼可亲老婆婆,还笑咪咪挥手向我们说再见。这是我的要求。

表面上,跟妖怪纠缠过这种糗事,我一个人承受就行了,阿祥不必有痛苦扭曲的记忆。实际上,我更不想被任何人知道我跟妖怪打过交道,包括阿祥,所以阿祥单纯保存我们在深山里遇到漂亮小姐的记忆,也就可以了。

"谢谢老板娘!再见!一定再见!"阿祥热烈挥手。

"嗯嗯,拜拜啦。"我故作轻松地挥别我的妖怪朋友。

在魔神仔的道别下,我们继续踏上前往大蛇祭的旅程。

走着走着,不禁有些感动。

想一想，我们这些所谓的人类，每天花在抱怨与烦躁的时间多到完全不可能为单纯的活着而开心，更不可能"以身为人类为傲"，至少我就没有听过有人跟我讲说"我觉得我是人，好棒喔好开心喔"这类不知所谓的话。

但这一些拥有高强神通的古灵精怪，明明比人还要厉害，却眼巴巴地想变成我们其中之一，修炼百年千年原来不是想成妖化仙，而是拼了命想变成平凡无奇的"人"，莫名其妙教人真有点感动。

或许吧？

或许真如魔神仔所说的，既然所有的妖怪都想修炼成人，一定代表"成为人"是一件很酷很跩的愿望，只是到底为什么"成为人"很酷很跩我还不知道。

但不知道，不代表不会感动。

既然我已经是这些妖怪修炼千年的愿望本身，是不是应该比现在更开心许多？

我不禁笑了出来。

这恐怕是我有生以来，第一次以身为人类为傲流露出的笑容呢！

第三章_
好多蛋的大蛇祭

1

在灿烂的阳光下拜别红山大旅舍，我们沿着绑着红布的大树一路走去。

阿祥的心情很好，一路走走停停不断拍照，拍山拍花拍草拍鸟拍树拍松鼠拍云拍影子，什么风吹草动阿祥都想按快门。

我真的搞不懂这种买了一台单眼相机就自以为是Discovery 摄影师的人的想法，比起来，那些在车展狂拍 showgirl 若隐若现激突的阿宅心态，我还觉得比较健康。

走到山谷底，还真让我们抵达了那一个神秘部落。

说它是一个神秘部落，其实真他妈的一点也不神秘，完全就是一个在花莲随处可见的小村庄，有看起来很像拷贝莱尔富的小杂货店，有邮局，有一间冒充 85℃ 的 58℃，有一间派出所，有一间看起来破破烂烂的温泉旅舍，还有原住民摊贩在产业道路边卖烤鸟蛋跟烤山猪肉……是的，明明就有一条偌大的产业道路开在村子旁边，我光是站在路边一分钟，就有两台沙石车从眼前飙过去。

王八蛋！开车可以到的地方，为什么网友给的地图要我们费神地翻山越岭？

"根本就是莫名其妙嘛！"我愤愤不平地将手中的地图揉成一团。

"看开点嘛，要是我们真的开车过来，就住不到红山大旅舍了啊，要是我们住不到红山大旅舍，这样是不是很损失！"阿祥倒是完全不以为意，"所以命运自有安排啦哈哈。"

我看他真是逆来顺受到变成真正的奴才性格了。

我们这两个外地游客来到这个村落，什么也不干，尽是东张西望，一下子就吸引到当地民众的注意。有一个看起来像是初中生模样的小鬼头朝我们冲过来，嘴里嚷嚷："你们是来参加大蛇祭的吧！刀大呢！刀大呢！我就是那个写信给刀大的网友啦！刀大刀大刀大刀大刀大刀大刀大！"

瞧他一副欣喜若狂，快要跑撞上我们的气势，我立刻泼了冷水："九把刀没空来，我们是他派来见识那个大蛇什么的典礼的……工读生。"

那个初中生紧急煞车，全身一震，崩溃大吼："干！为什么！"

正当我想随便安慰一下他时，那初中生超崩溃地用头撞我肚子，大叫："为什么！为什么刀大不自己来！为什么！为什么为什么为什么！为什么刀大不来！为什么猎命师出那么慢我真的好想看大蛇把刀大吃掉喔为什么为什么为什么！"他的头一直撞一直撞，撞得我的肚子都快出现腹肌了。

真的是草莓族，九把刀到底是有什么了不起，他不来给大蛇吃，你是不会把大蛇带去签书会吞九把刀啊？白痴。

"好了，我们都到了，九把刀叫我把大蛇祭好好记录下来，我们就速战速决吧。"我说，不耐烦把初中生的头从我的肚子上拔出来。

靠，他竟然崩溃到整张脸都哭爆了。

"为什么！为什么刀大要一直用同样的字占满画面为什么为什么！第一次用斩铁填满整页我还觉得超热血！第二次用就没创意！第三次用就老梗！第四次第五次用就是没品偷懒！为什么为什么为什么为什么为什么！为什么为什么为什么为什么为什么！为什么为什么为什么为什么为什么！为什么为什么为什么为什么为什

么！为什么为什么为什么为什么为什么！为什么为什么
为什么为什么为什么！为什么为什么为什么为什么为什
么！为什么为什么为什么为什么为什么！为什么为什么
为什么为什么为什么！为什么为什么为什么为什么为什
么！为什么为什么为什么为什么为什么！为什么为什么
为什么为什么为什么！为什么为什么为什么为什么为什
么！为什么为什么为什么为什么为什么！为什么为什么
为什么为什么为什么！为什么为什么为什么为什么为什
么！为什么为什么为什么为什么为什么！为什么为什么
为什么为什么为什么！为什么为什么为什么为什么为什
么！为什么为什么为什么为什么为什么！为什么为什么
为什么为什么为什么！"

"干我屁事啊。"我没好气地说。

"为什么刀大要放大字体混版面啊！"

初中生大崩溃，又把头撞过来。

就在初中生忙着用头狂撞我的肚子时，十几个乡民也围了过来，对我们再三打量，看样子大家都知道我们的来意了，这样很好，省了很多解释的麻烦。

几个小时前才刚刚对付完魔神仔，区区一个崩溃的初中生实在很不够看，我抓着初中生的脖子一拧，将他扔到一旁，笑笑地对围观的乡民们说："听说大蛇祭要等到我们到了才开始举行是吧？真抱歉我们在山上迷了路，折腾了几天，现在我们总算来了，这么隆重的祭典就不要再拖了吧？"

"我要坐最近的位子喔，我要用超特写把大蛇拍起来！"阿祥兴致高昂。

围观的乡民里面有一个派出所警察，他嚼着槟榔说："好啊，我先带你们过去洗个澡，洗完澡之后，等天黑我们就可以开始了。"一手搭我的肩，一手勾着阿祥的脖子，想热络热络似的。

"我真的好想看大蛇吃刀大喔！"初中生蹲在地上再接再厉崩溃大哭。

到底在乱说什么啊？我几乎要笑了出来。

2

我们在乡民的簇拥下，来到了一间被青山绿水环抱的小旅舍。

这间旅舍小归小，但规矩可是一点也不马虎，一个彬彬有礼的柜台先生将一本看起来非常厚的资料推到我面前，另外还递给我一本小册子，封皮上印着"恐怖绝伦！超惊悚大蛇祭导览"字样，附加一张看起来很假的大蛇图。

"住宿前，请先详细阅读这一份资料，读完后请在上面签个名。"柜台先生微笑，"谢谢您，祝福您，感恩！感恩！"

还真是头一次遇到住宿资料是一本电话簿厚度等级的瞎事，这旅馆到底有什么特殊之处还真是不想了解，总之不可能比魔神仔假造出来的红山大旅舍还要恐怖。我跟阿祥看也不看，直接翻到最后一页，就在底下签了名。

房间很普通，无须赘述的平庸陈设。

躺在硬梆梆的床上，我随手翻了翻刚刚柜台先生给我的小册子。

印刷还挺新的，内容不想细看，但就是一堆祭祀大蛇的流程，比如祭品要先剃光头、沐浴净身、食用豪华大餐之类的超蠢细节，以及关于大蛇在世界各地的种种传说记载，图案清一色由无敌拙劣的幼稚笔触完成，可信度零。

这本小册子，不禁让我想起了小时候去班级远足到了奇怪的小游乐园，总有一个展区挂上"不可思议的世界奇幻大展"，号称里头有外星人的尸体、海底怪鱼的标本、记录了飞碟声音的神秘录音带、长了头发的大石头、有两个头的变种乌龟、大脚怪踩在泥巴上的脚印拓……我们小朋友趋之若鹜，疯狂排队买票挤进去。其结果可想而知，就是极其失望地走出展场，唯一的安慰，就是再花 50 块钱在出口处抱着一条又肥又冷的黄金蟒合照。

"啧啧啧……这年头，这种乡下地方为了行销自己的地方特色，还真是无所不用其极啊。"我嗤之以鼻，将小册子扔在一边。

"不过看起来真有那么一回事耶，不然就不会大费周章等我们到了才开始啊，说不定，可以拍到惊人的照片喔。"同样躺在床上的阿祥津津有味地回顾着单眼相机里的照片。

"别说什么大蛇祭了，我看到时候连一条像样的蛇都看不到。"

"哈哈别那么说嘛，有看到就有看到，没看到就没看到啊！"

"什么没看到？好不容易才到了这里，至少要给我看到一条大一点的蛇。"

我们在床上有一搭没有搭地瞎聊，一股倦意袭上了眼皮，沉沉睡去。

不知道睡了多久，醒来时，我吓了一大跳，因为房间里满满的都是人。

这些乡民里有派出所警察、柜台先生、摊贩老板，当然还有那一个写信叫九把刀来的死初中生。大家都静静地看着我们，不晓得这种诡异的凝视已持续了多久，好像在演咒怨。

"你们怎么跑进来的！"我大叫，叫得阿祥也整个惊醒了。

"因为我有钥匙。"柜台先生晃晃手中的钥匙。

"这不是重点吧！"我怒气腾腾，"你们怎么可以随便进我的房间！"

"因为你签了同意书啊，感恩！感恩！"柜台先生皱眉，翻开那一大本几个小时前交给我们签名的厚厚大本不知所谓的住宿资料，手指着其中一页，"你看，这一条，本人欣然同意，如经过乡民集体表决，三分之二同意，则任何乡民都可以自由进出本人的房间。"

"……"我寒毛直竖，说不出话来。

这简直是王八蛋嘛！

"好吧，既然我们签了也就没办法了。"阿祥揉揉眼睛，打了一个长长的呵欠。

"肚子饿了吧，现在都已经晚上9点了。"一个坐在床边的大婶开口。

"？"身为九把刀的灵感特助，我感到很不对劲儿。

"我肚子是饿了。"阿祥则毫无警觉。

一个老人点点头，抠着眼角的褐斑说："也该是吃东西的时候了，我们带你们两位到楼下的餐厅吃东西，吃，豪华大餐。"

"不用了，我们自己去楼下杂货店买泡面吃就可以了。"我赶紧起身。

"泡面？"那个还穿着制服的派出所警察伸手按着

我的肩膀，"吃，豪华大餐。"

不只那一个警察大叔，坐在我床边的所有乡民全都用手按住我的身体。

看样子，这一场豪华大餐似乎是强制的。

3

我们在众乡民的包围下，走到楼下看起来实在不怎么样的餐厅。

一坐下，马上就有很多道热腾腾的菜从厨房端了出来，有蒸蛋、烤鸟蛋、水煮蛋、卤蛋、蛋花汤、皮蛋、咸鸭蛋、烘蛋、蛋饼、葱蛋、九层塔蛋、荷包蛋、炒蛋……哇靠，怎么通通是蛋？

"尽量吃，吃不够，厨房还有。"那个该死的初中生咬牙切齿地说。

太怪了，真的是太怪了。

"我想这些绝对是够了。"我拿起筷子，手指微微颤抖。

"可是……都是蛋耶。"阿祥总算也感觉到不对劲了。

我们默默吃着一堆蛋蛋蛋蛋，但这些乡民并没有加入饭局，全都站在桌子旁，瞪着我们跟满桌的蛋搏斗。这气氛真的是超诡异，没吃几口我就无法忍受。

"饱了。"我停下筷子。

柜台先生眉头一皱，再度拿起手中厚厚的住宿资料，翻到其中一页："不行不行，根据你自己签的第二百零七条房客条款，你本人欣然同意，当有任何乡民热情邀请你吃饭的时候，你无条件同意赶赴饭局。又根据第二百二十三条之二的规定，当饭局中经全体围观乡民表决，有三分之二认为你必须通通吃完所有的饭菜时，你便欣然同意吃完所有的饭菜，不得异议。感恩！感恩！"

此时，整间餐厅的乡民通通举手，岂止三分之二，根本就是全数通过。

"算了啦大明，签都签了啊。"阿祥无可奈何。

"那就大家一起吃吧？"我压抑怒火，扫视周遭的乡民，"不然我们两个人要吃到什么时候？"

乡民慢慢地摇头，完全不想理会我。

"算了啦，我就说签都签了嘛。"阿祥夹起一块葱蛋送进嘴里。

阿祥就是这样，每次在街上遇到假装要你填问卷的直销工读生，就忍不住签了一堆奇怪的营养食品回家吃，内容大同小异的百科全书也买了四五套，这种超容易被说服的烂个性不知道遇到什么事才会改。

足足又吃了一个小时，我们总算将桌上的蛋全都扫光。

我超饱的，蛋的气味从胃里不断翻涌而出，闻着自己打嗝的气味我都快吐了。阿祥看起来也很撑，瘫在椅子上动弹不得。

不过我知道事情还没结束。

根据我刚刚随便翻了翻的《恐怖绝伦！超惊悚大蛇祭导览》小册子，白痴到极点、却又让人不寒而栗的模糊印象……

"接下来，该不会是要我们洗澡吧？"我尽量保持最后的平静。

"是的，是我们这边很有名的蛋浴。"柜台先生微笑。

阿祥一愣，狐疑地说："蛋浴？"

"不洗可不可以？"我试着握拳，拳头却抖到无法握紧。

"根据……"柜台先生又开始翻住宿资料。

"靠！"我大声打断他的话，"我懂了，我了解了，我要报警！"

"报警？报警当然没问题啦，你是这个国家的合法国民嘛。"那个派出所警察立刻指着腰间的警用手枪，说，"只要三分之二的乡亲同意，你就马上可以跟我去派出所做笔录啦！"

想之当然，没有任何乡民举手。

"没有的话，那就不能报警，去洗澡。"派出所警察伸手按住我的肩膀。

顷刻间同时有十几个乡民按着我的肩膀，那股力道不只压住我的身体，也压得我的心情一沉，沉到了地狱的谷底。

难道这个由初中生提出的、蠢不可及的大蛇祭，果真会出现一条超级大蛇吗！

"那只蛇，很大……"那个死初中生按着我的头，咧开嘴："真的很大喔！"

九把刀的第六感实在可怕，这趟旅行实在是，危机四伏啊！

4

一直以来，我都以为恐怖漫画家伊藤润二笔下的古怪村庄、诡异庄园、充满传说与阴谋的小镇，永远只存在于幅员辽阔的日本、或是更大更奇怪的虚构国家，没想到台湾这么小，竟还是有如此诡谲充满压迫感的边陲地带——偏偏还让我身陷其中。

有，危险。

就在我们即将被押到沐浴净身的场地之前，我唯一能做的，就只有一件事。

"我想回房间拿个东西。"我开口。

"蛋浴什么都不需要，该有的我们都准备好了。"

"有个东西我是非拿不可。"我很坚持，"如果不拿，我就绝对不走。"

乡民面面相觑。

"大明，你想拿什么啊？那么急……"阿祥还在状况外。

"干你！就你！你立刻翻一下住宿资料！"我瞪着那一个柜台先生，"看看有没有一条规定写，如果我要上楼拿个东西再去蛋浴，竟然还需要三分之二以上乡民同意这种鬼话！"

柜台先生显然熟读了整本住宿资料，面有难色。

"没有的话，我就要上楼拿东西！"这点我绝不退让。

乡民再度面面相觑。

"就让他上楼拿吧，反正大家跟着他，他哪里也跑不了。"不知道谁开的口。

于是我跟阿祥在众乡民的团团包围下，再度回到了旅舍楼上。

在众人不耐烦的注视下，我拿出了我的背包，伸手在里头乱掏乱摸。

当然了，我肯定是要拿出九把刀送给我的救急锦囊。锦囊在红山大旅舍已经用掉了两个，都收到神效，只剩下最后一个。现在自是再度派上用场的时候！

我将锦囊牢牢抓在手中，霍然起身，对着乡民们大喊："还不退下！"

看着威风凛凛的我，乡民们完全呆住了。

"找死吗？还不退下！"我气势爆发，光眼神就足以杀人，"退下！"

"……"乡民们完全摸不着头绪，表情十分茫然。

"退下！"我有点慌了，语气更加凶狠。

"……"乡民持续迷惘，连一旁的阿祥也一脸不解。

"仔细看好！还不给我滚！"我用力挥舞手中锦囊，汗流浃背。

"白痴 白痴白痴白痴白痴白痴！"那个写信给九把刀的死初中生对着我大叫。

我完全傻眼了。

怎么可能？

前两个锦囊连魔神仔的幻觉结界都可以穿破，甚至能够反过来制伏魔神仔，第三个锦囊怎么连这一群无知无脑的乡民都搞不定？

我愣愣看着手中的第三个锦囊——典型的九把刀恶

作剧？

"拿到了就快走，蛋浴要认真洗一段时间啊！"派出所警察没好气地抓着我的肩膀，同一时间十几只手也抓住我的身体各处，将我抓向房间门口。

脑中瞬间一片空白的我，加上脑中一直都很空白的阿祥，就这么给带到一间老旧的公共大澡堂。等我恢复意识的时候，我全身都被剥了个精光，衣裤全给扔在我们脚边。

偌大的公共澡堂里早就挤满了乡民，我看这个场面，大概是整个村落的乡民都到齐了。现场完全没有肃静的气氛，一片七嘴八舌的闹烘烘，每个乡民的手里都捧着五颜六色的塑胶脸盆，脸盆里装的不是别的，是蛋。

通通都是蛋。

鸡蛋。

"好酷喔！"阿祥赤裸裸地站在完全没水的池子里。

"阿祥……"我很不安很不安很不安，全身狂起鸡皮疙瘩。

有必要做成这个样子吗？

有必要将两个游客当成虾子剥光光吗？

我在台湾耶，在文明与法治的台湾耶！

那个蠢不可及的大蛇祭……那个正发生在我身上的

大蛇祭，难道，真的会出现一条超级不合理的大蛇，把我跟阿祥生吞进肚吗？

此时，一个穿着写上"村长办公室"竞选背心的老人，拿着大声公对着大家喊："各位乡亲父老，多等了那么多天，大家都很烦了，是不是？"

现场齐声："是！"

村长朗声问："那么，赞成蛋浴立刻开始的乡亲，请举手！"

岂止超过三分之二，根本全场乡民都立刻高高举手。

"蛋浴开始！"

不知道谁喊的第一声，一颗蛋就稀哩呼噜飞到我的脸上，碎开，蛋液流出。

我还来不及惨叫，立刻就是成百上千颗蛋往阿祥跟我的身上砸来，如果由九把刀写一段际遇的话，他一定会无耻地用一千个咚咚咚字塞满整个画面骗版税，但我在现场，我还真的完全无法形容被上千颗鸡蛋轰砸全身的感觉。

"爽啦！"

"死都市人！烂天龙人！"

"看我的伸卡球！阿答阿答阿答！"

"中！中！又中！躲也没用啦！"

"妈！我刚刚打中他的小鸡鸡了耶！"

"我也要打他的小鸡鸡！"

蛋如雨下，我被砸到无法睁开眼睛，忽地被砸到睾丸，让我痛到整个人都弯曲了，为了表达我的痛苦，我象征性张口惨叫几声，立刻有好几枚鸡蛋冲进我的口中，逼得我表演一边呕吐一边闭嘴的高难度兼高矛盾的技术。

不知道这群疯狂的乡民砸了多久，但他们肯定是将脸盆里的蛋通通都砸光了才罢手，而阿祥跟我当然全身都是黏滑恶心的蛋液，以及细碎的蛋壳渣渣。

四周哄堂大笑。

我勉强用手指拨开了粘在眼睛上的蛋汁，看见阿祥同样狼狈地用双手拼命将脸上的蛋汁给抹开，他看着我，我看着他……

"大明，我们只是来看个大蛇祭，怎么会搞成这个样子啊？怎么办……我突然有种很害怕的感觉……"阿祥全身发抖，连这笨蛋也晓得害怕了。

"我……我也不知道。"我的牙齿直打颤，话都说不清楚。

"我的睾丸好痛！"阿祥哭丧着脸，"好像肿起来了。"

"我的……"我怕到差点都忘了痛,"也很肿。"

此时,一阵夸张的敲锣打鼓声后,一条大蛇从公共澡堂的布帘后蜿蜒爬出。

这条大蛇果然是有够大,也超级长。

问题是,这不是一条真正的大蛇——而是一群乡民披着蛇鳞皮状的长白布,摇头晃脑,以舞龙舞狮的方式将"大蛇"给舞了进来的假大蛇。

鞭炮在不断舞蹈的乡民脚边燃放,劈劈啪啪,挤在大澡堂里的全村乡民用力鼓掌喝采,气氛十分热烈。

"大蛇来啰!大蛇来啰!"村长用扩音器大喊,"咳!大蛇来啰!"

超级假大蛇弯来弯去,很快便穿过拥挤的人群,来到我们身边。

原来是么回事!!

我又好气又好笑地看着这一条终于逼近的超级大蛇,转头看着阿祥:"妈的,我差点被唬住了,原来是这种搞法!这哪来的爆笑风土民情啊?"

反应很慢的阿祥依旧惊魂未定:"还是很恐怖啊!"

"恐怖个屁!就当作被整就好啦!"我翻白眼。

大蛇张嘴,露出里面一个小学生乡民的脑袋瓜,看样子是这个村落的小学学生集体支援演出这一条烂大蛇，光是想象一群小学生苦着脸在操场排练的蠢样，我忍不住大笑出来。

"大明，笑点在哪里啊？"阿祥看起来还是很害怕。

"这条蛇全身上下都是笑点啊！"我哈哈大笑。

村长拿着扩音器大喊："一咬，阖家平安！"

全村乡民齐声大喊："阖家平安！"

只见这条张开大嘴的超级假大蛇，在阿祥的身上象征性咬了一大口。

村长拿起扩音器又喊："二咬，风调雨顺！"

全村乡民齐声大喊："风调雨顺！"

超级假大蛇换咬我一大口，我还听见几个不专心舞蛇的小学生在长布底下嬉闹，我趁机踹了舞头的那个小学生一脚。

村长拿起扩音器再度一喊："三咬，国泰民安！"

全村乡民齐声狂吼："国泰民安！"

这一吼，吼得整个澡堂差点崩溃，我的耳膜几乎爆炸。

但这一吼之后，不只我身边这条超级假大蛇以最快速度溜走，全村乡民也争先恐后拿着脸盆冲出澡堂，我眼睁睁看着他们将铁门从外面关上，还有一阵慌张反锁的铿锵声。

整间空荡荡的澡堂，就剩下满地的蛋壳蛋黄蛋液蛋臭，被剥掉乱扔的衣裤，还有我们两个浑身一丝不挂的蠢游客。

我们面面相觑，完全无法理解情势。

我尝试用手指抠着身上逐渐干掉的蛋液，那触感有够恶心。

"现在是怎样？"阿祥呆呆地看着我。

"我哪知道，就看他们什么时候放我们出去啊。"我看着手指上的蛋垢，恶。

"我们会在这里待一整个晚上吗？"阿祥捡起被丢在地上的手表，看了看。

"我跟你一样，我也是什么都不知道啊。"我打量这个颇有年代的大澡堂。

这里恐怕是日据时代就盖好了，乡民进行这个无聊又无脑的"大蛇祭"恐怕也有几十年的历史。虽然我对人类学没什么研究，但常识上，这种祭祀大概跟古老时代村民将处女丢进河里，宣称献祭给河神以祈求平安的道理，大同小异吧？

或许这个村庄以前遇到瘟疫肆虐、野兽伤人、山洪爆发等灾难，都是用这种象征性向山神进贡祭品的仪式，祈求山神赐福吧? 这个仪式令假大蛇咬了我们三口, 肯定就是以山神的巨嘴, 吞食掉满村庄的晦气吧?

而这里的山神, 就是大蛇? 也就是蛇神? 但为什么是用蛇神当山神啊? 大概以前真的有人见过一条很大的蛇所以穿凿附会吧? 还是蛇有什么特殊意义? 硬要扯远的话, 以蛇做神, 跟真武大帝脚下的乌龟跟大蛇的传说有没有关系啊?

我努力在这蛋气冲天的鬼地方思考, 好让我暂时忽略刚刚那一阵蛋洗的痛苦。

"大明, 现在都已经快 12 点了耶。" 阿祥皱眉。

"然后呢?" 我帮阿祥捡起他的单眼相机, 虽然没摔坏, 但整机都被蛋洗。

"我想我们要有心理准备在这里过夜。"

"在这里过夜?"

正当我不知道该怎么继续这种超弱智的对话时, 我隐隐约约听见什么, 挥手示意阿祥暂时不要说话。

"?" 阿祥不明所以。

我狐疑地看着阿祥, 压低声音: "你有听见什么吗?"

"听见什么?" 阿祥有些紧张。

"嘘。" 静声, 我仔细听。

不只我，这次阿祥也听到了。

是一种空气高速震动的细微声音。

不是吱吱。

……是呲呲。

在断断续续的呲呲呲呲声中，还有一股物体摩擦的、缓慢至极的爬梭声。

我们东张西望，想找到这些越来越近的声音来源。

很快的，阿祥跟我的视线合而为一。顺着彼此的视线，我们瞪着干涸的池子底——一个大到不正常的、犹如水井般的"排水孔"。

这里是公共澡堂的温泉水池，池底这个大排水孔平常肯定是给封住的，它的边缘都还留有圆滑的切边，十之八九是用大街上常见的厚实金属盘给盖住吧？

现在，它却空荡荡，直通深幽的地底。

"……"我全身颤栗。

"……"阿祥拿起单眼相机，颤抖地对准排水孔。

令人不安的呲呲声，缓慢到让人窒息的爬梭声，还有阿祥跟我的心跳声。

喀嚓。

　　答案揭晓的瞬间，阿祥的手指也按下了快门。

　　一条白色的大蛇，从直径至少一个成人手臂长的排水孔慢吞吞爬了出来！

5

这条大蛇，何止超级，简直是恐龙。

它吐信的舌头像一条红色长鞭，抽打着充满蛋臭的空气。

它的眼睛红通通，闪烁着赭红色的光芒。

纯白色的蛇鳞犹如接缝完美的盔甲，在地上刮出逼人暂时停止呼吸的声响。

至于它到底有多长，恕我无法奉告，因为它的巨嘴已经来到我们面前，其身躯都没完全爬出排水孔，不晓得还有多少藏在深邃的地底。

如此夸张巨大的蛇体已超出历史资料的既存记录，撕裂科学理解的范畴，颠覆乡民常识，突破现存的所有传说，凌驾电影特效，大幅击败 3D 效果眼镜的临场感。

超级大，无敌大，**恐怖大！**

就像小绵羊在河畔碰见大鳄鱼。

犹如毛毛虫在叶尖上撞见螳螂。

等同在房间打手枪妈妈突然开门进来问我要不要吃稀饭。

我们完全失去逃跑的力气，甚至连最低程度的尖叫都发不出来，只能呆呆地看着这只史前巨兽大白蛇，慢慢伸长爬起至天花板顶，其阴影完全将我们笼罩在底下。

蛋气弥漫，巨大的白蛇首从天花板顶缓慢垂下。

全身僵硬的阿祥转头，用一种我从没有见过的眼神看着我。

"……大明？"阿祥的脸，忽然被大白蛇的舌头抽舔了一下。

我看着阿祥将手上的单眼相机递了过来，一时还不明白。

"帮我拍。"阿祥的眼神超呆滞。

"啊？"我接过相机的手，几乎停格。

大白蛇的舌头又抽舔了阿祥的脸一下，其力道，就好像进食前玩弄食物般的温柔。

"不要开闪光，不然会不自然。"阿祥呆滞的眼睛里瞬间满出了泪水。

"啊？"我茫然了。

"手震的话，我永远都不会原谅你的。"阿祥的脸满
满都是大蛇的口水。

都什么时候了，他竟然还不忘拍照？

不过……

"我可没自信活到把照片上传到网络相簿啊。"我苦
笑，失禁了。

自从我当了为九把刀搜集灵感的助理之后，我好像
常常失禁。

不过这大概是我最后一次失禁了吧，哈哈，哈哈……
哈个屁啊我好想哭！

此时大白蛇温柔地张开大嘴，轻轻地含住阿祥的头。

阿祥的身体剧烈抽动了好几下，但露在蛇嘴外面的
手仍不忘朝我比 YA。

我赶紧拿起单眼相机，拼了命狂按快门。

我一边哭，一边失禁，一边遵守诺言帮阿祥记录下
他那执著的最后身影，直到阿祥只剩下两只脚丫子摇摇
晃晃，我依旧不断变换相机的角度，伸缩着镜头，尽其
可能地捕捉。

终于，阿祥消失了。

不，他没有消失，阿祥还卡在大白蛇的喉咙里，看

那个卡卡的怪形状，很明显阿祥还在摆 pose，如果他还
能说话，他肯定是想告诉我……

"我知道。"我按下快门，喃喃说道："继续拍是吧！"

终于阿祥的凸起 pose 越来越下沉、下沉、下沉，下
沉到离开我的视线，我才放下了相机，将它放在脚边衣
裤上。

大白蛇垂首，用它赭红色的眯眯眼凝视着我。

我知道，紧接着就是我了。

在我找到我爸爸被神秘液体溶解而亡的谜底之前，
我就要葬身在这个花莲小村的史前大蛇之谜里。我的人
生将尽前，果然还是在又哭又尿的悲惨情境下度过，如
果九把刀知道我是如何鞠躬尽瘁的，一定会，他一定
会……

"他一定会笑！"我勃然大怒，"他一定会笑到连眼
泪都流出来！"

被我这么一吼，大白蛇像是愣了一下。

我一拳打在大白蛇的脸上，大叫："不要用看食物的
眼睛看我！"

呲呲。

大白蛇纹丝未动，还用舌头在我的脸上舔了好大一
下。

我的求生意志，却随着我对九把刀的愤怒涌了上来，一拳又落："吐三小！"

这一拳没有打中，因为我踩到了满地黏滑的蛋液，整个滑倒。

我的脸重重贴地的那一瞬间，发生了两件事。

这两件事，一大一小。

先说大事，我的左脚，感觉给含住了。

我反射性回头一看，发现不是感觉，我的左脚是真的被大白蛇给含住了。

再说小事吧，我这一回头，赫然发现第三个锦囊被扔在我被脱掉的牛仔裤旁。

这一件芝麻蒜皮等级的小事，马上就变成我唯一能期待的潜在性大事，正当我被大白蛇含住左脚慢慢拖向后方时，我一把抓住第三个锦囊！

下一眨眼我已倒吊在半空中，大蛇含着我的左脚晃啊晃的，这个不自然的姿势害我感觉到骨盆跟大腿附近的位置好像脱臼了，我惨叫："痛死我啦啊啊啊啊啊啊啊啊！"右脚狂踹狂踢。

大蛇当然没理会，继续吞我。

"不要太过分啊！"我痛死了，将软趴趴的锦囊脱手一丢。

这一乱丢，意外丢中了大白蛇的两眼之间，却见大白蛇宛如被飞弹击中，整条蛇往后翻倒，而我也重重摔在地上。

顾不得屁股脱臼加左大腿严重抽筋，我马上用十万火急的速度将掉在蛋汁里的锦囊重新捡起，一个翻身，对着突遭重击的大白蛇大叫："哈哈哈！"

大白蛇弓起它露在排水孔外的巨长身躯，警戒地吐信示威，脑袋却又有些不稳地斜斜摇晃，很明显刚刚被锦囊击中的伤害仍在。

虽然我不知道这锦囊为什么刚刚对乡民没用、现在对大蛇却又很有效，但这一点也不重要，重要的是，这锦囊是我现在唯一能凭借的武器，我死抓着不放，装模作样地对大白蛇吼叫："来啊！来啊！"

此刻的对峙，比起今天中午我跟魔神仔的一挑一，形势更凶险了一百倍。

在我跟魔神仔摊牌之前，我们好歹也故作没事地相处了七天，大家有相处，魔神仔也会讲话，彼此就有沟通的基础，但眼前这条史前大白蛇，我们唯一的相处，就是我用单眼相机拍它吞掉我最好的朋友阿祥！

大白蛇的头顶着天花板，踞高而下。

"来啊！谁怕谁啊！"我挥舞着拳头里的锦囊，犹如挥舞圣火。

"呲呲……呲呲……呲呲……"大白蛇吐信的频率变高了，好像很生气。

我实在受不了这种恐怖的气氛，握紧锦囊，一个乱七八糟的箭步，用力踩着地上的蛋液往前，对着大白蛇的蛇腹就是一拳！

大白蛇吃痛，张嘴往下想将我一口气吞掉，我赶紧握住锦囊一个勾拳向上，刚刚好让我命中大白蛇下颚，那一瞬间，大白蛇竟给我这一拳轰成九十度后仰！

"！"

这种异样的感觉，就好像海贼王里的鲁夫突然学会了霸气，普通的拳力裹上了锦囊的威能，力量陡增一千倍似的！这一个超级大逆转连我自己也吓坏了，我忘了再补上几拳，就这么眼睁睁看着大白蛇痛苦地倒缩回那一个巨大的池底排水孔。

"……"我久久都说不出话来，只是干瞪着不断发出碰撞声的排水孔。

排水孔里渐渐没了声音，我想，大白蛇应该是知难而退了吧？

我就这样失魂落魄坐在地上，看着那个不晓得究竟通到哪里的排水孔。

"阿祥……"

阿祥被大白蛇给吞掉了，吃掉了，现在大概被消化到一半了吧，如果阿祥还有知觉，一定希望我拍下他变成浆糊状的模样，白痴的他一定觉得很酷。

我想学那些假文青，哀伤地对带走阿祥的排水孔说点什么感伤的话，但我一句对白也想不出来，更悲惨的是，天啊我竟然没有办法哭出来，我还无法相信阿祥真的被大白蛇给吃掉了……如此脱离现实的事。

过了许久，我终于意识到这里是澡堂，于是我找了一个水龙头，加上一块干瘪的水晶肥皂，将自己跟衣裤彻底冲洗了个干净，湿淋淋地等待天亮。

终于，鸡鸣了。

当乡民一大群喜孜孜地将公共澡堂反锁的门打开后，看见我还活着，每个人都傻到说不出话来。

我跟乡民之间也没什么好说的，所以我就送他们每人一句干你娘，随后便带着阿祥遗留下的单眼相机，趁乡民来不及反应，就火速跳上一台急驰而过的沙石车，离开了那个糟糕透顶乱定法律的烂村庄。

"你们这些——王八蛋！"我在车顶沙石上，高高向他们用力比中指。

我躺在被盗采的沙石上，刺眼的阳光螫得我睁不开眼。

两个人来爬山，一个人离山。

一阵悲怆，突然想写几句新诗献给无法与我一起回家的好朋友，阿祥。

Old，Friend，

你在蛇肚里，过的，好，吗？

冷？

还是，太黏？

是不，是，觉得，很挤？

手机，没有，跟着，被，吞，吧我想，

所，以抱歉，我，无法打给你，唉，

单眼新，的，我收，下，了，

帮你，好好，地用，似乎也是我，的，新责任，吧。

谁叫我们是 friend 呢？

阿，祥，

再见。

祝，你早，日变成一颗，

蛋。

第四章_
嘴角他妈的的鞋带

1

回到了台北，满脸是灰的我考虑要不要去报案。

虽然阿祥被史前巨兽级的大白蛇吞掉，这么扯，扯到去警察局做笔录时一定会被笑死，但我手中可是握有相当程度的证据，也就是二十几张阿祥被大蛇活吞的连续照片，这些照片即使送去科学鉴定也没有问题，因为都是货、真、价、实！

然而比起报案，有件事我急着想知道。

还没换下一身臭味的衣服，我立即搭计程车冲去找九把刀。

刚刚拍完电影《那些年，我们一起追的女孩》的九把刀，正在后期公司台北影业忙剪接，我难得看到那个大烂人一脸疲惫地瘫坐在沙发上，好像连打了十次枪，委靡不振。

"讲完了就快滚，我们还在剪电影最后十分钟啊。"穿着拖鞋的九把刀蓬头垢面，连鼻毛都没时间剪，皱眉瞪着我，"哇靠，你好臭！"

"老板，你快告诉我，你给我的三个锦囊，装的到底是什么？"我握拳。

"装大便。"

"不是，我是认真的，锦囊里装的到底是什么！"

"装大便。"

"老板……我一点也不是在开玩笑！"

"装大便。"

他妈的我最气我认真跟别人讲话的时候，却一直被乱敷衍，我气急败坏地拿出那三个神秘锦囊，用蛮力乱扯，终于把锦囊的布扯破，里面装的三个黑黑的东西掉了出来。

我握在掌心，仔细端详。

这三个黑黑软软的东西似曾相识，我一闻，竟然有一股熟悉的臭味。

"这东西……"我抽动鼻子，近距离确认锦囊里黑色物质的气味。

"就跟你说是大便。"九把刀不耐烦地说。

"谁的大便？"我闻到了恐惧。

"还有谁？"九把刀一副理所当然，"当然是我的大便。"

我傻到完全说不出话来了。

这个王八蛋老板，在锦囊布里装了三坨大便，然后交给我当护身符？

"为……为什么？"我失神，手中的大便差点掉在地上。

"我不是在非洲肯亚的游记里说过吗？"九把刀没好气地说，"自己去我桌上的稿子翻一翻。"

我想起来了，九把刀曾说过，由于动物常常用排泄物的气味划分地盘，所以在荒野旅行的老行家，常常会特意搜集猛兽的排泄物，如狮了，如熊，如豹的干掉的大便，晚上扎营烤火时，先烧一点，将猛兽的气味发散出去，入夜的时候，再将剩余的排泄物散放在帐篷外圈当作地盘示警，如果有别的动物接近，闻到了这些猛兽的排泄物气味，就不敢侵入，于是旅人便能安心入睡。

基于这个逻辑，一向幻想自己是地球上最强生物的九把刀，竟然将大便装在锦囊，叮嘱我危急时刻拿出来解围——这种超自大的思考逻辑！

九把刀，他真的病得不轻！

"不过，那不是普通的，我的大便。"

"！"

"那是我特地挑在阳年阳月阳日的全阳时间，在我家阳台上，屁股晒着中午太阳拉出来的大便，拉出来后，还在太阳底下晒了七七四十九天才算制作完毕，彻底吸收太阳的精华，绝对就是超级无敌龙大便，遇鬼杀鬼，遇魔降魔！"

"……这种制程是从哪听来的？"

"全阳时辰，跟一口气搞他七七四十九天，不就是所有灵异人士的共识吗？"

我真的是超傻眼的。

这种毫无道理的蠢事，就只有九把刀这种白痴兼自大狂才干得出来！

暂时撇开九把刀是不是唬烂，这三个锦囊的的确确有斥退魔物的奇效，第一个锦囊将我拉出了妖怪的幻觉迷雾，第二个锦囊成功压制住魔神仔，第三个锦囊则硬是狠狠击退了那条史前大白蛇！

是大便也罢，不是大便也罢！

我暂时不想去想了，但我也不想再屈辱地拿着九把刀的大便了，我泄恨似的用手将三块早已被我握烂的大便黏在电影后期公司的沙发上，反覆擦拭，在这个过程中九把刀竟然打了个盹。

"老板！醒醒啊老板！"我沉痛不已，"故事还没说完……"

"嗯啊？你还没走？"

悲痛莫名的我赶紧告诉九把刀大蛇祭血腥的真相，高潮迭起，句句血泪。

"喔，真的假的啊？阿祥被那条大蛇给吞了？"九把刀看起来很提不起劲。

"阿祥死了！"我哽咽，拳握紧。

九把刀打了一个很臭的呵欠："真可怜，不过……阿祥是谁啊？"

看样子这王八蛋其实根本不信，没关系，我拿出阿祥的单眼相机，从照片库里按出那些惊悚直击，每一张照片都足以登上国家地理频道杂志的封面，最烂也可以拿去上刘宝杰的关键时刻。

只见九把刀面无表情地看完那些蛇吞人的图片，抬起头来看着我。

"那条蛇很大耶。"九把刀将相机还给我。

"蛇……很大？"我难以置信他的无感，接过相机的时候手还在发抖。

"嗯啊。"九把刀揉着布满血丝的眼睛。

"老板，那个村庄全部的乡民都是变态！他们集体谋杀了阿祥！不只这样，他们还涉嫌非法制定违反宪法的烂法律，非法限制我们的人身自由，更非法将我们全身剥光，再非法用鸡蛋砸我们，还瞄准我们的小鸡鸡！对了，他们非法逼我们吃很多的蛋！满桌子的蛋！那种烂村庄就是这样坑杀游客的，我相信这种变态的太蛇祭一定不只办过一次，他们肯定涉嫌伙同大蛇谋杀了几百个游客，这是一桩残酷的历史大屠杀啊！"

"蛋蛮好吃的啊。"九把刀的注意力迥异于常人。

"老板！那是满桌子的蛋！都是蛋！我跟阿祥都吃到快吐了！"我咆哮。

"不过……阿祥是谁啊？"

"阿祥是我最好的朋友！"我很激动，这家伙到底有没有在听啊。

"被吃了，挺牛×的啊。"

"牛×？老板！这是一条人命啊！我最好的朋友的命啊！"

九把刀摇摇晃晃从沙发上站起，从报架旁的自动研磨咖啡机里倒了两杯热咖啡，一杯给我，一杯给自己。

"王大明，你还蛮会唬烂的嘛。"九把刀杵着下巴。

"唬烂！我从不唬烂！"我快爆炸了。

有这种不重视生命的老板，我拿的钱也是脏的！我继续干下去也没意思了！

"那你看看，站在你后面的人是谁？"九把刀的视线射向我的背后。

我霍然转头，脖子差一点给吓断。

阿祥！

阿祥就站在我后面，歪着脖子，好奇地打量我。

"！"我吓到完全说不出话来。

"从刚刚你一坐下，他就站在你后面听你鬼扯。"九把刀不以为然地看着我。

为什么！

阿祥明明就给大白蛇吞进肚子了，照道理说现在应该变成了一条大便，可为什么又活生生出现在我面前？难道过去几个小时发生的一切都是我的幻觉吗？难道我都在做梦吗？

拿起热咖啡，九把刀慵懒地说："就是这样，王大明，做一份事领一份钱，你别想我会为你又烂又假的故事付一毛钱啊。"

"这种事……怎么可能……"我勉强吐出这几个字。

阿祥看着我，但眼神令我陌生。

"你不是阿祥！"我脱口而出。

等我意识到我刚刚说的那句话有多可怕的时候，一阵寒意才爬上我的头皮。

"我、是、阿、祥……呲……呲……"阿祥以极为缓慢的速度说话。

那眼神，根本就不是阿祥的眼神。

不，那根本就不是正常人的眼神！

"老板！他不是阿祥！"我惊叫。

"啊？为什么？"九把刀闻着热咖啡的蒸气，一副事不关己。

"他讲话后面加了呲呲呲的怪声！"我尖叫。

"我是阿祥，呲……呲呲呲呲。"那个不是阿祥的阿祥，脸色奇怪地呲呲呲。

很故意！

"原来呲呲呲是阿祥的口头禅啊？"九把刀恍然大悟。

"不是！"我大叫。

"我是阿祥，呲呲呲。"阿祥瞪大眼，微微吐舌。

"你看！他的眼睛红红的！那根本就不是人的眼睛！"我指控。

阿祥的眼睛不只红通通的，仔细一看，还闪烁着不正常的光。

"原来阿祥经常熬夜啊？"九把刀点点头。

"不是！不是！不是不是不是不是！"我大叫："他
不是阿祥！"

够了！

够了！

原来这一切还没有结束！

2

原以为一切的恶梦，在我不顾一切逃离了那个变态村庄后就会结束。

但，是我太天真了。

离开了电影后期公司，不管我走到哪，"阿祥"就跟到哪。

不，他不是阿祥，他只是一个长得很像阿祥的人。

我故意去百货公司地下街吃饭，"阿祥"就跟我去地下街吃饭。我吃着打卤面，他就面无表情坐在我前面，眼皮眨也不眨地看着我吃完整碗面。

"看三小……叮当啦！"我嘴巴挑衅，心底却狂起疙瘩。

"呲呲呲，呲呲呲。"阿祥发红的眼睛盯着我。

我故意去汤姆熊玩投篮机，"阿祥"就跟我去汤姆熊看我投篮。我连续投了二十几次，他就一根紫竹直苗苗地看着我投了二十几次。

"阿你是没地方去喔！别跟着我！"我超不爽，作势拿球砸他。

"呲呲呲，呲呲呲。"阿祥又是那一副死样子。

最后我故意去电影院看二轮电影，"阿祥"就站在戏院门口等我看完电影出来。据戏院门口卖卤味的老板说，"阿祥"竟站在那里一动也不动，站了整整两部片的时间。

老实说，被"阿祥"这种魂不附体的跟法，我真的不敢去人少的地方，更别提回家。

依照我长期看"关键时刻"受到的启发，再加上我不负责任的判断，这个一直死跟着我不走的"阿祥"，很可能是被某种怪物给"掉包"了，或至少，也是被幽灵附身了。

一想到这两个可能性，我根本不敢落单，当机立断决定睡在人来人往的行天宫门口柱子旁，让关老爷保佑我一觉到天亮。

天要亮不亮，我就被寒气冻醒。

我揉着眼睛哆嗦醒来的时候，第一眼就看到了"阿祥"。

"阿祥"就站在我面前，看着貌似流浪汉的我睡了一整夜。

我又倦又累，一股无奈压过了火气。

"你到底想怎样？"我坐了起来。

"呲呲呲。"阿祥还是超白目地呲呲呲，"我是阿祥。"

"你不是阿祥，但你到底想怎样？"

"我要当阿祥。呲呲呲。"

"你不是阿祥。"

"我要当阿祥。呲呲呲。"

"……"

我总算听清楚了。

这个假装阿祥的家伙，说要当阿祥，意思等同他承认了自己并不是阿祥。

暂时，还不是。

我当然心知肚明他不是阿祥，但他直承不讳，还是让我打了一个冷颤。

幸好大爷我就坐在行天宫前面，背后有关老爷当我靠山，正气无限。

"我听不是很懂。"我指着他，微怒，"反正你承认了你不是阿祥，是吧！"

"我要当阿祥，呲呲呲。"阿祥面无表情地说，"呲呲呲。"

"那你告诉我，真正的阿祥去哪里了！"

“呲呲呲，吃掉了。”阿祥双眼发出淡淡的红光。

是啊，我这不是白问吗？

阿祥正是在我眼前被吃掉的，当时我只顾着拍照！

“好，吃就吃了，那你为什么要扮成阿祥的样子？”我握拳。

“我吃了阿祥，所以我要当阿祥，呲呲呲，呲呲呲。”

“什么！竟然就是你吃的！”我跳起来。

“呲呲呲……”阿祥用吐舌头的死样子，承认了他就是那条凶手大蛇。

我们两个，一个人，一个人妖，就这么样在行天宫前呆呆看着对方。

说是对峙，并不精确，我几乎无法用语言抓准这种你看我我看你的茫然气氛，“阿祥”的红眼并没有透露任何敌意或杀气，而我的心情陷入极度的错乱。

站在我面前的，不仅仅是一个假扮成阿祥的妖怪，更是吞吃阿祥的凶手。

这个可能性在这个妖怪自己说出口前，我并不是完全没有想过，而是一直回避这样的念头在我脑海滋生。因为我知道我不仅没种报仇，即便有种也没本事报仇，假使有本事报仇、但报仇肯定会让我自己陷入两败俱伤的危机，十之八九我也会畏缩不敢报仇。

所以我的心中一直暗暗祈祷这个"阿祥"千万别是吃掉阿祥的凶手，否则我就被迫陷入某种道德危机——不知道凶手是谁也就罢了，但凶手就在眼前，不帮朋友报仇的话，就是没义气！

现在好了，我一不小心就让这个妖怪承认了他就是吃掉阿祥的凶手，逼我自己陷入了窘境。

不行，我得找回立场。

"我不相信，你就是那条大蛇。"

我一边冒冷汗，一边冷笑："这一点都没有道理，根据质量守恒定律，一条那么大的蛇，怎么可能变成这么小的一个人？重量都到哪里去了？我看，你只是一个假冒阿祥的流浪汉吧，还呲呲呲咧！"

"我可以变给你看，呲呲呲。"阿祥微微歪头，一副说变就变的模样。

"等等，变也没用，别以为你变成了大蛇，我就会相信你就是那一条吃掉阿祥的大蛇。"在诡异的压力下，我开始说教起来，"在那种鬼地方，大蛇肯定不只一条，而是有千千万万条大蛇，就算你们之间有一条蛇吃掉了阿祥，你们长得通通那么像，谁分得清楚哪一条才是真正吃掉阿祥的那一条？"

"只有吃掉那一个人，才可以变成那一个人。呲呲呲。"

"是喔？你说了我就要信啊？告诉你！我这个人就是有一分证据说一分话！"

"呲呲呲……"

"不要在那边给我呲呲呲！"

我乱七八糟跟眼前这个杀阿祥凶手辩论起来，就是不肯接受残酷的事实——我是一个很糟糕的没义气烂朋友。话说，世上最远的距离，就是吃掉朋友的妖怪就在眼前，但我却只能假装自己不是一个孬种！

我甚至不敢走过去给他一拳！

渐渐的，一大早就来拜拜的香客多了起来。

我开始后悔，为什么昨天去电影后期公司找九把刀的时候，知道了锦囊的真相，没有拉下脸跟他再多要几个干大便，害我现在毫无筹码。

"你到底想怎样？"我试图保持冷静，"是不是想等我走到没有人的地方，再忽然把我吃掉！"

"我说了，呲呲呲，我想当阿祥。"阿祥重复着同一句话，"教我，当阿祥。呲呲呲。教我，当阿祥……"

忽然，我从阿祥的赭红色的眼睛底，看见了真诚的渴望。

这一份渴望，我依稀在魔神仔的眼窟里见过……

3

现在的场景，是麦当劳。

我的桌上摆了一堆薯条，以及一排刚刚从便利商店买来的鸡蛋。

薯条是给我吃的，而那一排鸡蛋，当然是给"阿祥"吃的。

在接下来的一个多小时里，我总算强迫自己听明白了"阿祥"的故事。

上一篇游记里说过了，花东深山里山精鬼怪尤其多，许多都幻想着总有一天可以幻化成人，这点我是亲身经历。至于这条一不留神就活了上千年的大蛇，也不例外。

比起没有形体也没有原貌的魔神仔，这一条超级大白蛇可是结结实实地活了非常久，久到有一天，它的躯体大到可以吞掉一整个人的时候，它就真的吞了一个人。它觉得，比起其他动物，人吃起来的感觉很不一样。

"很不一样？"我咬着薯条。

"人会，说话，呲呲呲……"阿祥吞了一颗蛋。

的确，人会说话。

不像其他的动物所发出的单调声音，其竭尽所能也不过就是"声调转换"的程度，人类在挣扎惨哭时所嚎叫出来的"语言"充满了各式各样的音阶与潜在的表达意义，令大蛇深深着迷。

它心想，这种拥有千奇百怪的"语言"的物种，究竟为什么如此与众不同呢？他们临死之前所发出来的叫声，除了求饶，还有什么其他意义吗？

为了得到答案，它就一直吞一直吞一直吞。

直到一整个部落都被它默默吞掉。

直到两个部落都埋葬在它的肚子里。

为了对抗贪吃的大蛇，不同部落间的原住民勇士开始集结讨伐，用弓箭与砍刀试图夺回老祖宗遗留下的猎场，却前仆后继地消失在森林里。狼狈的生还者，则成为大蛇传说的一部分。

起先大蛇只是原住民历代相传的魔物，后来汉人呼朋引伴进了山区伐木，也糊里糊涂走进了大蛇的五脏庙。眨眼过了两百年，日本军队的太阳旗挥舞进了花东，也有好几支部队在深山里遭遇到了大蛇的强袭，子弹一排排钉在它坚韧的鳞片上，仓皇失措的武士刀向它挥舞……

带来了蛮横的死亡，却同样吞噬了强敌，大蛇被误植了山神的称号。

它的身子越来越大，某种模糊的答案也悄悄地在它的肚子里孕育成形。

它开始听得懂粗糙的语言，于是它总算听明白了来自人类部落的乞饶，出于好玩，也出于想知道"这么做的话会有什么样的结果"，它接受了来自人类单方面的约定——它一年只造访红花部落生吞两个人，换来人类五体投地的崇敬。

吞的人少，却被当成神祇，大白蛇觉得很新鲜。

其余不吃人的时间，它就吃吃别的东西，但渐渐地它发现自己不吃东西也不感到特别饥饿，或许灵性的增长慢慢地抑制了食物之于生存上的需求。而它也开始跟深山里其他想幻化成人的精怪对话。

"对话？"

"没错，对话。呲呲呲！""阿祥"露出极难得的得意神色。

基于食物链牢不可破的关系，原先不同的动物之间是鲜少对话的，即使碰了面，也只会发出大大小小的"声音"做最基本的生理沟通——警告、求偶、害怕、虚张声势、主张地盘，诸如此类，远远不是聊天。

是的，聊天。

人类的语言包涵的意义太丰富了，意义丰富到满出来，满到衍生出很多累赘的用法，仔细想起来，聊天的确是一种很奇妙的状态，泛指与延续生命基本无涉的、意义不明的、纯粹打发时间的沟通，这种沟通仅会发生在具有灵性的动物身上。例如，这些不约而同想成为人类的精怪上。

发现这一点之后，大白蛇便爱上了这种漫无边际的对话，只要遇到了那些山精湖妖，大白蛇就开始练习语言。

说起来讽刺，人类的语言，跨越了精怪之间的物种障碍，成为大家共同的桥梁。同时透过这些对话，大白蛇也迅速接受了来自其他精怪的愿望——成为人。

大蛇毫无疑问地将这种愿望挪为己用。

大家都想成为人，所以它也要成为人。

"这种白痴想法我从魔神仔那里听过一遍了，真是不可理喻。"

"……我觉得，成为人，很好。呲呲呲。"

"哪里好？"

"可以使用语言。"阿祥吐吐舌头，说，"呲呲呲，就像现在。"

除了可以使用语言，大白蛇也很喜欢这一个不只是想要吃东西跟拉屎的自己。

它觉得，自从想成为人之后，自己的的确确跟其他的动物不一样了，也跟以前那一个整天只想吃东西跟找树洞冬眠的那一条自己，大大的不一样了，因为它首次有了不仅仅是想活下去的"愿望"。

它觉得自己与众不同。

多半是"愿望的魔力"在体内发酵，从它想变成人类的那一天起，它就一直很努力把自己变成人，这中间的变化过程近乎不可思议，连它也搞不清楚自己哪来的"法力"可以让身体产生如此剧烈的改变。

最后它发现，自己似乎可以变成任何一个自己曾经吃过的人。

"是基因吧，被你吃过的人的基因，都变成你身体的一部分了。"

"基因……不是灵魂吗？呲呲呲……"

"灵魂？"

"虽然并不清楚，但我可以感觉到，呲呲呲，那些人还活着。"

假阿祥的表情非常认真，那股认真令我怔住。

"被你吃掉的人，还活着？"

"呲呲呲，大家都拼命的，在我身体里，呲呲呲，活着。"

"真是了不起的自我安慰啊，干。"

每一年它都持续进食着由大蛇祭提供的倒霉人类，它可以变幻的人越来越多。

可大白蛇虽然可以变成人，却一直无法延长自己变成人的时间。

有时它仅仅能变成一个小时的人，有时它却可以变成三天分量的人，但从来没有维持过人形超过一个月以上。忽然之间，无预警的，它就会从人的躯体变化成巨蛇的原始状态。

它想过，是不是它吃的人不够多。

它也想过，是不是它想变成人的愿望不够强烈。

它更想过，会不会有可能是它根本还没抓到如何变成人的诀窍。

它不知道，为什么。

"你问我为什么？我怎么知道，我打从一开始就是
一个人。"

"你没有想过，要变成其他动物吗？哔哔哔……"

"我干吗想变成其他动物？"

"哔哔哔……"

是啊，我虽然常常抱怨身为一个人的悲哀，抱怨我
爸爸被溶解的悲哀（还有读者在乎这点吗），抱怨身为
九把刀灵感助理的悲哀，但我的确没想过变成其他的动
物。

有时候我会听到别人感叹："啊，如果我是一只鸟就
好了。"

嗯啊，如果你是一只鸟，就可以飞翔在高空上，飞
呀飞呀……感觉很爽。但你必须冒着一不留神就被老鹰
吃掉的危险，忍受每天都要吞毛毛虫果腹的悲哀，当然
了，你从此以后都看不懂海贼王最新进度。

偶而我也会听到有人对着大海叹息："唉，若能化身
海豚，该有多自在？"

嗯啊嗯啊，要是你变成了一只海豚，当然可以整天
游泳，想游去哪就去哪，但你打不过鲨鱼，躲不过鱼网，

每天还要忍受跟另一只海豚亲热的感觉。万一被抓进海洋公园就更凄惨，每天都要负责跳火圈用鼻子顶气球带给所有小朋友欢笑。对了，身为一只海豚，你也看不懂海贼王最新进度。

那些整天感叹想变成另一种动物的人，都只是嘴巴说说，都只是在写诗。

没有人真心真意想变成人类之外的动物，这也就难怪，其他的动物都眼巴巴地想变成人。

"你说你不晓得什么时候会再变回蛇，也包括现在吗？"

"是的，呲呲呲……"

"所以你随时都会变成一条超级大蛇？"

"很有可能，呲呲呲……"

"那我现在正式告诉你，如何永远变成人，这个问题我无法解决。"我严肃地用薯条指着假阿祥，又指了指自己，"我是谁？我不过就是一个很普通的人，我没有办法让你一直 hold 在人的状态。"

"呲呲呲……"

"你会呲呲呲，我也会呲呲呲，但我没有办法让你 hold 在人的状态，again ！"

我郑重告诉假阿祥，就是不想我们之间有任何误会。

如果这个世界上真有一个人可以帮助这条蛇精永远变成人类，那一个人，也不会是我，不可能是我，绝对不会是我，百分之百不会是我，至少刘宝杰跟许浩平甚至是张友骅的等级都在我之上。

"……你是第一个。"假阿祥开口，"呲呲呲。"

"第一个什么？"

"第一个，可以让我感到害怕的人类。呲呲呲。"

我楞了一下。

"喔，是这样吗？"

"你挥出的拳头，呲呲呲，打得我，很痛。"

假阿祥的脸竟皱了起来，好像我那一拳的劲道还残留在它脸上似的。

虽然假阿祥对那一拳的力量有所误解，厉害的并不是我，而是九把刀的大便，但这个梗我不能说破，万一被假阿祥发现我并没有揍倒它的力量，说不定等一下它就会将我拉到麦当劳的厕所吞掉。

为了在这个妖怪面前挺直腰杆大声说话，我得好好守住这个屎级的秘密。

"虽然身为人类的超级强者，但关于一条蛇怎么变成一个人，我还是没有头绪。"我情不自禁地拔着头发，"既

然妖怪都会人的语言，你没问过其他的妖怪怎么确实变
成人吗？"

"大家，都没有答案。呲呲呲……"

"倒也是，其他的妖怪好像都没有你厉害。"

想起我跟阿祥在红山大旅舍遇到的那个魔神仔，他
聚集了一大堆乱七八糟的妖怪，在废墟里施展妖术，说
穿了，也不过就是在特定的结界范围内将人迷昏，让人
产生幻觉，将恶心巴拉的死青蛙、蚯蚓与泥巴汤当作山
珍海味吃下。

但其实，那些妖怪根本无法变成人形，他们只是用
法术（是法术吗？）改变了人脑内的意识，让旅人以为
自己看到了人，可他们根本还是原来的模样。这种幻觉
还仅限定于在特殊的地界里才有效，逊得要命。

相较之下，这条大蛇妖可以变成一个确确实实的人，
而不是单纯搞幻觉，它的道行一定比魔神仔高了七八层
楼高，改天还得靠它向山里那些精怪传授如何变成一个
人的方法，而不是倒过来。

"我不想只是可以变成人，呲呲呲，我想成为一个，
真正的人。"假阿祥不忘吐舌头，"呲呲呲。"

"我知道，但我一开始就是一个人，所以我不知道

怎么变成一个人。"我紧皱眉头，假装思考，"这么说好了，我连怎么从人变成一条狗一只猫我都不知道。"

"有没有可能，呲呲呲……我每天都吃一个人，就可以一直当人？"

"你问我，我问个屁？"

"那，怎么办？"

"我哪知道？但我非常确定一件事，那就是，如果你hold 不住，在都市里突然变成一条大蛇，百分之百会被警察乱枪射死，要不然就是被抓进动物园关一辈子，如果这里是美国，你还会被太空总署关起来做研究，总之，你千万不可以突然变回一条蛇。"

"我尽力。"假阿祥吃着蛋，"呲呲呲。"

"不是尽力！是一定要做到！"我握拳。

我们继续聊。

我吃光了薯条，而假阿祥也吃光了蛋。

基本上，我答应竭尽所能帮假阿祥想办法维持住人的状态，毕竟真阿祥某种程度也变成了这个假阿祥身体的一部分，那么，我帮假阿祥，就等于帮真阿祥。尤其我想到了真正的阿祥还有家人，而他的家人一定无法接受阿祥从此以后都回不了家的事实。

基于交换条件，假阿祥应允我，它必须努力扮演好真阿祥的角色，它必须常常回家跟真阿祥的父母相处，它甚至必须努力工作好拿钱回家，总之，它要让自己以阿祥的身份努力活下去。

就当作，我眼前的这个阿祥，是阿祥 2.0 版本好了。

"我答应你，呲呲呲……"假阿祥吐吐舌。

"就这么说定了。"我淡淡地说，轻轻捏住了拳头，"唯有你继续阿祥的生命，我才可以忍住不替好友报仇的冲动，否则，我一拳灌爆你的脸！"

"了解，呲呲呲。"

不过，详细到底要怎么令假阿祥变成一个真阿祥呢？光是外表像是远远不够的，要当真阿祥，我得花很多时间跟他说阿祥是一个什么样的人，做过什么事，读过什么学校，喜欢吃什么不喜欢吃什么，阿祥关于拍照上的兴趣，等等等等的太多太多。

又聊了好一会儿，假阿祥慢慢站了起来，进了麦当劳的洗手间。

我心想，原来蛇变成了人也晓得大小便，只是……不知道现在这个 2.0 版本的阿祥，拉屎拉尿的功能是不是也跟人类完全一样，还是略有不同？话说，我好像不知道蛇是怎么大便的？

几分钟后，假阿祥摇摇晃晃从厕所走了出来，捧着肚子在我对面坐下。

"对了，有一件事我不明白，就是你刚刚是怎么小便还是……"

"……咯。"假阿祥没有呲呲呲，而是打了个嗝。

我话说到一半，就不由自主停住，因为假阿祥那个嗝吹出来的气实在太腥太臭了，整个喷在我的脸上，竟令我有些晕眩。

而假阿祥的嘴角，挂着一条长长的东西。

那条长长的东西当然不是面条，因为麦当劳他妈的没有卖面条。

那条长长的东西有些脏，样子有点眼熟，好像是……好像是……

"鞋带？"我怔了一下。

"呲呲呲……嗝！"假阿祥又打了一个嗝，照样命中我的脸。

我几乎快被臭到晕倒。

而假阿祥这一口嗝，不只吹出了浓浓臭气，还吹出了几条黑丝。

那些黑丝轻轻飘落在桌上，我定神一看，发现是……

"头发？"我瞪着桌上的黑丝，抬起头，又瞪着假阿祥。

假阿祥满脸无辜地看着我。我这时总算注意到，从刚刚起假阿祥就一直捧着的肚子，干，真的是有够大，大到很不自然，大到像有一颗篮球藏在衣服底下。

"……"我看着假阿祥。

"……"假阿祥看着我。嘴里，还衔着一条鞋带。

一个年轻妈妈在麦当劳里走来走去，脚步越来越急，她走进喧闹声此起彼落的儿童游乐区，随即又快步走了出来。她开始询问每一个坐在位子上的人，有没有看见她的儿子。

"对不起，请问你有没有看到我儿子？"年轻妈妈来到我身边。

"儿子？"我镇定地看着她。

"大概这么高，刚刚还在这里的。"年轻妈妈焦急地用手比了一下，大约是一个六岁小童的高度。

"喔？"我面不改色，摇摇头。

"他刚刚一个人去厕所，一下子就不见了，怎么会这样呢……"

年轻妈妈丢下这句话，看我没回应，就跑下楼找店经理去。

我看着假阿祥。

我看着，嘴角衔着一条烂鞋带的假阿祥。

在感到毛骨悚然，与感到怒不可遏之间，我选择
了——

"阿祥！"我用力拍桌。

"呲呲呲……"假阿祥像是吓了一跳，"咯！"

"你到底是想当人！还是想当妖怪！"我很愤怒。

"呲呲呲呲呲呲呲呲呲呲呲呲呲！"假阿祥表情
僵硬。

我用力拉着假阿祥嘴角的那条鞋带，用力一拔，就
这么将那条该死的鞋带拔出来！但那一个被生吞进去的
小孩子，当然不可能跟着这条鞋带被我一并拔出！

这真的是，太血腥！太暴力了！

假阿祥不过去了洗手间一趟，就在里头吞了一个小
孩！

小孩！小孩！就连好莱坞的恐怖电影都对小孩特别
礼遇，不管是大白鲨大鳄鱼食人鱼大海怪大蟑螂，根本
不可能有小孩被这些变态怪物干掉！因为！没有人可以
接受天真无邪的小孩遇害！

这只妖怪，简直就是毫无良心！

"不可以！吃小孩！"我压低声音，却气到发抖，"绝
对不可以吃小孩！"

"……"假阿祥好像被我的气势震慑住，连呲呲呲都忘了，"为什么？"

"你知道！那个年轻妈妈有多可怜吗？她辛辛苦苦养大了孩子，结果却被你吃了！这是什么道理？就因为你是妖怪，所以就可以吃人吗！"我快气哭了。

"不可以吃小孩。呲呲呲……"

"对！那个妈妈很可怜！从此以后她就见不到那个小孩了！"

"我懂了，呲呲呲。"

那个年轻妈妈在店里走来走去，问来问去，我看了真的很不忍心。

但我无法真的用神级的暴力制裁这个妖怪，只能动之以理。

与其说，我要教这个妖怪怎么当阿祥，不如说，我得先教他如何当一个人。

我要教一个妖怪慢慢用最合情理的方式渗透进人类社会，否则他不但不会是一个活得像人的假人，而是一个披着人皮不断造孽的妖怪。

"听好了，人类跟动物最大的区别，就是人类有道德感！"

"道德感？呲呲呲……"阿祥陷入沉思。

"要当人，要懂得体贴别人的心情！"

"我懂了呲呲呲。"

"要当人，就要知道有些事可以做，有些事却万万不能做！"

"我懂了呲呲呲。"

"你要成为一个人，就不能用蛇的脑袋去想人的事！"

"我懂了呲呲呲。"

阿祥站了起来，在我还没会意过来前转身走下楼。

我不懂，阿祥到底知道了什么才果断下楼，但不久后阿祥回来，我马上知道阿祥它完全不懂。因为阿祥它的肚子比刚刚大了两倍，走路都一拐一拐的。

"……"我的心跳加速。

"呲呲呲。"阿祥打了个嗝，"咯～～"

"你做了什么？"

"我下去把那个女人吃了，这样，他们就可以在我肚子里相遇了。"

"嗯，呲呲呲？"

"是的，呲呲呲。"

我感到很晕眩。

我想，我跟阿祥 2.0 之间的沟通，还有很多的路要

走……

第五章_
外星人的烂实验

1

持续为您报道，我是助手王大明。

这几天我一直在网路上帮忙搜集毒药的知识，因为大烂人九把刀要写一篇关于杀人的没营养奇幻小说，要我帮忙整理一些稀奇古怪的杀人法。

"为什么要杀人这么麻烦？呲呲呲，让我吃掉不就好了。"

说话的，当然是阿祥2.0。

这几个礼拜，除了安顿好阿祥外，我还帮他找到两份辛苦但简单的工作。

第一份工作是在公园旁的路口帮房地产业者举大字报，就是上面写着"三峡的价格，信义区的享受"、"尊荣体验、富贵一生"、"台商返乡极致首选"之类字眼的大字报。

第二份工作是在精华地段的骑楼里发印有候选人照片的面纸包，面纸包上面除了印有恳请支持的字样外，当然还有一张被 Photoshop 修到连他妈都不认得的候选人照片。

这两个工作，是我觉得只要有基本的勤劳就可以干得起来的内容，不仅让阿祥有事做，也可以帮助阿祥适应人类的社会。

"呲呲呲，为什么我需要工作？"

晚上阿祥拿着我帮他拿到的工资，一脸不解。

"因为工作可以赚钱。"我喝着思乐冰。

言简意赅是我的强项。

"为什么我需要赚钱呲呲呲？"阿祥看着我喝思乐冰。

废话连篇则是阿祥的特色。

"因为有了钱，就可以买很多人类需要的东西，你可以买衣服穿，买东西吃，你可以找地方睡，有很多钱的话你就可以买车子，有更多钱的话还可以买房子，有超多钱的话还可以潜规则女明星……有爆多钱的话，哇靠你一定要分给我！"

"我可以吃很多不用钱买的东西……"阿祥很困惑。

不等阿祥呲呲呲，我赶紧打断："等一下，你不能吃人。"

"不是，最近我吃了几只在路边走来走去的狗，呲呲呲，还有猫，还有几只鸽子。对了呲呲呲，本来我还想吃一只老鼠，但它跑太快一下子就不见了。"

"……"

虽然乱吃路边的流浪动物很不可取又没爱心，但阿祥暂时没再吃人我已经很感动，现在就不先跟他计较。然而一时之间我也找不到话可以说服阿祥，毕竟当他还是一条大蛇的时候，本来就在深山里狂吃很多不值钱，喔不，是不要钱的东西。

"我不会冷，不需要穿衣服，我也不用开车，我也可以睡在路边，呲呲呲，我不知道钱可以拿来做什么。"阿祥想了想，又说，"晚上我常常看有些人睡在路边，他们可以，我也可以，不是吗？呲呲呲。"

"那些睡在路边的人是马英九的问题，不是你的。"我皱眉，努力解释，"基本上你当然可以睡在路边，但是呢，如果你想当一个真正的人类，是不是应该学着跟大部分的人类一样，过大部分人类都在过的生活？"

"那我可以吃了睡在路边的人吗？呲呲呲，他们看起来很好吃。"

"不行不行不行，要我说多少次啊，我们人类跟动物最大的区别，就是我们……我们不会吃掉自己的同类。"

178

我猛抓着脑袋，忽然想到一件很重要的事，"我不是叫你每天看报纸认识一下人类的社会吗？"

"我看不懂人类的字，我只会听。"阿祥面无表情，"呲呲呲。"

"对喔……我怎么没想到这一点？看样子我得帮你报名小学的注音符号班，从基础开始学起。总之，虽然我们不会吃掉自己的同类，但我们人类有时候会为了钱，违反原则去杀了另一个人，可见钱非常重要，既然钱对人类非常重要，你要当人，就得好好去赚钱，从赚钱的过程中慢慢体会钱为什么对人类很重要。"

"好吧，呲呲呲，希望我可以学到钱的重要。"

把握机会教育，我继续说："我跟你说，人呢，是一种不只是想要活下去的动物，人也很多奇怪的欲望需要满足，钱呢，就是满足那些欲望最重要的东西。"

"欲望？呲呲呲，我以前是一条蛇的时候，最大的欲望就是想当一个人呲呲呲，但人最大的欲望又是什么？"

"说得好，通常呢，一般人的最大欲望就是想要有很多钱。"

"有钱可以买到什么比成为一个人更好的东西呢呲呲呲？"

"干，钱可以拿去买蛋，你喜欢蛋吧？"

"呲呲呲。"阿祥露出罕见的高兴表情。

"那就对了，你拿你自己赚到的钱，去买蛋，这样是不是很有意义？"

"呲呲呲，很有意义。"

诸如此类，令我不耐的对话不停上演，因为我得不断解释很多我根本觉得不需要解释的东西，让这条蛇好好了解身为一个人类，终其一生都必须做很多徒劳无功的瞎事，至于这些瞎事的背后究竟有什么意义……这种大哲学家都未必有正确答案的东西，我也没有义务知道，于是我就胡乱搪塞过去，反正只要阿祥不吃人，慢慢他就会体会到，身为一个人有很多很多很多的无奈。

虽然阿祥是一个危险人物，但我无法时时刻刻陪在阿祥身边教导他。我叫阿祥晚上去看电视肥皂剧练习人类使用语言的方式，以及人类是怎么过日子的。

比起跟我相处，我相信每天看 8 个小时以上的电视会更有用。

我错了。

"我最近在看一个电视剧，呲呲呲，我有很多地方不懂。"

"什么地方不懂？"

阿祥坐在天桥阶梯上，手里拿着一盒有机生鸡蛋，吃得津津有味。

我拿着一杯热咖啡。

"有一个男的人类明明喜欢一个女的人类，却跟另一个女的人类生下另一个人类小孩，而那一个人类小孩长大后喜欢上另一个女的人类，呲呲呲但那一个女的人类是他妈妈跟另一个男的人类生下的女的人类，他们发现之后自认无法进行更近一步的交配，因此非常痛苦甚至想要结束自己的生命，为什么？"

这种落落长的句子我当然听得一头雾水，但经验告诉我，这是个老梗。

"因为他们是兄妹。"我肯定是猜对了。

"呲呲呲为什么兄妹不能交配？在山里根本没有这种问题。"

"人跟动物最大的不一样，就是人不会近亲繁殖，也就是说人类不会跟自己的父母兄弟姊妹儿女交配，除了因为近亲繁殖很奇怪很不卫生之外，最重要的是近亲繁殖会让下一代的基因变得很烂。"我说着一般初中生也明白的生物课内容。

"基因？"

这是我第二次跟阿祥提到基因了。

于是我又花了 5 分钟用粗制滥造的方式解释基因是什么东西。

"既然不能交配，就找别人交配就好了，呲呲呲为什么要那么痛苦？"

"很好的问题，其实真相当然就是去找别人交配就可以解决问题了，有时候我们还会找很多不同的人交配，真实世界里大家也很少有这种烦恼，但电视上演的剧情本来就很夸张，通常不是人类真正的生活方式，简单说，就是电视乱演。"

"为什么电视上演的东西，呲呲呲不是人类真正的生活方式？"

"因为人类喜欢假的东西。"

"为什么人类喜欢假的东西呲呲呲？"

"真实世界令人难受啊阿祥，你知道人类跟其他动物最大的区别是什么吗？"

"人类不吃自己的同伴呲呲呲。"

"错。"

"人类不会近亲繁殖……呲呲呲人类有道德观……"

"错了，人类跟其他动物最大的区别，就是我们人很会自我欺骗，我们会强迫自己相信一些根本不可能的事，好让我们觉得好过一点。包括人不吃人，这点其实也是假的，是我们自己骗自己用的，因为我们觉得人如果可以吃人的话，这个世界就太恐怖了，但其实人偶尔还是会吃自己人的。"

"所以我可以吃人了吗呲呲呲？"

"不行，我刚刚只是举一个极端的例子。"

为了不使阿祥走上邪路，我非常努力地解释："比如我们人类其实大部分的人都没什么爱心，但我们很喜欢拍一些有爱心内容的电影跟电视剧，比如大部分的人都很孬种，但我们拍了很多关于勇气的电影跟电视剧，又比如我说过人类跟动物最大的差别就是人有道德观，但其实大部分的人都没什么道德观，我们之所以说自己有道德观是怕被别人发现我们其实没有道德观，所以我们拍电影或电视剧的时候常常都拍一些很有道德观的作品，这就是一种集体的自我欺骗。"

阿祥的表情有点痛苦，有点烦恼，又有点不大理解。

"人很矛盾……呲呲呲？"

"这点倒是说对了，人类真的是一种很矛盾的动物。"

我点点头，心里却猛摇头，我真是太天真了，居然会叫阿祥多看那些俗烂的八点档！很多对人类的观点都会被奇怪的剧情给误导，我得小心应付这类问题。

这时我的手机响了，来电显示是"假装被外星人实验的老伯"。

哇靠，几个礼拜之前"在钓虾场浪费掉的那一个晚上"迅速在我脑袋里重播，我冷笑了一下，接了起来，真希望那个年轻有为的老伯看到我现在的表情。

"请问是九先生的助理王先生吗？"话筒里的声音有点怪怪的。

"是的，我就是王大明本人，请问要干三小叮当？"我没好气。

"王先生啊，人无信用是畜生，还记得你答应过我要去让外星人做实验吧？今天晚上9点来钓虾场集合啊！记得！记得啊！要依照约定把实验费通通交给我，这是——"

"这是天经地义，我完全了解。"我忍不住吐槽，"但你故意怪腔怪调是怎样？"

"是这样的，前几天我去做实验，外星人在我的喉咙抹上一种奇怪的药膏，之后就开始在我们间做交换喉结的手术，手术非常复杂，历经了整整三天时间，幸好除了那个日本人以外大家都顺利完成了，所以我现在的喉结是新的，暂时有点不适应也是天经地义。"

虽然百分之百是唬烂，但我还是忍不住多问一句："那个日本人手术不顺利，是怎样？"

"没有喉结。"

"嗯……没有喉结。"

"幸好她原本就是个女人，所以没有喉结，但新的喉结没有成功移植到她的喉咙里，还是算手术失败，那些外星人都很遗憾，唉。"还重重叹了一大口气。

我真的很后悔问了那个智障问题，好像我也变得很智障。

此时我看了一眼身边表情呆滞的阿祥，灵光一现："对了，我有一个朋友也想去开开眼界，不晓得报名还来得及来不及？"

"啊？你的朋友智商很高的吗？"

是喔，我都忘了那个"实验"的对象，其先决条件是智商高。

"放心吧，大不了外星人给的智力测验过不了，他就自己回家。"

"那关于你那一位朋友的推荐费跟实验费……那个实验费他可以自己拿，但推荐费应该算在我这边是吧？毕竟你只是顺便问了我一下，但真正向外星人推荐的还是我，是吧是吧？"

"总之晚上 9 点钓虾场见。"

"钓虾场见！"

挂掉电话。

我看着在一旁默默吃蛋的阿祥，我也不知道为什么想邀他跟我去钓虾场，或许是怕他无聊，也或许是我直觉让阿祥认识一下人类世界里的愚蠢跟诈骗，也是一个很好的机会教育。

"阿祥，晚上别看电视了，我带你去看一堆笨蛋。"

阿祥眼睛一亮："我可以吃掉那些笨蛋吗？呲呲呲？"

"不行，笨蛋是一种不能吃的蛋。"

"笨蛋不能吃，知道了呲呲呲。"

2

灯光昏暗，空气混浊。

对阿祥来说，钓虾场也是一个非常新鲜的体验，所以早在晚上 8 点我们就提前到了钓虾场，堂堂正正地钓虾等外星人。

还不到约定的 9 点，我已钓到了 5 只虾，而阿祥则钓了整整一桶虾。

啧啧，没想到阿祥是一个钓虾界的绝世高手。

"呲呲呲，为什么人类要用这么……"

阿祥眼睛盯着水面，话说一半，就陷入绞尽脑汁的语塞。

"没有效率。"我猜测。

"是的，呲呲呲，为什么人类要用这么没有效率的方式，吃虾子？"

阿祥这么说的时候，正好叼着烟的钓虾场老板拿着两桶活蹦乱跳的虾子，熟练地往池子里泼洒，正在钓虾的客人纷纷叫好。

对阿祥来说，钓虾已经够白痴了，先将想要钓起来的虾子往池子里丢，再千辛万苦把虾子钓起来煮了吃，实在是蠢到了极点。

"人类跟其他最大的不一样，就是人类经常做各式各样徒劳无功的事。"

"为什么？"

"好问题，我想是因为……人类是一种闲不下来的动物，如果太快完成一件事，就会节省太多的时间，如果有太多时间却不知道要做什么，人就会很无聊。"我只是随便说说，"阿祥，你知道人类是一种非常长寿的动物吗？活太久却不知道要干什么，是一件很恐怖的事，所以人类会努力把非常简单的东西给复杂化，好掩饰自己其实是在浪费时间的真相。"

"呲呲呲，我开始理解了。"阿祥似懂非懂，顿了顿，说，"我在电视看到很多人很努力将一口就可以吃掉的食物，用非常复杂的方式烹煮它，这也是想要顺利浪费时间，对吧呲呲呲？"

"可以这么说。"我鼓励阿祥，"你想要当一个真正的人类，除了要努力工作赚钱之外，也要好好学习如何浪费时间，这样才可以将工作赚到的钱连同时间一起浪费掉，知道吗？"

"我会努力的，呲呲呲。"阿祥显得有点高兴。

9 点到了，老伯出现了。

我站了起来，被我交代不要随便乱讲话的阿祥也站了起来。

老伯的身边亦步亦趋跟着一个外星人，外星人一看到我就赶紧递上名片："你好，你一定就是大名鼎鼎的九把刀先生的助理，王大明先生了吧？"

名片上写着：西喇玛星系 8-G107 区，第三行星，刺刺武国国家研究院研究员，撒拉八客——百分之百，这绝对是我拿过最潮的一张废物名片。

"不好意思因为我没有通过外星人的智力测验，这次只能推荐，不能跟你们一起实验，希望你们等一下可以顺利通过考试，这样我才可以快点拿到两位的推荐费跟你的实验费，银货两讫，天经地义。"老伯的怪腔怪调明显就是装的，还装得非常不像。

"嗯嗯嗯嗯这个都没问题，你可以滚了。我唯一想问的是……"我看着那位彬彬有礼的外星人，说，"请问这位……"

"撒拉八客。"外星人微微鞠躬。

"是的，请问这位撒拉八客先生，身为一个外星人，你不觉得你长得跟我们地球人未免也太没有什么不同了吗？"

我会这样说，是因为这位外星人根本就是百分之一百的地球人，完全不需要我多花一个赘字形容来自另一个星球的访客模样，不折不扣，他就是一个会用中文的洋鬼子。

"关于这个问题，我们可以上车慢慢说。"

"上车？不是上飞碟吗？"

"不是的，这件事说来话长，但我们刺刺武国来到地球的方式并不是搭乘交通工具，而是曲速传送空间，这个科技有点难以用地球的语言说明，简单说就是用高浓度珈玛雷射束以每秒三亿的频率稳定交错，借此在宇宙空间击破次元孔制造反引力磁场，再用反物质次列光引导时间在空间轴上重新排序，排序完成后，接下来的银河座标就采用第三十六星等计算法就可以标记完成了。"

"讲解得真是浅显易懂。"我谦虚地微微鞠躬，"欢迎来到地球。"

3

我跟阿祥跟着那位外星人来到钓虾场外，撒拉八客左手一挥，没有从天际冲出一道反物质曲速传送光束，而是从巷口冲来了一台计程车。

"在地球，我们得好好学习人类的生活方式。"撒拉八客微笑为我们开门。

"呲呲呲……"阿祥有点高兴地表示同意，"我也正在学习。"

那位年轻有为却被移植喉咙的老伯向我们挥手道别。

在计程车上，那位远道而来的撒拉八客先生解释道，他们之所以能够穿越宇宙来到地球，科技当然是比地球还要高个七八层楼，但为什么选中这么落后的地球进行研究，跟他们长得非常像地球人很有关系。

也就是说，西喇玛星系 8-G107 区，第三行星上的居民，其模样跟地球人极度类似，虽然高矮胖瘦一样存在着个体间的差别，但大家都是两只眼睛一个鼻子一只嘴巴，还都长在大致一样的地方，开膛剖肚后，脏器的位置与功能好像也没有太大的差异。

"这就非常奇怪了。"撒拉八客严肃地说。

"为什么奇怪？"我心不在焉地附和。

"因为我们星球的环境跟地球并不相似，却发展出极度类似的主生命体，你不觉得，这一切都非常地不可思议吗？明明第四行星的星体环境跟我们第三行星相距不远，两个星球的主生命体却有不小的差距，你不觉得，这也很奇怪吗？相反的，我们两个星球距离如此遥远，即使用光速旅行也要30万年的时间，彼此却孕育出高度相似的主生命体物种，这种遥远的羁绊，真正是宇宙的浪漫啊！"撒拉八客微笑。

"喔，那很好啊。"我竖起大拇指比赞。

真是辛苦了，不知道是哪家精神病院跑出来的妄想症。

"但我们没有黑人。"撒拉八客皱起眉头。

"陈建州吗？"我大方地说，"那我们送你啊！"

"不是，是黑皮肤种族的人。"撒拉八客苦恼地说，"我们一直觉得很奇怪，我们的星球上也有白人黄人红人之别，却偏偏没有黑人，这是为什么？我们不知道，为什么你们有黑人我们却没有，到底是演化上出了什么分歧点，还是黑人的生理构造与地球环境有什么特殊的联系，这点也是我们的实验重点之一。"

"呲呲呲，为什么呢？"阿祥歪头。

"喔，那很好啊。"我打了一个呵欠："……随便啦！"

不只是想弄清楚为什么地球有黑人，西喇玛星系 8-G107 区第三行星却没有黑人，这群外星人也想知道地球人的身体构造是否完全跟他们的星人一模一样，还是存在微小的差异，或许那些为小的差异便是西喇玛星系 8-G107 区第三行星上没有盛产黑人的个中原因。

所以他们做了很多奇奇怪怪的实验，都在于想更加了解地球人的身体，实验的项目五花八门，撒拉八客快速说了一些，就跟钓虾老伯说的差不多，全都是一些毫无学术价值的烂手术。

为了加速研究的进行，他们总共派遣了十几组研究团队在全世界各地进行研究，在台湾，这群外星人已经深耕了五年时间，实验项目也越做越细，各组之间互相较劲、比赛谁先找出为什么地球盛产黑人的原因。

虽然我一句话也没相信，但基于礼貌我还是勉为其难地比了个赞。

"研究人类好玩吗？呲呲呲？"阿祥的眼睛倒是闪闪发亮。

"这是一个非常神圣的领域啊。"撒拉八客庄严地结束话题。

我们抵达一点也不神秘的巷弄深处时，计程车跳了245块。

依照刚刚弯进巷子前我看到的最后一个街牌，这里是永和四号公园一带，一条挤满机车的窄小巷子底，我想这里的居民压根都没想过西喇玛星系 8-G107 区第三行星星人暂时就住在附近搞人体实验吧。

下车前计程车司机向我偷偷使了个眼色。

"嗯？"我不懂。

"要不要帮你报警？"计程车司机压低声音，瞥了一下车外的撒拉八客。

了解，真是好心的司机大哥啊。

"不用了，应付神经病在我工作的范围内。"我心头暖暖地关上车门。

这个社会真是温暖。

不过不是我在臭屁，神经病我超会应付的，在上一本《上课不要看小说》里面我已经示范过种种危机应变的技巧，还能从与神经病的相处中取得重要的写作资料，眼前这一个领我上楼、自称外星人的中年男子，怎么说也不可能比那一个超会踩脚的文慧还要凶狠吧？

4

所谓的实验室位于公寓五楼的顶楼加盖。

楼梯间的气氛很怪，由于这里是一层两户，而外星人租下的这一户人家对面的另一户人家的门口，那户人家从门口到楼梯间排了好几个背着可称是全副武装登山设备的男人，而门缝里不断传来女子淫荡的叫春声，叫得欲仙欲死好不快活。

我多看了一眼，只换来那几个登山客的白眼。

"看三小？"一个登山客瞪着我。

我注意到他的眼睛只剩下一只，很恐怖。

"没有啊。"我的耳根子一定红了。

"还看！"另一个登山客发怒指着我。

我发现他的手指少了两只，好少只。

"……"凶屁啊？

我只敢在心里回这一句。

"到了，请进。"撒拉八客将所谓的实验室门一开。

哇靠，里头完全没有实验室的感觉，房屋里的摆设就是一间装潢没有格调也毫无风格可言的死样子，完全没有必要花字数描述空间感。

倒是已经有好几个人挤在沙发区，或站或坐或蹲，正都聚精会神填写一份试卷，我想那一定是传说中的智商测验题了。

像撒拉八客那样身穿全套黑色西装、一脸"干我就是外星人啦"的假外星人，大概还有五位，他们带着略显僵硬的笑容，在那些正在做测验的人旁走来走去，监考吧我猜。

"那么，先请你们填写这一份问卷，通过了我们再开始实验。"

撒拉八客发给我们考卷，一人一张，说："半个小时内请作答完毕。"

我最讨厌写考卷了，但这份考卷的第一题就吓到我，害我忍不住认真起来。

*****

西喇玛星系 8-G107 区第三行星，高阶智力测验试卷，地球版。

请各位同学发挥你的高智商，在半小时内作答完毕。

姓名：＿＿＿＿＿＿＿＿＿＿＿＿

1. 道德行动题

如果你在公共厕所里大便，却发现墙上的公共卫生
纸用完了，请问该怎么做，才是最聪明的决定？

打电话向朋友求助？

牺牲袜子或内裤取代卫生纸？

跟隔壁的便友商借卫生纸？

直接用湿湿的屁眼在墙壁上写字？

间接用湿湿的手指在墙壁上挥毫？

不管了直接穿上裤子走人？

冒险走到洗手台用手取水清拭屁眼？

其他？

试论证原因。

2. 科学应变题

如果你独自一人在太空旅行中遇到曲速引擎遭破碎
星体击毁，动力失去四分之三，可预见不久后机体有焚
烧的危机，你应该怎么做，才有最大的生存机会？

加速航行到最近的星体，发送信号等待救援？

设定自动驾驶，然后试图自行维修？

为避免机体爆炸马上停驶，在宇宙空间自然漂流，思考下一步？

利用最后的能源发射等负离子光束，搜寻周遭最近的飞行器，设定自动拖曳？

趁动力尚足时，一口气暴冲进入曲速跳跃，试图回到母星基地附近？

以尚未验证的光能萨满假说为基础，随机进入宇宙空间的平行虫洞？

其他？

试论证原因。

3. 冒险犯难题

一个人在荒野中行走，在前方遇到四条岔路，分别为 A、B、C、D。

A 路有一只刚吃饱的孟加拉虎，B 路有四只快饿死了的藏獒，C 路有一只狮子跟一只熊正忙着打架，D 路为食人族经常出没的猎人头路线。

请问你应该选择哪条路，才是最合理的决定？

试论证原因。

4. 分析能力题

请问孔子、秦始皇、五月天阿信、达文西、叶问、汤姆克鲁斯、织田信长、牛顿、林肯、林书豪、尾田荣一郎、麦可乔丹、周星驰，这几个人有哪一个共同点？

试论证原因。

*****

*****

西喇玛星系 8-G107 区第三行星，高阶智力测验试卷，地球版。

请各位同学发挥你的高智商，在半小时内作答完毕。

姓名：王大明

1. 道德行动题

如果你在公共厕所里大便，却发现墙上的公共卫生纸用完了，请问该怎么做，才是最聪明的决定？

打电话向朋友求助？

牺牲袜子或内裤取代卫生纸？

跟隔壁的便友商借卫生纸？

直接用湿湿的屁眼在墙壁上写字？

间接用湿湿的手指在墙壁上挥毫？

不管了直接穿上裤子走人？

冒险走到洗手台用手取水清拭屁眼？

其他？

试论证原因。

答：用自己的卫生纸

答：因为我有带

2. 科学应变题

如果你独自一人在太空旅行中遇到曲速引擎遭破碎
星体击毁，动力失去四分之三，可预见不久后机体有焚
烧的危机，你应该怎么做，才有最大的生存机会？

加速航行到最近的星体，发送信号等待救援？

设定自动驾驶，然后试图自行维修？

为避免机体爆炸马上停驶，在宇宙空间自然漂流，
思考下一步？

利用最后的能源发射等负离子光束，搜寻周遭最近
的飞行器，设定自动拖曳？

趁动力尚足时，一口气暴冲进入曲速跳跃，试图回
到母星基地附近？

以尚未验证的光能萨满假说为基础，随机进入宇宙

空间的平行虫洞？

其他？

试论证原因。

答：马上去买一台新的飞碟

答：因为新的比较好

3. 冒险犯难题

你独自一个人在荒野中行走，在前方遇到四条岔路，分别为 A、B、C、D。

A 路有一只刚吃饱的孟加拉虎，B 路有四只快饿死了的藏獒，C 路有一只狮子跟一只熊正忙着打架，D 路为食人族经常出没的猎人头路线。

请问你应该选择哪条路，才是最合理的决定？

试论证原因。

答：往回走

答：啊不然咧？

4. 分析能力题

请问孔子、秦始皇、五月天阿信、达文西、叶问、汤姆克鲁斯、织田信长、牛顿、林肯、林书豪、尾田荣一郎、麦可乔丹、周星驰，这几个人有哪一个共同点？

试论证原因。

答：都是韩国人
答：全世界都是韩国人发明的

*****

别说半小时了，我一分钟就交卷。

我天资聪颖写超快不意外，意外的是阿祥也跟我同一时间交卷，而其他人都还在振笔疾书，将考卷的空白处写得密密麻麻，有的还将考卷翻过去写，上面还有非常复杂的图案辅助。

我忍不住看了一下阿祥的答案。

*****

西喇玛星系8-G107区第三行星，高阶智力测验试卷，地球版。

请各位同学发挥你的高智商，在半小时内作答完毕。

上课不要
烤香肠

姓名：黄豪祥

1.道德行动题

如果你在公共厕所里大便，却发现墙上的公共卫生纸用完了，请问该怎么做，才是最聪明的决定？

打电话向朋友求助？

牺牲袜子或内裤取代卫生纸？

跟隔壁的便友商借卫生纸？

直接用湿湿的屁眼在墙壁上写字？

间接用湿湿的手指在墙壁上挥毫？

不管了直接穿上裤子走人？

冒险走到洗手台用手取水清拭屁眼？

其他？

试论证原因。

答：吃掉大便
答：因为大便可以吃

2.科学应变题

如果你独自一人在太空旅行中遇到曲速引擎遭破碎星体击毁，动力失去四分之三，可预见不久后机体有焚

204

烧的危机，你应该怎么做，才有最大的生存机会？

加速航行到最近的星体，发送信号等待救援？

设定自动驾驶，然后试图自行维修？

为避免机体爆炸马上停驶，在宇宙空间自然漂流，思考下一步？

利用最后的能源发射等负离子光束，搜寻周遭最近的飞行器，设定自动拖曳？

趁动力尚足时，一口气暴冲进入曲速跳跃，试图回到母星基地附近？

以尚未验证的光能萨满假说为基础，随机进入宇宙空间的平行虫洞？

其他？

试论证原因。

答：变成一颗蛋

答：因为我可以变成一颗蛋

3. 冒险犯难题

一个人在荒野中行走，在前方遇到四条岔路，分别为 A、B、C、D。

A 路有一只刚吃饱的孟加拉虎，B 路有四只快饿死

了的藏獒，C 路有一只狮子跟一只熊正忙着打架，D 路
为食人族经常出没的猎人头路线。

请问你应该选择哪条路，才是最合理的决定？

试论证原因。

答：B→A→C→D
答：最好吃的留到最后吃

4. 分析能力题

请问孔子、秦始皇、五月天阿信、达文西、叶问、
汤姆克鲁斯、织田信长、牛顿、林肯、林书豪、尾田荣
一郎、麦可乔丹、周星驰，这几个人有哪一个共同点？

试论证原因。

答：都可以吃。
答：都可以吃吧？

*****

"阿祥，没想到你答得蛮不错的嘛！"我拍拍阿祥

的肩膀。

　　"普普通通啦，吡吡吡。"阿祥有点难为情。

　　虽然这份考卷很智障，但我们的答案也不遑多让，我觉得我们马上可以滚了。

5

过不久，所有人都交卷了。

在等待考卷批改结果出炉时，我们这群彼此都不认识的人之间的气氛有点尴尬，你不看我，我不看你，避免交流彼此的视线，说真的，大家被哄被骗来参加假外星人的智力测验，本身就非常侮辱自己的智商！

不久后，撒拉八客公布测验合格的人选。

"本次智力测验难度极高，各位龙争虎斗，战况激烈，比赛过程精彩绝伦，但胜负在所难免，难免有遗珠之憾。现在公布智商测验合格的人选，听到的人请举手——陈志荣。"

"啊？又！"一个还穿着黑猫宅急便制服的大叔惊慌失措地举手。

"陈王佳惠。"撒拉八客宣布。

"是！"一个肥胖大婶闪电举手，脚边还放着一个菜篮。

"黄绮君。"撒拉八客宣布。

"……"一个戴着红色胶框眼镜的女大学生，脸色不悦地举手。

"江启斌。"撒拉八客宣布。

"干！"一个土流氓模样的男人瞪大眼睛，"真的假的？"

"王大明。"撒拉八客宣布。

"！"我的反射神经一时会意不过来。

"王大明？"撒拉八客看向我。

"干！"我大惊举手。

那戴着红色胶框眼镜的女大学生瞪了我一眼。

"最后一位，黄家祥。"撒拉八客宣布。

"是。"阿祥缓缓举手，吐舌，"呲呲呲。"

撒拉八客满意地点点头，轻轻鼓掌："恭喜以上的六位高智商杰出人类，即将协助我们展开意义重大的新实验，现在，就让我们为入选的人开心，为落选的人惋惜，让我们，珍、重、再、见。"

在零零落落的掌声中，我着实惊魂未定，光是我跟阿祥那种瞧不起人的烂答案也可以合格，就足以证明这是一份无效的智力测验啊！

送走了那些智力测验不合格但一脸也不遗憾的人

后，那几个假外星人走进厨房说要准备实验器材，留下我们这六个入选者坐在客厅里干瞪眼。

倒是阿祥先开了口。

"所以我是一个高智商的人类了吗？呲呲呲！"阿祥有点高兴地看着我。

"肯定不是。"我斩钉截铁地否定。

"希望实验不要搞太久啊，我等一下还要回家陪老公睡觉。"买菜大婶担心。

"我入选还可以解释，但为什么是你们跟我一起入选？"女大学生语气不满地说，一副高高在上，"你们到底在考卷上回答了什么？"

"我也没写什么太了不起的东西，我只是尽力而为而已。"宅急便大叔抓抓头，一脸不好意思，"Just do it, mission impossible."

"我干你娘。"土流氓冷冷地看着女大学生。

"你凭什么骂我？"女大学生气急败坏地瞪着土流氓。

"我说，我在考卷上写干你娘。"土流氓得意洋洋地补充，"我就一直写干你娘写到连考卷翻过去都还在干你娘！"

女大学生气到涨红了脸，显然不信。

但我当然是信的，百分之百的信，因为我的答案没有比满纸干你娘高明到哪里去，而我也坐在这里成为一个出类拔萃的高智商人士。

"现在怎办？等一下真的会有实验吗？"我转移话题。

"呲呲呲。"阿祥凑热闹。

"管他什么实验，有钱拿就对了。"土流氓从鼻子吹气，"敢不给钱的话，等一下我就抄一堆兄弟过来，把他们通通干一干，干完了再抓去填海！干！"

"对对对对，就是赚外快嘛。"买菜大婶又看了一次手表，神色焦躁。

真是个超矛盾的大婶，现在都已经几点了，买菜哪有人买到这么晚的？如果这么晚还没回家老公都没发现，那就真的不需要回家了好吗大婶。

"不管等一下是做什么实验，大家互相帮助，有个照应总是好的。"宅急便大叔抓抓后脑袋，腼腆地说，"Like a bridge over trouble water，哈哈，哈哈……"

"我干你娘讲三小英文！"土流氓超不屑。

"呲呲呲？"阿祥有点不懂现在的气氛。

"你可不可以嘴巴放干净点，不要说什么都一直带脏话？"自视甚高的女大学生语气尖锐，针对土流氓，"对人有一点基本尊重，OK？"

"关你屁事！"土流氓翻白眼，展开经典的别三抖脚。

"你说什么！"女大学生气得头发都快竖起来了。

"我说关你屁事！"土流氓的脚越抖越快："干！"

我虽然讲话低级兼没水平，但土流氓的这种说话方式还是让我觉得很超低级超没水平。此时撒拉八客与其他五个黑衣人笑容可掬地从厨房走了出来，他们手上闪闪发亮的银色钢瓶令这一连串超没水准的争吵戛然而止。

"那我们就开始实验吧。"撒拉八客说。

语毕，他们同时戴了封闭式面罩。

在我们都还没意会到戴那些面具代表什么意思的时候，银色钢瓶里喷出的高压气体已笼罩我们。

接下来诚如你想，那一瞬间我们就昏死过去。

6

醒来时，第一个感觉是冷。

"好冷。"我打了个哆嗦。

"没穿衣服当然冷啊干你娘！"土流氓啐了一口痰。

没错，我们全身都被剥光光，全身赤裸地大字型摊在彼此面前，不仅如此，我们的双手被紧紧铐住，双脚也被强制撑开，在宛若十字架的奇特刑具上一点也无法反抗。

面对这个逆境，我首先注意到刚刚那一个瞧不起众生的高贵女大学生，她美妙的裸体也毫无保留地暴露在我们面前，我的嘴角情不自禁地扬起。

"看什么看！"女大学生咬牙切齿，"非礼勿视没听过是不是！"

"我干你娘！"土流氓还是维持他的经典台词。

"啊怎么会被脱光光呢？现在到底是 What's wrong with everybody 啊？"宅急便大叔不断扭动想缩起光溜

溜的身子，但当然是徒劳无功。

"这到底是什么实验啊？很快就结束了吗？"买菜大婶羞红了脸，但没人想看。

"呲呲呲。"阿祥也是一脸刚刚醒来的朦胧。

"等等！……阿祥，你的老二呢！"我大吃一惊。

哇靠！阿祥的老二不见了！

才睡一觉，老二就从阿祥的两腿之间凭空消失了！

难道这个变态的外星人实验内容，就是切除高智商的人的性器官吗？

"不是，呲呲呲，我没有老二。"阿祥自己倒是很冷静。

"什么叫没有老二？"我吓坏了。

"我是母的，呲呲呲。"

"什么叫你是母的？"

"我是一只母蛇，呲呲呲。"阿祥认真地解释，一点也不避讳在场还有别人，"我试过把老二变出来，但我猜它是人类雄性至阳之物，我的道行还不够，呲呲呲，就是变不出来，呲呲呲……"

哇，我从来没想过那条巨蛇的性别，对我来说，或者对很多人类来说，蛇就是蛇，哪会去想蛇是公的还是母的？打从这个大蛇妖用阿祥的身体重新出现在我面前的那一刻，我就把它当成一个男的，一个拥有老二的，百分之百的雄性！

现在！它原来是条母蛇！

"听不懂什么蛇不蛇？反正你的朋友没老二就是阴阳人啦干！"土流氓超不屑我们之间的对话。

"现在是讨论你朋友为什么没有……没有老二的时候吗！现在是怎样！脑子都不清楚吗？"女大学生气到奶头都尖了起来，"还看！头转过去！"

"啊，sorry！sorry！"宅急便大叔赶紧道歉。

"还有你！还看！"女大学生对我咆哮。

"啊看一下是会死喔？"我忍不住回嘴。

"是不是我成为一个完全的人类的时候，我就会有老二了呲呲呲？"阿祥根本不管现在是什么状况，依旧非常执著。

"阿祥，人类跟其他动物最大的不一样就是，我们人类会看状况决定什么是当下最重要的事，而现在最重要的事，绝对不是你要怎么样才可以长出一条活蹦乱跳的老二，而是，我们到底要怎么脱困！"

"喔，你们误会了。"

主导这场诡异实验的撒拉八客当然又出现了。

他与他身后的五个黑衣人，手上全都戴上超薄型手术手套，他们脸上超专业的制式化笑容让人不寒而栗，我们全都闭嘴。

"你们误会了，各位并不是受困，你们是主动参与我们的人体实验，这一点在你们来之前就已经充分被告知了，不过各位别担心，实验很快就结束，在你们离开这里之前，也将获得一笔让人满意的报酬。"

"……我干你娘。"土流氓第一个回话。

撒拉八客向土流氓点头示意，接着道："就如同各位所知道的，今天的实验完全针对高智商的地球人所设计，实验的主题是，高智商人类的肛门在经过异体交换后，是否会影响智商的变化。"

六个黑衣人一字排开，手里拿着似乎一点也不高科技的焊枪。

焊枪喷嘴射出青色火焰，烤着另一只手上所拿的一点也不高科技的手术刀。

"什么！你想用手术将我们的 Ass 换来换去？"宅急便大叔大惊。

"我现在就告诉你！不会！"我惨叫，"换肛门不会影响智商！"

"我干你娘！"土流氓这次终于应对得体了。

被干你娘的撒拉八客不为所动，依旧笑容满面："如果各位在今天实验中表现良好，将有机会参加我们一周后的进阶主题：高智商人类与低智商人类的肛门进行交换后，是否会产生智商互换的情况。"

"不会！铁定不会！"我惨叫。

"我也保证！I promise 肛门跟智商一点关系也没有！Nothing's gonna change my love for you！"宅急便大叔也慌了。

"你们到底是什么人！快点放我们出去！"女大学生屈辱地大叫。

"我想回家大便。"买菜大婶也哭了。

"干！你！娘！"土流氓奋力挣扎："谁也别想动老子的屁眼！干！"

"呲呲呲，呲呲呲？"阿祥看起来满脸疑惑，完全不知大难临头。

不理会我们的哭天抢地，撒拉八客有条不紊地维持他的实验说明顺序。

他说，为了让这项实验有丰富的资料前后对照，除了刚刚用测验卷了解了我们的智商外，我们的肛门也得建立完整的资料库，因此……

"因此怎样！"女大学生全身都快爆炸了。

　　"因此我们得先调查各位的肛门。"

　　撒拉八客嘉许地看了女大学生一眼："不过各位不要过度担心，为了避免肛门遭到伤害，我们会将各种营养丰富的蔬菜水果塞进各位的肛门，并记录你们的肛门针对不同特质的蔬菜水果产生的刺激与反应，等到肛门交换手术完成后，我们再以相同营养质量的蔬菜水果塞进各位的新肛门，记录肛门在不同的宿者身上是否仍有相同的感受，或是有全新体验。当然了，那时候也会再做一次智力测验，一切过程都十分科学，敬请期待。"

　　"期待个屁！"我真的快疯了，"超不科学！"

　　"我想回家大便。"买菜大婶一直哭。

　　"我干……"土流氓惨叫，"你……"

　　土流氓并没有正确无误地把你的娘干掉，因为一颗苹果已经以时速一公里的速度滑入了他的屁眼，土流氓的表情瞬间揪结起来，好像圣斗士的小宇宙喷发。

　　"江启斌先生，请问你现在有什么感受？"一个黑衣人非常专业地问，手上拿着纸笔等待。

　　"喔喔喔喔喔喔喔……我干……"

　　"觉得很干？"

　　"喔喔喔喔喔喔喔喔喔喔……"土流氓的表情扭来扭去，就是说不清楚。

"是表达的词汇不足，还是感觉就是喔喔喔？"

"喔喔喔喔喔喔喔喔喔喔喔喔喔……"

"了解。"黑衣人点头速记。

我的天啊，这根本就不是实验，从头到尾我都没有看到任何属于外星人的高科技设备，也没有看到一个长得不像地球人的外星人！我只看到一颗苹果塞进一个没水准的屁眼！

这简直是 SM 嘛！

另一个黑衣人拿着一颗柳丁，慢慢接近张口结舌的宅急便大叔。

"等等！Wait a moment！"宅急便大叔急了，"能不能打个商量不要 put that 柳丁 in my ass？！我们可以文明一点！OK！"

"实验是神圣的。"

"那能不能换小颗一点的橙子？ Change！Change！"

当然是不能 Change，随着那颗柳丁以秒速五公分的动能进入宅急便大叔的 ass，宅急便大叔的人生也在这一刻进入了新的境界。

黑衣人详细记录着大叔中英杂交的感想，我则完全不想听。

　　擅长险中求胜的我忙着注意实验桌上的蔬菜水果里有芹菜、小黄瓜、香蕉、莴苣、火龙果、山药、荔枝、龙眼、甘蔗、香菇、红椒、水梨、高丽菜、一串鱼蛋、红萝卜、仙草还有一颗非常显眼的西瓜跟……凤梨。

　　托 A 片之福，如果是香蕉或小黄瓜之类要插我屁眼倒还可以想象，鱼蛋虽然不是蔬菜水果也无所谓，但绝对！我绝对不能让那颗西瓜跟那团凤梨接近我！

　　我在心中暗暗祈祷。

7

现在我们把镜头交给棚内的买菜大婶。

"我想回家大便。"买菜大婶还是哭。

"实验结束后就可以回家大便了。"

黑衣人温馨地向她保证,一边将那串还在冒烟的鱼蛋塞进她颤抖的屁眼。

"陈王佳惠女士,请问你现在有什么感觉?"黑衣人专注地观察。

"我想大便。"买菜大婶脸色一沉。

只见那串消失的鱼蛋又出现了。

大便也像挤牙膏一样出现了。

原来那串莫名其妙被归在蔬菜水果类的鱼蛋,是被大便排山倒海的力量给推挤出来的,真所谓"精诚所致,金石为开",就是这个道理。

"喔!"黑衣人啧啧称奇,仔细记录下这一切过程。

阿祥就太不幸了。

那一颗让我非常担心的凤梨，已经被阿祥的屁眼给认养了。

"请问黄家祥先生，你的肛门现在有什么感觉？"黑衣人照样访谈。

"痛，呲呲呲。"阿祥眉头紧皱，发表感想，"人类跟其他动物真的有好多地方都不一样，呲呲呲……"

"阿祥！撑住！"我只能给予精神支持。

阿祥真的是一个很奇妙的衰人。

在以前还是宅宅的那一个版本的阿祥，他的命运悲惨到被一头大蛇给吞了，说出去谁也不信。而现在这一个只是拥有阿祥躯壳的 2.0 版本阿祥，还是同样命运乖违，屁眼活吞了一颗没剥皮的大凤梨。

女大学生那一边，则是誓死抵抗到底，非常贞烈。

"我警告你！你们如果在我身上进行这种下流手术，我出去一定会告死你们，一定！"女大学生好屈辱，明明眼泪都爬满了脸，却还是义正辞严。

"黄绮君小姐，请你放松，请配合我们的实验，这是个很严肃的事情。"

"我拒绝！"女大学生凄厉地说。

如果这是一部正常的英雄小说，那么小说里最正的正妹有难时（屁眼快被塞莴苣了，应该算是超有难吧），英雄便会登场，在千钧一发之际出手解救美女……的肛门。

真高兴，这不是一本英雄小说。

甚至这不是一本正常的小说。

"啊啊啊啊啊啊啊啊！我恨你们！我恨！我恨！！"

在莴苣的凌辱下，女大学生彻底崩坏了。

异常的，她没有哭，也不再吭声。

她的眼神陷入一种很冷酷的意境，这意境太高深了我看不懂。

如果这是漫画猎人，女大学生已经强制自己成长变成一个爆气的老女大学生，

但幸好这也不是漫画猎人，所以这个女大学生只是一个屁眼含着一团莴苣的崩溃女大学生。

剩下我了。

黑衣人站在摆满蔬菜水果的实验桌上，端详着该拿什么插我好。

身为一个职业作家的帮手，我真的完全没有想象过帮九把刀寻找故事灵感会危险到哪里，所有我曾遭遇过的危险与困境，都让我觉得未来不可能更糟，再糟，也不可能糟过文慧的铁脚，不可能糟过乔奶大婶的自爆，

不可能糟过大蛇的吞噬，不可能糟过魔神仔的恶烂大餐，不可能糟过住满猛鬼的自杀旅舍……

现在，我的屁眼战栗不已。

"那就这个吧。"

黑衣人慎重地拿起一盘仙草，慢慢走向我。

仙？

草？

"哈哈哈哈哈哈哈哈哈哈哈！我是仙草！我是仙草！"我乐坏了。

真的！

这辈子我就这一刻最快乐最爽最无敌了！

"你们看！我是仙草啊！"我拼命大叫，简直笑出眼泪了，"我是仙草！"

买菜大婶、女大学生、土流氓以及宅急便大叔，全用一种极度憎恨的眼神看着我。那种眼神里包含的高浓度怨毒，实在是让我爽翻天啦！

于是那位黑衣人奋力地将那盘仙草塞进我的屁眼里，哈哈完全 OK 啦，我超配合地扩张我的肛门，好让仙草进入。老实说我觉得屁眼有点痒，有点凉，有种奇异的滑稽感让我一直科科科笑个不停。

"仙草！我是仙草哈哈哈哈哈！我是仙草！仙草哈

哈哈哈哈哈！”

黑衣人塞仙草的动作却停了。

“报告长官，仙草塞不进去，一塞就碎掉，接下来该怎么办？”黑衣人叹气。

“还怎么办！想办法啊猪头！”我骂道。

撒拉八客想了想，说：“那就用西瓜吧。”

西瓜！

“等一下！可以用汤匙啊！用……用吸管把仙草吹进去啊！”我大惊。

撒拉八客与黑衣人对看了一眼，像是在考虑我的提议。

“用！西！瓜！”女大学生凄厉地大叫。

“Watermelon！ GO WATERMELON！”宅急便大叔也怒吼了。

“喔喔喔喔喔喔喔喔喔喔喔喔～～”土流氓龇牙咧嘴。

“我！要！回！家！大！便！”买菜大婶也尖叫了。

我慌了，我真的慌了：“把我的手松开，我自己来，我自己来，我愿意配合，我一定积极配合！”

撒拉八客皱眉：“好吧，把他的手松开。”

“用！西！瓜！”女大学生嘶吼着。

撒拉八客又皱了皱眉，说："等等，那就用西瓜吧。"

"仙草！"我绝不退让。

"仙草不是蔬菜！"女大学生大爆炸了。

"鱼蛋也不是啊！"我怒了。

"西瓜！"女大学生超级大爆炸了。

"西瓜！"宅急便大叔也爆炸了，"西瓜西瓜西瓜西瓜！"

"我要回家大便！"买菜大婶依然没有放弃她的理想。

"喔喔喔喔喔喔喔喔喔喔……"土流氓终于说出完整的单字，"西瓜！"

"就西瓜！"撒拉八客拍板定案。

黑衣人立刻双手捧起那一颗大西瓜，步步逼近。

我霍然转头看向状况外的阿祥，大叫："阿祥！马上吃掉这些外星人！"

阿祥不解："呲呲呲，但人类跟其他动物最大的不一样，不就是人不吃自己的同类吗？呲呲呲？"

西瓜持续逼近我的肛门，我大叫："你白痴啊！我不是跟你说过，人类跟其他动物最大的不一样！那就是！人会为了自我欺骗而造假！我说我们人不吃人其实是骗你的！人！人一直都会为了自己牺牲其他的同类！"

"呲呲呲，那，人什么时候会牺牲自己的同类？"

西瓜已经顶到了我的肛门，我的屁眼慢慢扩张，情势万分紧急。

真捅下去，我的余生都会有走路走到一半自动漏粪的毛病啊！！！

"保护地球和平，即使牺牲同类也是身为人类的责任啊！"我惨叫。

"保护地球和平？呲呲呲，什么时候？"阿祥疑惑。

"现在！"

就在我大吼的同一时间，西瓜逼近我的肛门只有半根指头的距离。

绑住阿祥的手铐裂开了。

阿祥是怎么变成一条超级大蛇的，没人看清楚过程。

只知道一条凶猛的白色大蛇在几个眨眼间就吞掉了所有穿着黑衣服的外星人，像一阵非写实的风，像一幢幢电影特效般的鬼影，像睁眼放映的恐怖恶梦。

　　然后在没有人看清楚个中变化的情况下，巨大到足以撑破整个客厅的大蛇莫名消失了，只剩下一个捧着大肚子、没有老二、屁眼含着一颗凤梨的赤裸阿祥。

　　阿祥打了一个很臭的嗝。

　　"……"所有人都呆住了，买菜大婶更是昏厥过去。

　　对他们来说，刚刚那一幕足以超越不久前发生在他们屁眼上的悲剧。

　　"外星人好吃吗？"我保持镇定。

　　"一次吃太多了。"阿祥答非所问，又打了个嗝，"呲呲呲……"

　　我四肢垂软，看着地上那一颗滚来滚去的大西瓜。

　　结束了。

　　我的屁眼安全了。

　　不断打嗝的阿祥解开了每一个人的手铐脚铐，彼此帮忙把屁眼里的蔬菜水果拔出来，整个过程都没有人讲话，之后也各自默默回家。我想不会有人报警。

　　那一阵子我才有点理解，说不定偶尔大家在电视新闻上看到有人去医院拔出塞在肛门里的怪东西，如酒瓶，如手机，如羽毛球拍，如保龄球瓶，非常可能是参加了疑似假外星人的烂实验吧？

"阿祥，你刚刚吃的那些人，口感跟以前吃的那些人，有任何不一样吗？"

回家的路上，我忍不住疑神疑鬼起来。

"呲呲呲，我也不知道。"阿祥有点不好意思，"我都用吞的。"

有很长一段时间，我都无法确定撒拉八客等人到底是真的外星人、还是得了失心疯的地球人。毕竟真正可以证明他们拥有超高科技的交换肛门手术（这种手术虽然很糟糕，但应该很难搞吧）还来不及发生，我就命阿祥以最自私的暴力强行结束一切。

直到后来发生了另一件事，我才知道，原来那天晚上阿祥的大暴走，大大影响了地球的命运、以及我自己卑贱的人生，而阿祥究竟能不能顺利在这个世界里成为真正的人类……

当然，那又是另一个故事了。

第六章_

蒸汽缭绕的浴缸

1

不得不说，九把刀是一个很容易躺着也中枪的笨蛋。

这个礼拜他无奈陷入在 Makiyo 殴打计程车事件的大混战中，我在旁边观察他，忍不住觉得他有一点点可怜，不管是记者还是乡民都超爱问他各式各样的社会问题，他不回答，大家就爱猜他心里想什么，可只要他回答了，不管说了什么都会引起一阵天下大乱，然后九把刀就得没日没夜窝在电脑前不断发文澄清，满背是箭。报应啊报应！

不过他可怜，我更可怜，连续好几天都在跑可能增进小说灵感的新闻事件，比如有一个超唬烂的新闻说，在澳洲有一个人晚上在沙漠尿尿，结果阴囊被躲在暗处的毒蛇咬了，他痛到冲进房里请室友帮他吸阴囊里的毒，室友拒绝（不晓得考虑多久喔），但还是带着他开了40分钟的车冲到医院打血清，终于救回这个老二被咬的衰人一条命。

这种低级新闻九把刀最爱了，但这种在 ptt 八卦版就可以找到资料的新闻，九把刀只会付我一瓶牛奶的钱，所以我得为了其他更有低级潜力的新闻上天下海，好搜集到一般记者无法接触到的新闻幕后。

有时忙到我常常忘记，我来担任九把刀的助理并不是真的想帮助他成为天杀的故事之王，而是想借用这个大烂人的资源去调查我爸爸被神秘液体溶解之谜。

而阿祥2.0，在吃了六个"号称外星人但看起来很像地球人的人"之后，在我出门寻找灵感时足足在家大睡了一个礼拜。

他以人形缩在房里角落捧着大肚子，消化的声音非常难听，还不时打着超臭的嗝，那些臭嗝凝聚不散，终于从门缝底下飘出。一个礼拜后住在隔壁的房客怀疑是尸臭（某种意义来说，也的确是尸臭），终于忍不住打电话叫房东处理。

一听疑似尸臭，房东就腿软了，马上找来管区警察跟他一起开门。

当时我不在现场，但据说门一打开的瞬间，首当其冲的两个警察立刻昏死过去，而那个房东远远吸了一口臭嗝的结果，则是丧失嗅觉一个月，失去胃口半年。

2

　　我到派出所做笔录的时候，阿祥还没醒来，只是不忘打嗝。

　　笔录只做了5分钟，派出所里都是尸臭的味道，所有人都戴着医疗等级的口罩，唯一一个没有戴口罩的人是铐在椅子上的小偷，而他已经吐到不省人事。

　　"你朋友怎么都叫不醒啊？又没有闻到酒味，是不是嗑了药啊？"负责笔录的管区警察口起很差，脸色更差。

　　"我哪知道，想知道就抓去验尿啊。"我态度不佳，因为我也很无奈。

　　"就赌你朋友嗑药！来！抓去验尿做业绩！"管区警察大怒拍桌。

　　于是昏睡中的阿祥就被抓去厕所验尿了。

　　3分钟后，负责验尿的小警员慌慌张张从厕所冲出来。

"报告长官……他……"小警员上气不接下气。

"他什么啊！说说！"管区警察瞪着他。

"这位黄家祥先生没有老二！"小警员神色惊慌。

"什么叫没有老二！"

"报告长官……就是……就是没有老二的意思！"

管区警察疑神疑鬼地跟小警员进去厕所里面看，不久后两个警察气冲冲走向我。

"你朋友为什么没有老二！"管区警察气急败坏质问。

"我怎么知道？我朋友好好跟你们去了厕所验尿，结果尿还没验，老二就不见了，我没怪你，你怪我？！"我反过来咄咄逼人，"把我朋友的老二交出来！"

"……所以他是阴阳人还是变性人？"管区警察一时语塞，"讲清楚嘛！"

"跟你说我不知道啊！我只知道我朋友跟你们去验尿，然后老二就不见了，他醒来的话一定告死你们。"我冷笑，"告到你们当铺去当老二才赔得起！"

经历过大风大浪，区区一个烂笔录怎么难得倒我。

我们之间无法沟通，但验尿还是继续验，然而阿祥大概是进入了蛇类的类冬眠模式，所以怎么也叫不醒，要催尿也不得其门而入，但他一直在厕所里打嗝，近距离拿纸杯等尿的警察们纷纷呕吐，半小时后终于结束了这一场闹剧。

继续狂睡的阿祥被扔在我旁边，一张酸痛药布不偏不倚贴在他的嘴巴上。

"不验了，依我多年的专业经验，你朋友是习惯性嗜睡。"管区警察一屁股坐下。

"我不知道，反正他在你们厕所丢了老二。"我抖脚。

"别血口喷人啊！"管区警察气势一弱，改口，"警民好好合作嘛。"

他问了我一些基本资料，我无关痛痒地随便回答。

"你朋友到底平常都吃什么，怎么打嗝那么臭！"管区警察口气很差。

"我哪知道，我又不是他的谁。"我抓头。

"是不是吃了大便啊！"管区警察愤慨起来。

"不就是尸臭嘛？我看吃了人肉还差不多。"我不甘示弱。

"听好了，你朋友醒来后叫他多吃青菜啊！要不然就多喝蔬果579啊！总之管管你朋友嘛！卫生习惯那么差，以后怎么还有人敢把房间租给他啊？"管区警察嫌恶地说，"该说的我都写下来了，你没说的我等一下自己脑补，在这里签个名，快点把你朋友带回去！"

"等等……他不能回去！"一旁昏倒的房东摇摇欲坠地举手，"他太臭了，我没有叫他付房间消毒的钱已经不错了，他一回去的话，隔壁两边的房客都会马上搬走！"

"房间他付了钱的。"我反对。

"合约里面有规定，房客卫生习惯太差的话，房东有权收回。"房东开始哀求，"拜托你们行行好，别把我的房客都赶跑了，这个月的房租我就不跟你们算了，快搬快搬。"

唉，这倒是阿祥理亏了，我可没有想为难无辜房东的意思。

我只好无奈地扛起阿祥叫了计程车，把阿祥扔到天空地阔的大安森林公园，在他身上放了一张纸条和两张百元钞票叫他醒来找我。

阿祥只是狂睡觉，我想应该不会有人为难他吧。

3

满身草屑的阿祥来找我，已是三天后的事。

没地方住的他只好跟我挤一个房间，我别无选择，幸好阿祥的日常花费奇低无比，顶多就是一天一盒鸡蛋的程度，没有造成我什么负担，睡觉的时候床当然是我自己睡，而阿祥则将身体蜷曲睡在浴缸里，这点我倒不觉得委屈了他，他也没有抱怨。

他变得超宅，几乎不想出门。

不想出门，阿祥倒有大量看电视的需求，特别是偶像剧，越是缠绵悱恻不切实际的剧情他越爱看，偶尔遥控器切到电影台，也是以爱情电影为主。

每天我出门，阿祥都正襟危坐在和室地板上看着电视。

我回家的时候，阿祥都还维持一模一样的姿势，好像纹丝未动。

有一天我回家，阿祥的表情特别古怪。

"我觉得，我好像越来越不了解人类了，呲呲呲。"

阿祥专注的脸上都是电视荧幕的蓝色反光。

"怎么说？电视剧又太难懂了吗？那就看卡通啊。"

我将排骨便当放在和室桌上，随手递给阿祥一盒生鸡蛋。

"太难理解的东西，太多太多了，人类真是太复杂了，呲呲呲。"

阿祥的眼睛一动也不动地盯着电视重播的东京爱情故事完结篇，一手默默接过生鸡蛋，却没有立刻打开盒子吞，而是好好地放在和室桌上。

看电视比吃东西重要？看样子阿祥已经进入了小学儿童的境界了。

我猜想，从虚伪的电视里、从那一些被文青批评得一文不值的偶像剧跟乡土剧里面，阿祥所学习到关于人类的一切，或许比真正的现实世界还要更贴近我们对人类的想象……宅在家里看电视比发传单更容易了解人类在想什么吧。

我们一起吃便当跟蛋，一起看东京爱情故事倒数第二集的最高潮，男主角永尾丸治在故乡来回奔跑、到处问人有没有看过照片上的女孩，都没有结果，最后独自一人在足球场上惆怅摆烂时，女主角赤名莉香才偷偷从他的背后出现，一转头，还连续来个特写镜头三连发，非常俗气，但非常……非常……让人激动得想哭啊！

"丸子！"赤名莉香笑道。

"……"我的视线又模糊了。

这一段我已经看过好几遍重播了，每一次我都会哭得很崩溃，可今天有阿祥在我旁边，我强忍住像娘炮一样狂哭的冲动，只令几滴眼泪滑落。

"你在哭，为什么？呲呲呲？"阿祥疑惑。

"这就是人性啦！"我觉得有点丢脸。

"人性就是……哭？呲呲呲？"

"对啊，就很感动啊。"

"哭，我看过的每一个电视剧，都会有人哭呲呲呲，通常都是雌性的人类哭，而且一哭就停不下来。但现在你是一个雄性，你也哭，呲呲呲为什么？"

"就跟你说这是人性啊，只要是人，就一定会被爱情给感动，一感动，就算是没人性的九把刀也会虎目含泪啊！"

"……呲呲呲，爱情啊？"阿祥若有所思。

"对啊，爱情很特别啊，你想想，原本没有任何关系的两个人，彼此爱上了对方，或者！一开始男的不喜欢女的，或女的不喜欢男的，又或者更惨，两个人彼此讨厌，甚至痛恨对方！但不管，总之这原本陌生的一男一女历经千辛万苦终于在一起，从此以后他们就是世界上最亲密的两个人，或许他们还会生下两个小孩，然后那些小孩长大后，还会去认识别的陌生的男孩女孩，然后又历经另一段千辛万苦的爱情，然后又……"

"然后又生下更多的人类小孩，呲呲呲。"阿祥接着说。

"没错，这样的爱情不值得感动吗？"

"可是，爱情一定要一男一女吗？呲呲呲，我之前在电影台看了一部片，有两个外国人在很美的山上交配，感觉上那部电影也是在讲爱情，但他们之间的交配并不会繁衍下一代，呲呲呲这种无法繁衍的感情也可以称为爱情吗？"

啧啧啧，除了怎么戒也戒不掉的呲呲呲外，我注意到阿祥可以用的词汇越来越多，语句也开始复杂起来，电视可以教的东西还真不少，阿祥真不愧是一条很有灵性的千年蛇妖。

那么说起来，我应该也可以用一些比较复杂的字眼啰？

"喔，你看的应该是断背山吧？你已经在看那么进阶有深度的同志电影啦？那正好，我觉得爱情当然不分男女，如果我们逆向思考，今天两个男的谈恋爱了，他们的爱却不是为了繁衍后代，而是更单纯的喜欢对方，那样的爱情不是更伟大吗？不是更感人吗？"

"……呲呲呲，好像有点道理。"

"不是有点道理，是超级有道理。反正男的跟男的，女的跟女的，都可以谈恋爱，就算是人跟鬼之间也可以爱来爱去，比如……最经典的就是倩女幽魂这系列的电影，有机会你切到纬来电影台或东森电影台，他们常常重播，你就会看到爱情跨越人鬼之间的隔阂，那是非常猛的感动喔！"

"也会哭吗，呲呲呲？"

"会啊，一定哭的啊！"

阿祥沉默了片刻，眼睛看着电视，眼神却没在看电视。

许久，他开口："是不是等到我了解爱情以后，我也能成为真正的人类呢？呲呲呲？"

"非常有可能。"我胡乱保证。

"那我就能哭了吗？"阿祥的眼神泛着异光，"呲呲呲。"

"……一定没问题的。"我点头。

此时阿祥将手放在我的手上，我登时全身僵硬。

只见他表情无比认真说："呲呲呲，那我们两个来谈恋爱吧。"

我大惊，但没吓到失去理智："当然是不要啊。"

"为什么？呲呲呲？"

"你是男的耶！"

"我其实是一条母蛇，呲呲呲。"

"但你长得就是我的好朋友阿祥的模样啊！不但是男的，还很丑！"

"你不是说，呲呲呲爱情也可以发生在两个雄性人类之间吗？"

"那也要我喜欢你才可以啊！"

"你不是说，爱情也可能是一开始彼此并不喜欢吗？这样历经千辛万苦的爱情，更加令人感动，不是吗，呲呲呲？"

"我们之间绝对不可能！阿！祥！"

"所以以后历经的重重困难，会让我们的爱情更加辛苦吗？"阿祥跃跃欲试。

"不会！干完全不会！"我非常坚持。

"我们可以从接吻开始吗呲呲呲？"阿祥认真地看着我，"我看过好几个偶像剧，里面的一个雄性人类跟

雌性人类常常从一个不小心跌倒的吻，展开了人类所谓
的爱情呲呲呲？"

说完，阿祥把嘴嘟了起来，嘴角还有一点蛋黄！

干我超想一拳朝他的脸灌下去的！

"阿祥！你冷静！你听我说！"我握紧我的拳头，不
让我的小宇宙爆发。

"还是我们从一不小心喝醉然后就上床开始……我
们的爱情？呲呲呲？"

"不要！你休想跟我上床！"我往后摔了两步，"我
们之间真的不可能！"

"这句话我也常常在偶像剧里听到，呲呲呲，这算
是一种暗示吗？"

阿祥点点头，他脱下了裤子。

顿时就知道他想干什么了，我赶紧说："我出去几
天！你先冷静一下！"

我反射性地夺门而逃，留下没穿裤子示爱的阿祥。

4

还是失控了。

其实我并不怪阿祥，也可以理解阿祥想尝试变成人类的决心，毕竟成为人类是每一个妖怪的最高志愿，原因不明，极可能是集体盲从，但我理解这种盲从到底的坚定决心。

但我理解阿祥，不代表我愿意牺牲自己成全他。

回不了家，我只好在九把刀家里打地铺打了三天，直到九把刀用好神拖将我扫了出去，我才勉为其难地回去。

该面对的还是要面对。

我在巷子口便利商店买了一打台湾啤酒跟两盒鸡蛋，以及一本宫本喜四郎所写的《偶像剧里的荒谬爱情大揭露》，打算好好彻夜开导阿祥，让他迷途知返。

没想到一开门，就看到一个年轻女孩正坐在我家和室地板上看 A 片。

"！"我怔住，差点以为开错门。

那个年轻女孩长得清纯可爱，眼睛大大的清澈无辜，嘴角有两个小小的梨窝，一头乌黑俏丽的短发，最重要的是——我根本就认识她！

她是我最常意淫的日本 AV 女优，椎名素子！

"我是阿祥，呲呲呲……"椎名素子吐着舌头。

"阿祥？！"我一震，几乎要腿软。

"我变成这个样子，呲呲呲，你喜欢吗？"椎名素子，喔不，阿祥说。

"你……你把话给我说清楚！"我扶着墙，这才阻止自己昏过去。

"呲呲呲。"阿祥看起来很得意。

原来我夺门而逃的这三天，阿祥除了持续在电视上看偶像剧外，也开始胡乱摸索我电脑里的影片，偏偏我的 A 片档案夹霸占了一半桌面，他全都点开来看，发现影片都是人类的交配大全，就沉迷研究下去。

由于我搜集了我最爱的椎名素子超过三十部 A 片，所以阿祥看最多的 AV 女优也是椎名素子，于是原本就是一条无法变出老二的母蛇的阿祥，决定试着用自己吃过的几百个女孩的灵魂（我想阿祥的意思应该是基因，或 DNA 之类的吧），拼凑出椎名素子的模样，然后在镜子前面慢慢微调。

他办到了，从他变成了她。

"阿祥，你这样让我不知道该怎么办。"我的脑子很乱。

"我这样，你不喜欢吗呲呲呲？"阿祥眨眨眼，无辜地嘟起嘴。

看来阿祥也认真学习过模仿人类女孩装可爱的方式，我超想揍下去的。

"喜欢个屁！"我很火大。

"可是你有很多她的影片，呲呲呲。"阿祥模仿出椎名素子的招牌笑容。

"你这样真的不行，阿祥，这样真的很怪！"我大声说，但我其实也不知道自己在乱讲什么。

阿祥穿着从我衣柜挖出来的运动 T 恤，还有一条小短裤，找不到内衣穿的"她"当然胸前大激突，整个人散发出令我手足无措的少女气息。

"哪里怪？呲呲呲？"阿祥撅起嘴。

"我们是朋友，记得吗？"我握拳，试着冷静。

"记得，呲呲呲。"阿祥用力点点头，"所以我们是从朋友关系开始的爱情。"然后越靠越近，越靠越近。

"不是这样！虽然你……你的确是我朋友了，但你之前可是吃了我另一个朋友，也就是真正的阿祥！"我有点恼怒起来，"所以我们之间是完全不可能的！"

"我知道，我什么都知道呲呲呲。"阿祥挨着我，撒娇地在我耳边说，"我原来是一条蛇，所以我们是人蛇两隔。我吃了你的好朋友，所以我们一开始是敌人，你很讨厌我呲呲呲。但我们一起经历了奇怪的实验，有了共患难的基础。前几天你跟我吵了一架，所以我们之间有了冲突的高潮呲呲呲……"

我伸出手，却推不开她。

我……我嘴巴说不要，身体却很诚实地抱住了阿祥。

好热，我的身体好热好热。

曾对着电脑荧幕看了无数次的女神就坐在我旁边，穿着我宽宽松松的衣服和裤子，还娇羞地投怀送抱，这不就是我的梦寐以求吗？

不，或许我在梦里也不敢求过这个画面。

阿祥将她的头埋在我的怀里，听着我快要爆炸的心跳。

她的呼吸声，她的气息，都让把我逼疯了。

"现在，我们差不多应该……呲呲呲？"阿祥柔声。

"应该怎样？"

"应该交配……不，呲呲呲，我们应该一起睡觉了，对不对？"

5

为了表示我跟喜欢斩铁的九把刀的格调有很大的不一样，我拒绝用大量的象声字填满整整两页的稿纸糊弄读者。而且我想这本小说出版的时候，肯定不是限制级，所以我拒绝哗众取宠，很有职业道德地大幅省略我跟阿祥接下来半个晚上发生的事。

总而言之，言而总之，半个晚上后，筋疲力竭的我们用仅剩的力气爬到了浴室，虚弱地将水龙头慢慢旋开，将热水注满浴缸。

我们曲着膝盖，在小小暖暖的浴缸里喝着早已不冰的啤酒，我试着让大量的酒精麻痹我的理智。而阿祥明显看起来很高兴，不仅跟我一起喝光了啤酒，很久没吃蛋了的她还一口气吞了整整两盒蛋。她打嗝的时候竟然会将头别到一旁，还用手羞答答地捂着……哇靠。

暂时我不想讨论刚刚发生在我们身上的异变，我自然而然地说起不着边际的事。不知不觉，我聊起了我为什么会跟阿祥一起去深山的原因。我是一个畅销作家兼王八蛋九把刀的助手，为了一封读者的古怪来信，千里迢迢将自己送入荒谬的险境，还把自己最好的朋友送进一个刚刚跟我那个那个的母蛇的胃里。

"呲呲呲这就是缘分吗？"阿祥幽幽听着。

"反正这一切都是从九把刀那边开始的。"我避重就轻。

"那你为什么要当九把刀的助理呢呲呲呲？"

"因为我要解开，我爸爸当年被神秘液体溶解的谜。"

我只好话说从头，聊起我小时候的惨事。

然后我又聊到了我怎么通过九把刀超烂的面试，聊到我第一个出的任务，聊到了我其实是一个拯救全台北市免于核爆的无名英雄，聊到我虽然经历过很多大风大浪，却还是没能接近我爸爸被溶解之谜……唉，至今为止我都还没进入我人生的冒险主题，真是没用。

我聊着，她听着。

在蒸气缭绕里，阿祥看起来很美很美。

"大明，我喜欢跟你睡觉，呲呲呲。"印象中，这是她头一次这么叫我。

"嗯。"我有点尴尬。

"所以我是不是又更接近人类一点了呢？呲呲呲？"

阿祥眨眨眼。

"我不知道。"我沉默片刻，又说，"应该是吧。"

"这几天我注意到，人类跟其他动物最大的不一样，可能也包括了，呲呲呲虽然自己不一定做，但人类也很喜欢看不是自己进行的交配。"阿祥舔着嘴角的蛋黄，甜甜地说，"我也很喜欢看人类交配，所以我比以前都更接近人类了呲呲呲，我……好高兴。"

说完，阿祥将头埋进了热水里，我情不自禁打了一个冷颤。

这混账家伙，真的把人类研究透彻了。

我叹了一口气。

"阿祥，其实人类跟其他动物最大的不一样，就在于人类常常会自以为自己跟其他动物很不一样，其实，人类跟其他动物没有什么不同。"

阿祥好像没有听到，持续潜在热水里。

或者我这么说，其实不是她想要得到的答案吧？

许久，阿祥的脸才浮出水面。

"总有一天，我会学到哭吗？"阿祥楚楚可怜地看着我。

"会的，一定会的。"我有气无力地伸出手，摸摸她红通通的脸。

"那，在我学会哭之前，我先陪你找到你爸爸被溶解的原因，好不好？"

"好啊。"

阿祥抱住我。

我抱住阿祥。

我不知道这是不是谈恋爱。

但，拥抱是真的。

我喜欢这个拥抱，也是真的。

"……你刚刚忘了说，呲呲呲。"

"这样不是比较像人类吗？"

"呲呲呲，比较像你。我喜欢听你说呲呲呲。"

"呲呲呲。"

（完）

版权登记号：01-2012-2537

图书在版编目(CIP)数据

上课不要烤香肠 / 九把刀著. —北京：现代出版社，2012.6

ISBN 978-7-80244-468-3

Ⅰ. ①上…　Ⅱ. ①九…　Ⅲ. ①长篇小说—中国—当代　Ⅳ. ①I247.5

中国版本图书馆CIP数据核字（2012）第086970号

本书由大众国际书局股份有限公司授权。

本书仅限于中国大陆地区发行，不得销售至其他任何海外地区。

作　　者	九把刀
责任编辑	刘春荣
出版发行	现代出版社
地　　址	北京市安定门外安华里504号
邮政编码	100011
电　　话	010-64267325　010-64245264（兼传真）
网　　址	www.xiandaibook.com
电子信箱	xiandai@cnpitc.com.cn
印　　刷	北京诚信伟业印刷厂
开　　本	890mm×1240mm　1/32
印　　张	8
字　　数	129千字
版　　次	2012年6月第1版　2012年6月第1次印刷
书　　号	978-7-80244-468-3
定　　价	25.00元